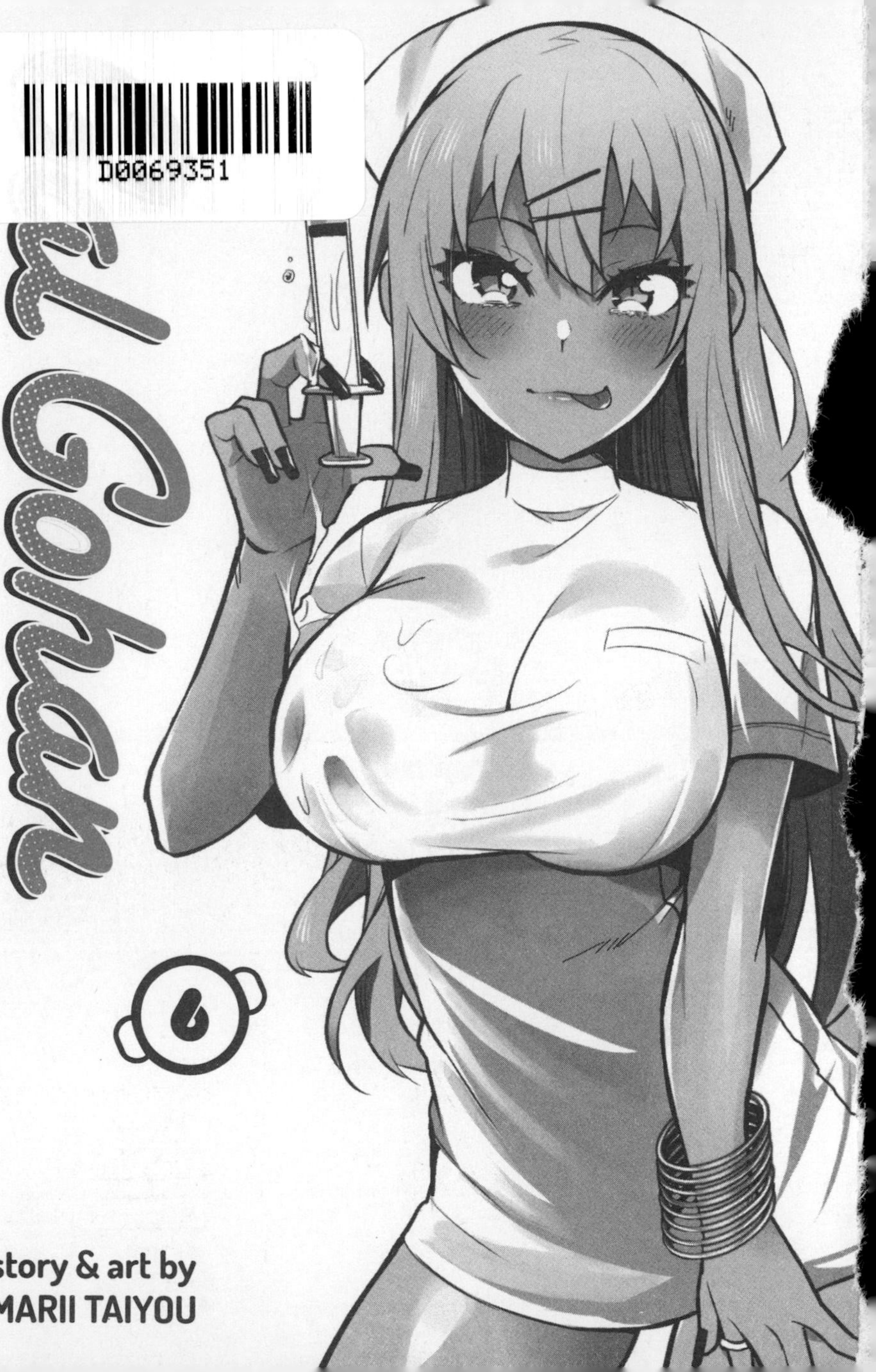
l Gohan
6

story & art by
MARII TAIYOU

contents

Gal Gohan

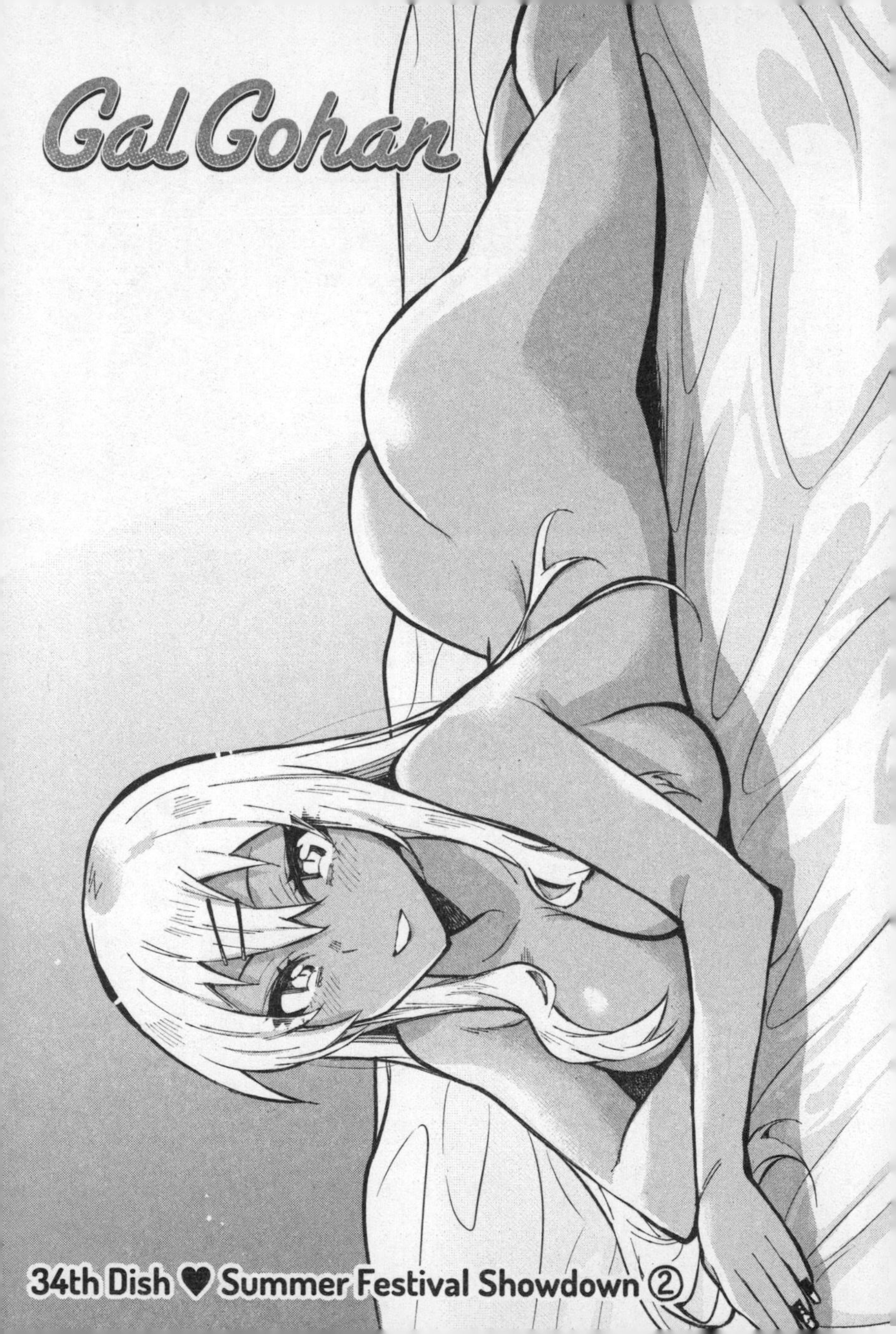

34th Dish ♥ Summer Festival Showdown ②

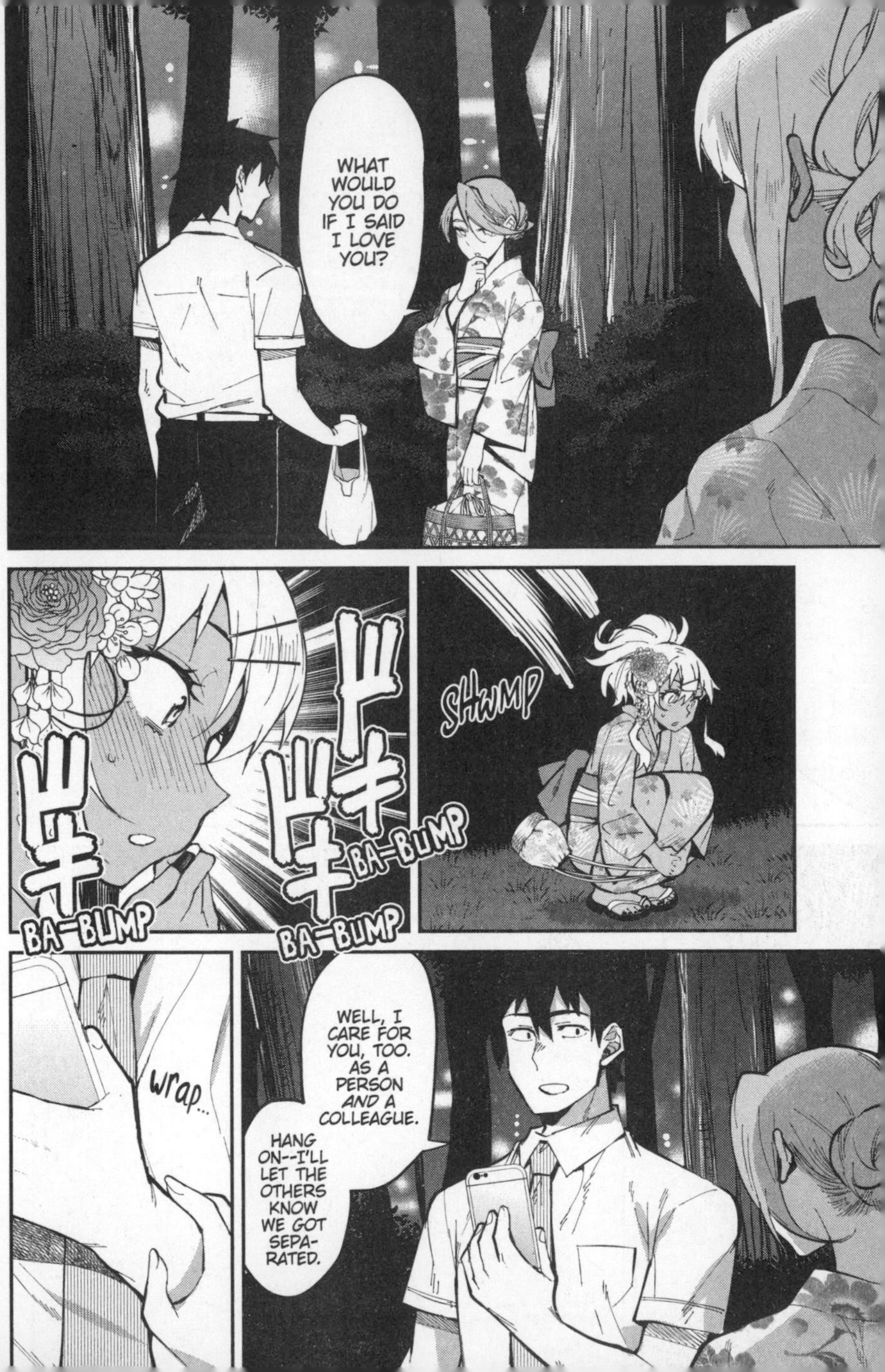
WHAT WOULD YOU DO IF I SAID I LOVE YOU?
SHWMP
BA-BUMP
BA-BUMP
BA-BUMP
WELL, I CARE FOR YOU, TOO. AS A PERSON AND A COLLEAGUE.
HANG ON--I'LL LET THE OTHERS KNOW WE GOT SEPA-RATED.
wrap...

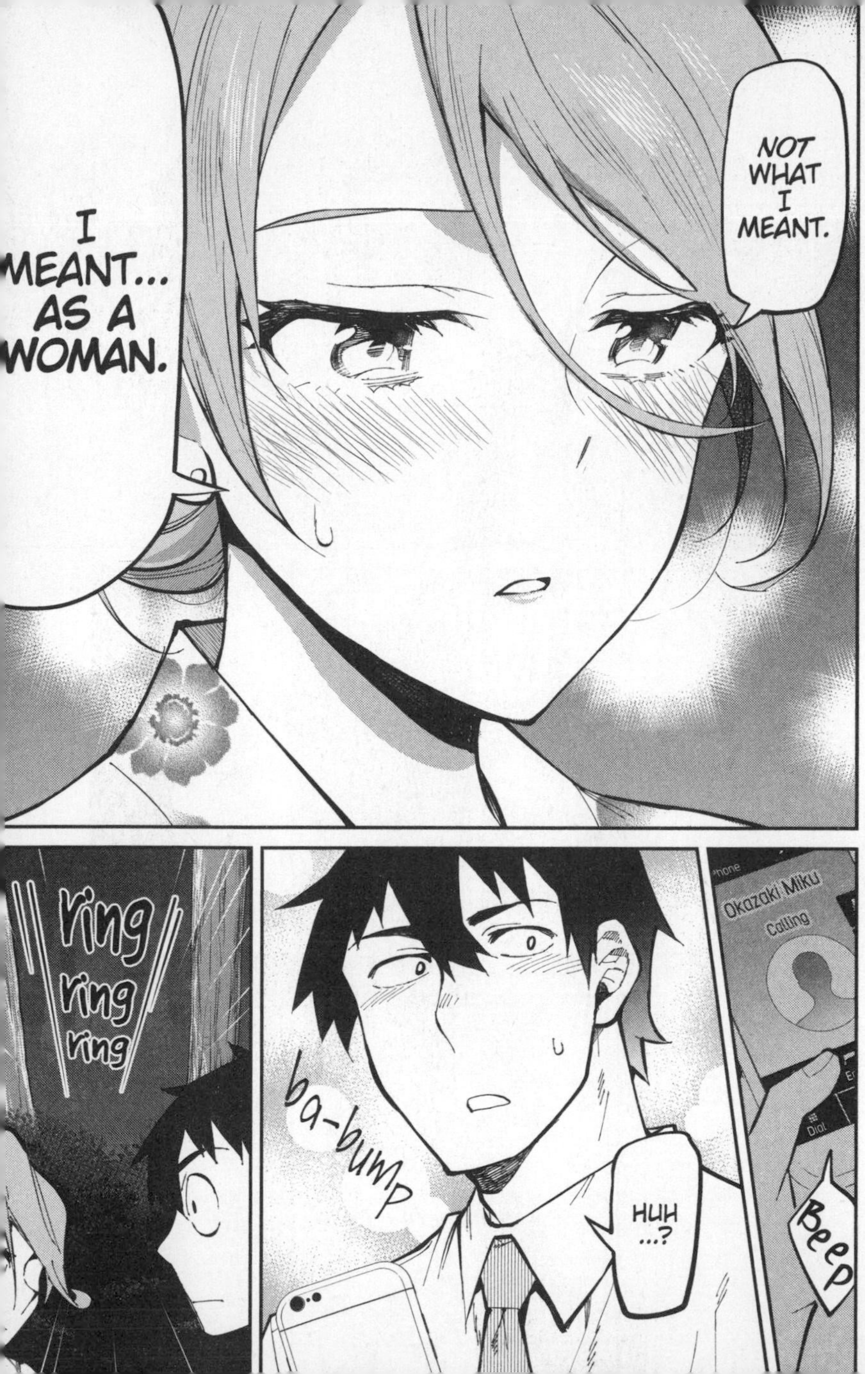
NOT WHAT I MEANT.
I MEANT... AS A WOMAN.
Okazaki Miku
Calling
Dial
Beep
ba-bump
HUH ...?
ring
ring
ring

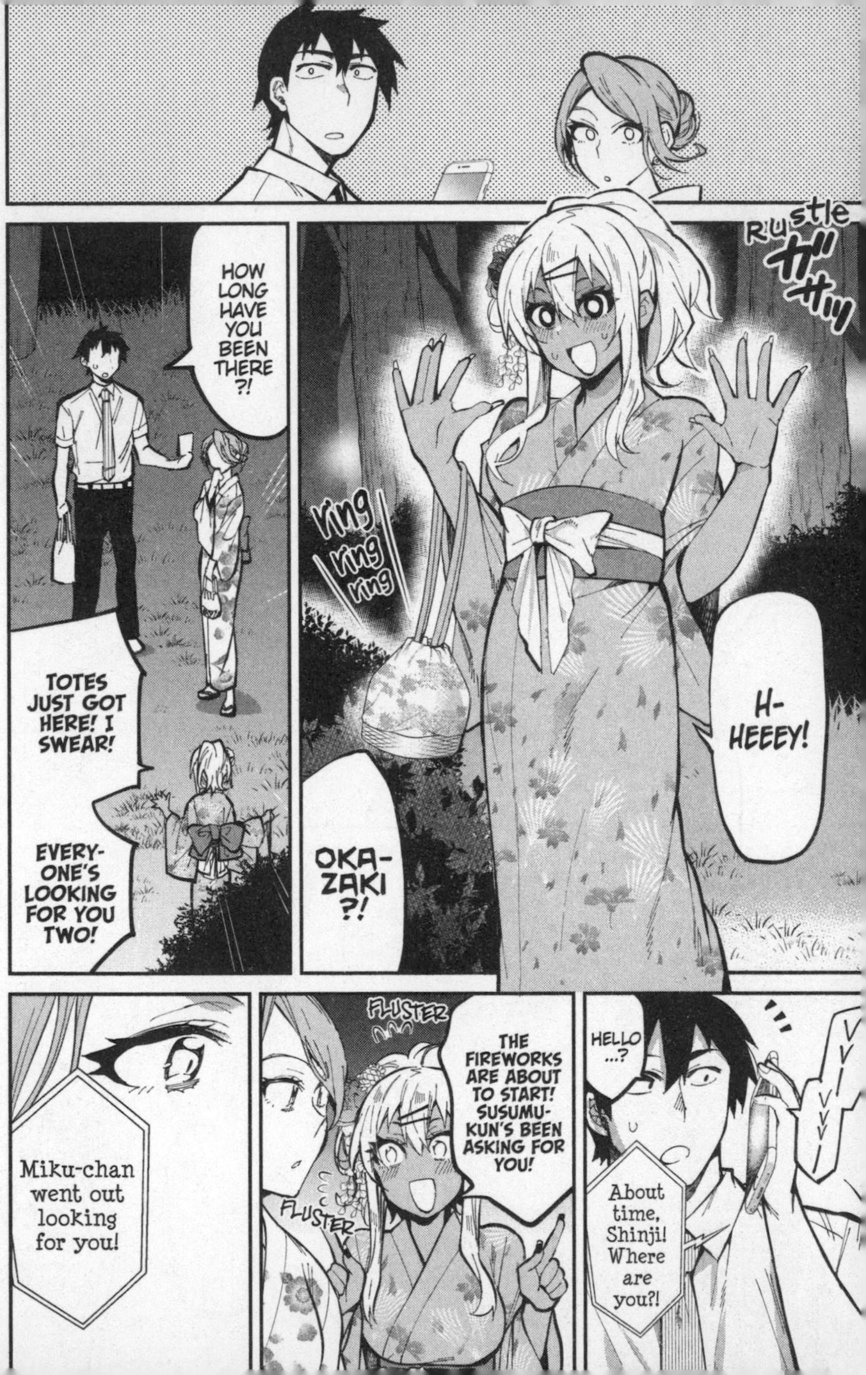
RUSTLE
H-HEEEY!
ring ring ring
OKA-ZAKI ?!
HOW LONG HAVE YOU BEEN THERE ?!
TOTES JUST GOT HERE! I SWEAR!
EVERY-ONE'S LOOKING FOR YOU TWO!
HELLO ...?
About time, Shinji! Where are you?!
FLUSTER
THE FIREWORKS ARE ABOUT TO START! SUSUMU-KUN'S BEEN ASKING FOR YOU!
FLUSTER
Miku-chan went out looking for you!

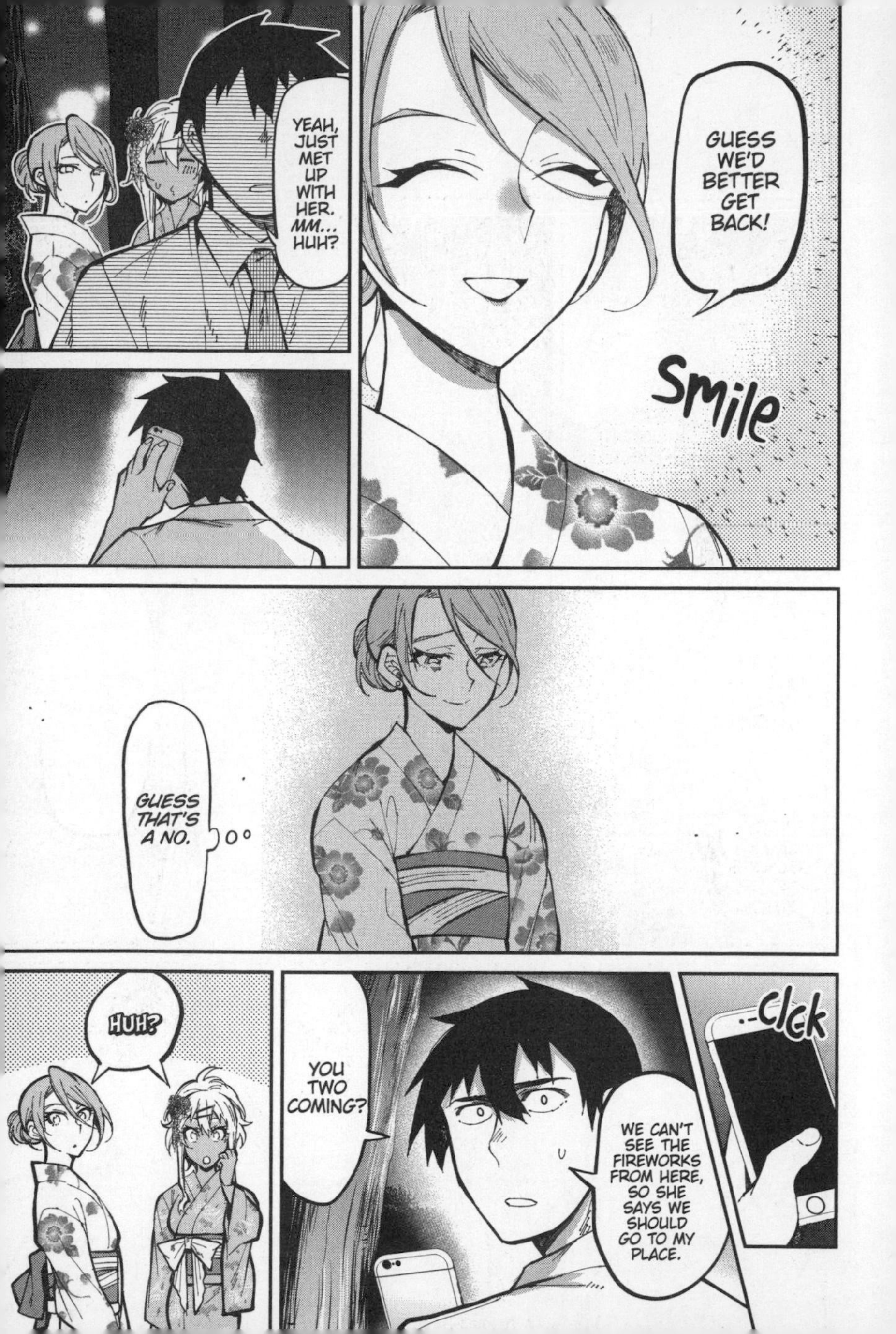
GUESS WE'D BETTER GET BACK!
Smile
YEAH, JUST MET UP WITH HER. MM... HUH?
GUESS THAT'S A NO.
..Clck
WE CAN'T SEE THE FIREWORKS FROM HERE, SO SHE SAYS WE SHOULD GO TO MY PLACE.
YOU TWO COMING?
HUH?

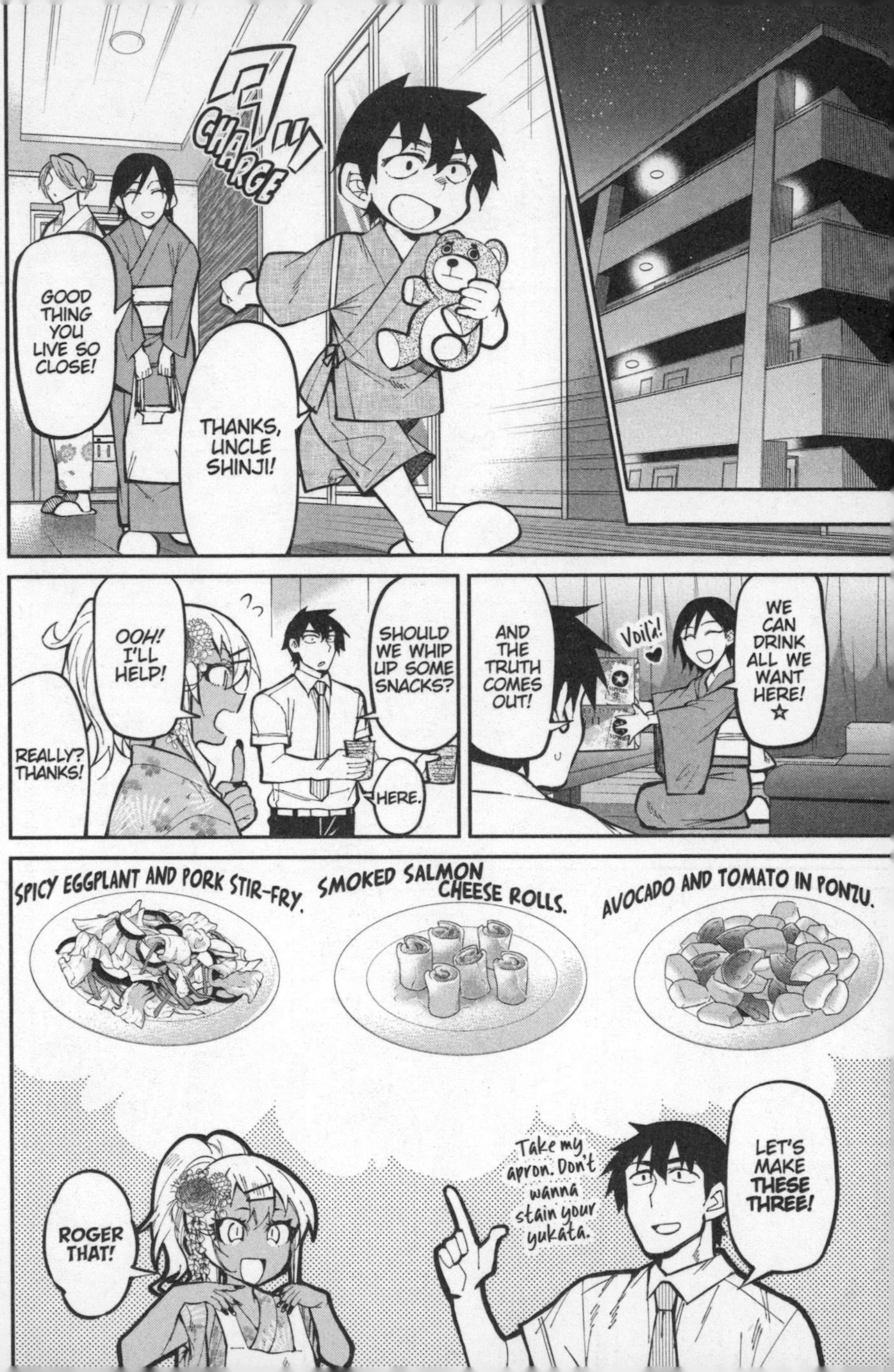
CHARGE
THANKS, UNCLE SHINJI!
GOOD THING YOU LIVE SO CLOSE!
WE CAN DRINK ALL WE WANT HERE! ☆
Voilà! ♥
AND THE TRUTH COMES OUT!
SHOULD WE WHIP UP SOME SNACKS?
HERE.
OOH! I'LL HELP!
REALLY? THANKS!
AVOCADO AND TOMATO IN PONZU.
SMOKED SALMON CHEESE ROLLS.
SPICY EGGPLANT AND PORK STIR-FRY.
LET'S MAKE THESE THREE!
Take my apron. Don't wanna stain your yukata.
ROGER THAT!

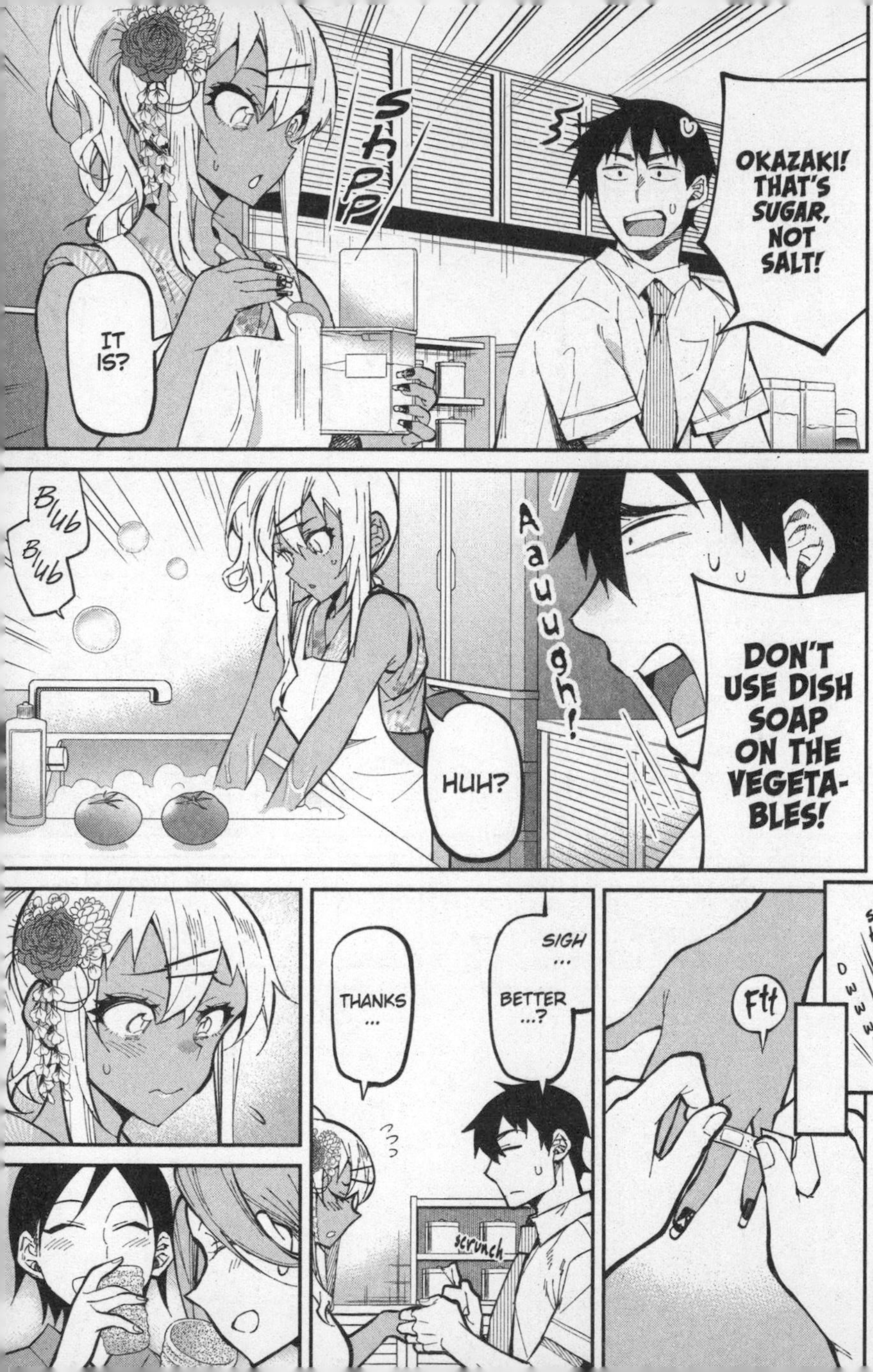
OKAZAKI! THAT'S SUGAR, NOT SALT!
Shpp
IT IS?
Aaugh!
DON'T USE DISH SOAP ON THE VEGETA-BLES!
Blub Blub
HUH?
shirk
Owwwi!
Ftt
SIGH ... BETTER ...?
THANKS ...
scrunch

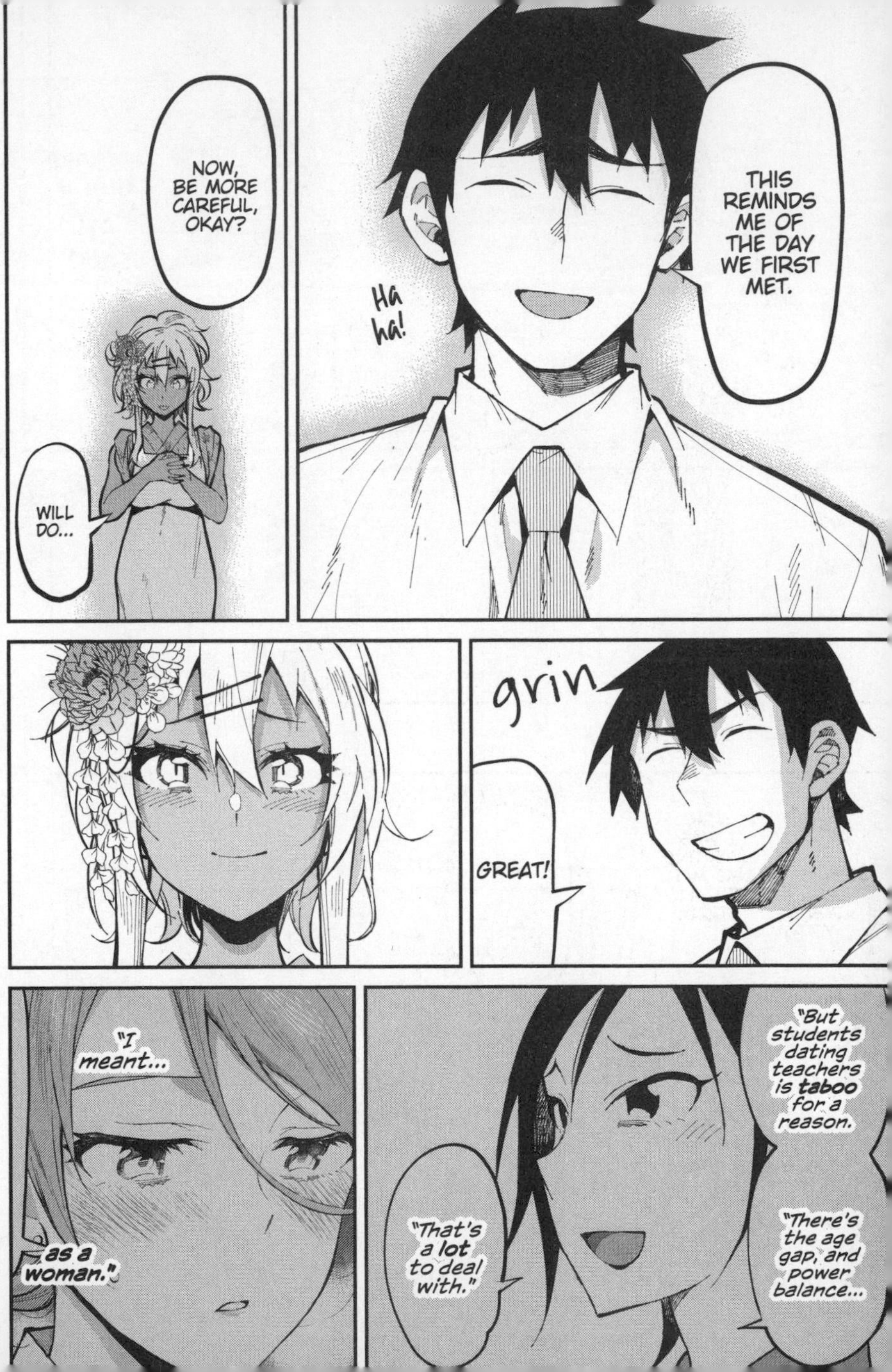
THIS REMINDS ME OF THE DAY WE FIRST MET.
Ha ha!
NOW, BE MORE CAREFUL, OKAY?
WILL DO...
grin
GREAT!
"But students dating teachers is **taboo** for a reason.
"There's the age gap, and power balance...
"That's a **lot** to deal with."
"I meant...
as a woman."

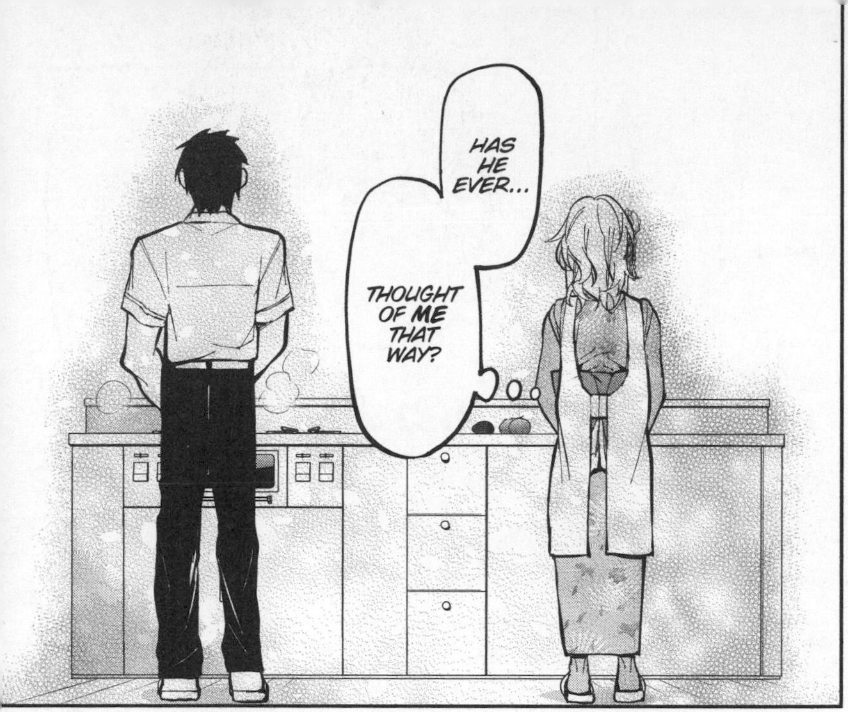
HAS HE EVER...
THOUGHT OF ME THAT WAY?

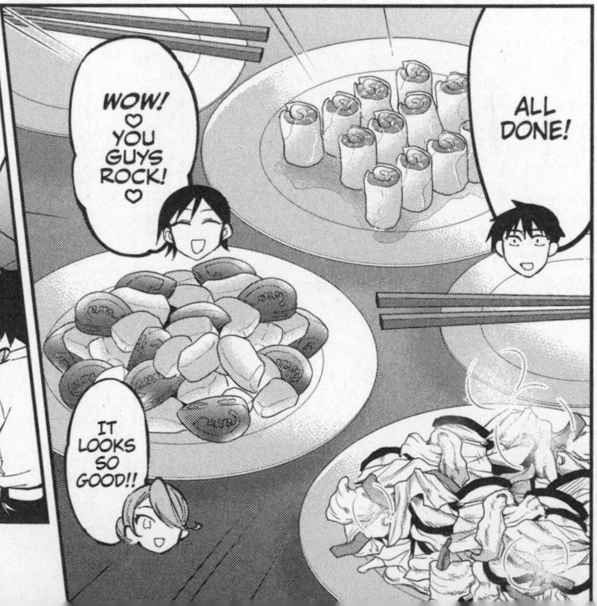
ALL DONE!
WOW! ♡ YOU GUYS ROCK! ♡
IT LOOKS SO GOOD!!

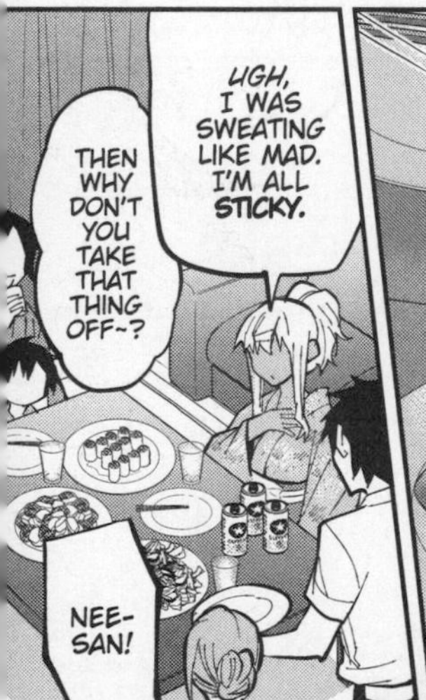
UGH, I WAS SWEATING LIKE MAD. I'M ALL STICKY.
THEN WHY DON'T YOU TAKE THAT THING OFF~?
NEE-SAN!

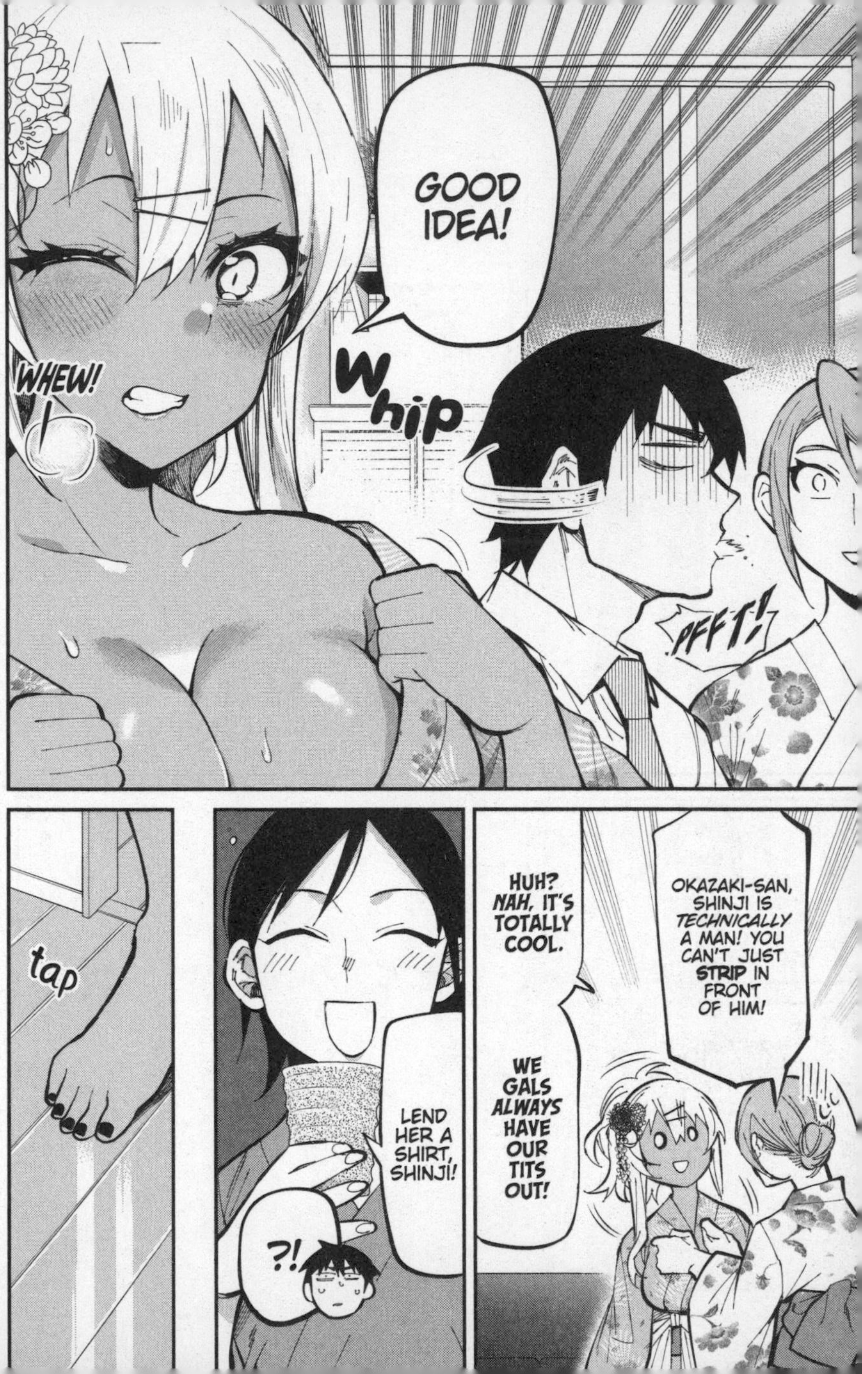
GOOD IDEA!
Whip
PFFT!
WHEW!
OKAZAKI-SAN, SHINJI IS TECHNICALLY A MAN! YOU CAN'T JUST STRIP IN FRONT OF HIM!
HUH? NAH, IT'S TOTALLY COOL.
WE GALS ALWAYS HAVE OUR TITS OUT!
LEND HER A SHIRT, SHINJI!
?!
tap

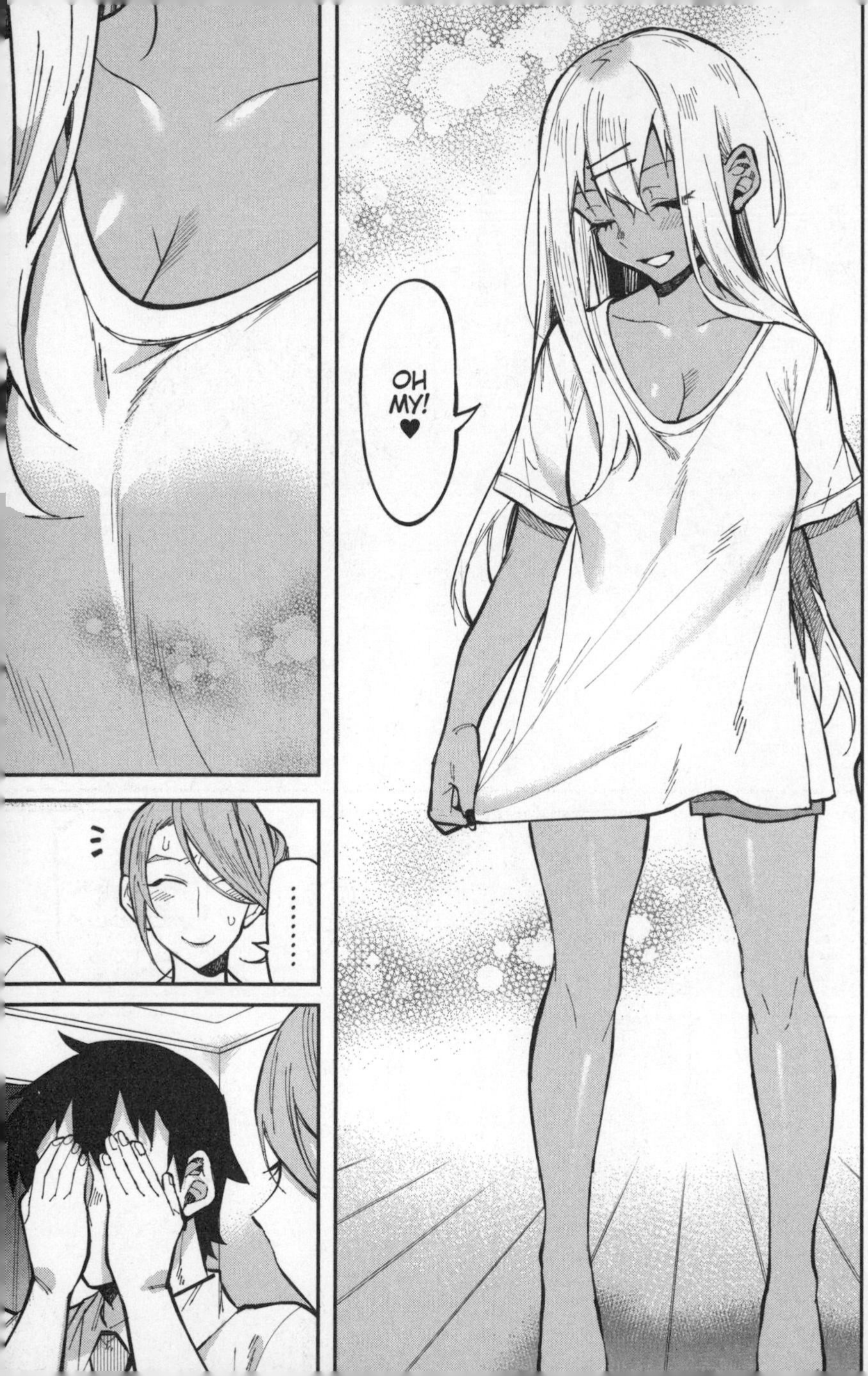
OH MY! ♥
......

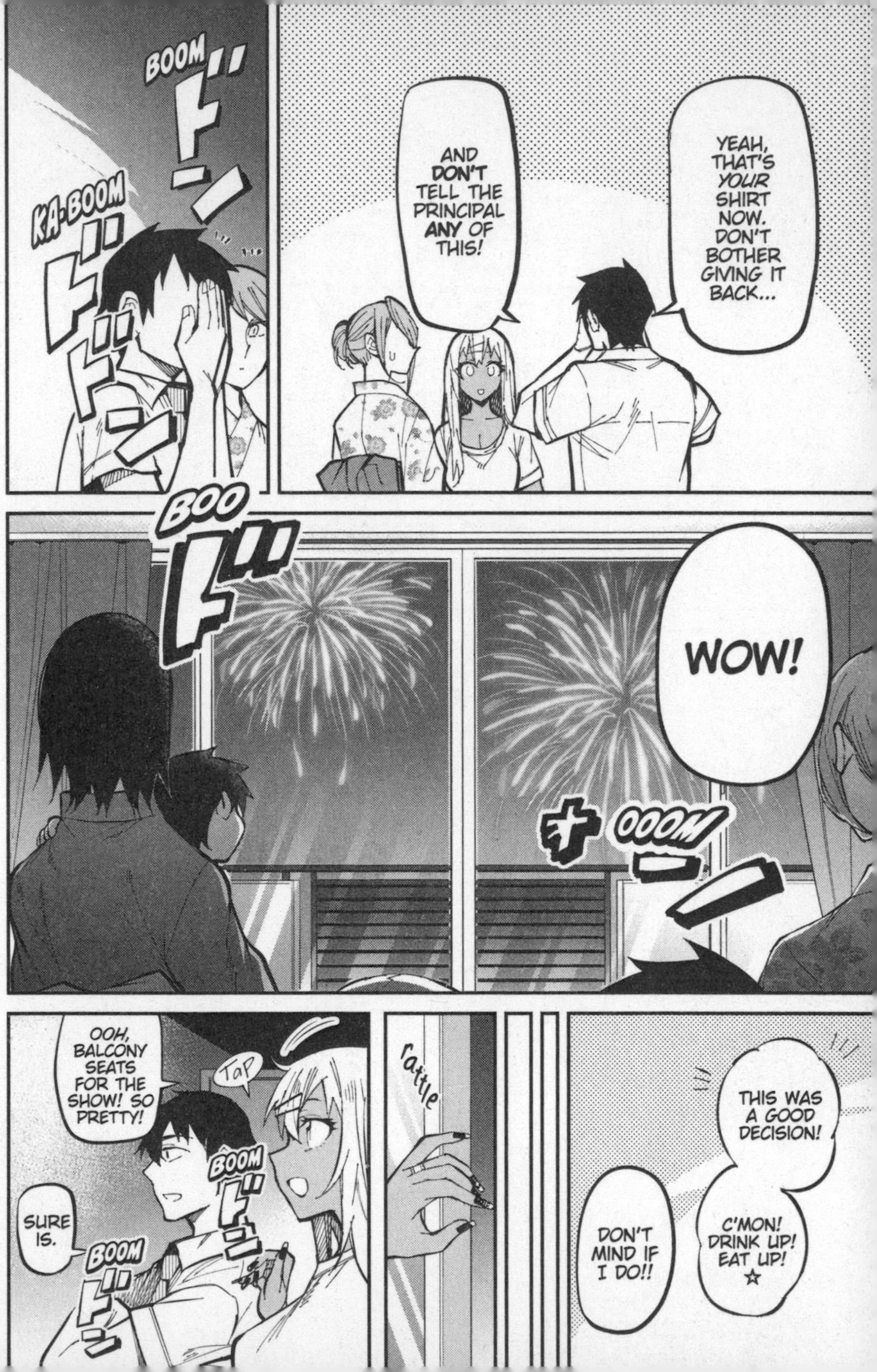
YEAH, THAT'S YOUR SHIRT NOW. DON'T BOTHER GIVING IT BACK...
AND DON'T TELL THE PRINCIPAL ANY OF THIS!
BOOM
KA-BOOM
WOW!
BOO
OOOM
THIS WAS A GOOD DECISION!
C'MON! DRINK UP! EAT UP! ☆
DON'T MIND IF I DO!!
rattle
OOH, BALCONY SEATS FOR THE SHOW! SO PRETTY!
Tap
BOOM
SURE IS.
BOOM

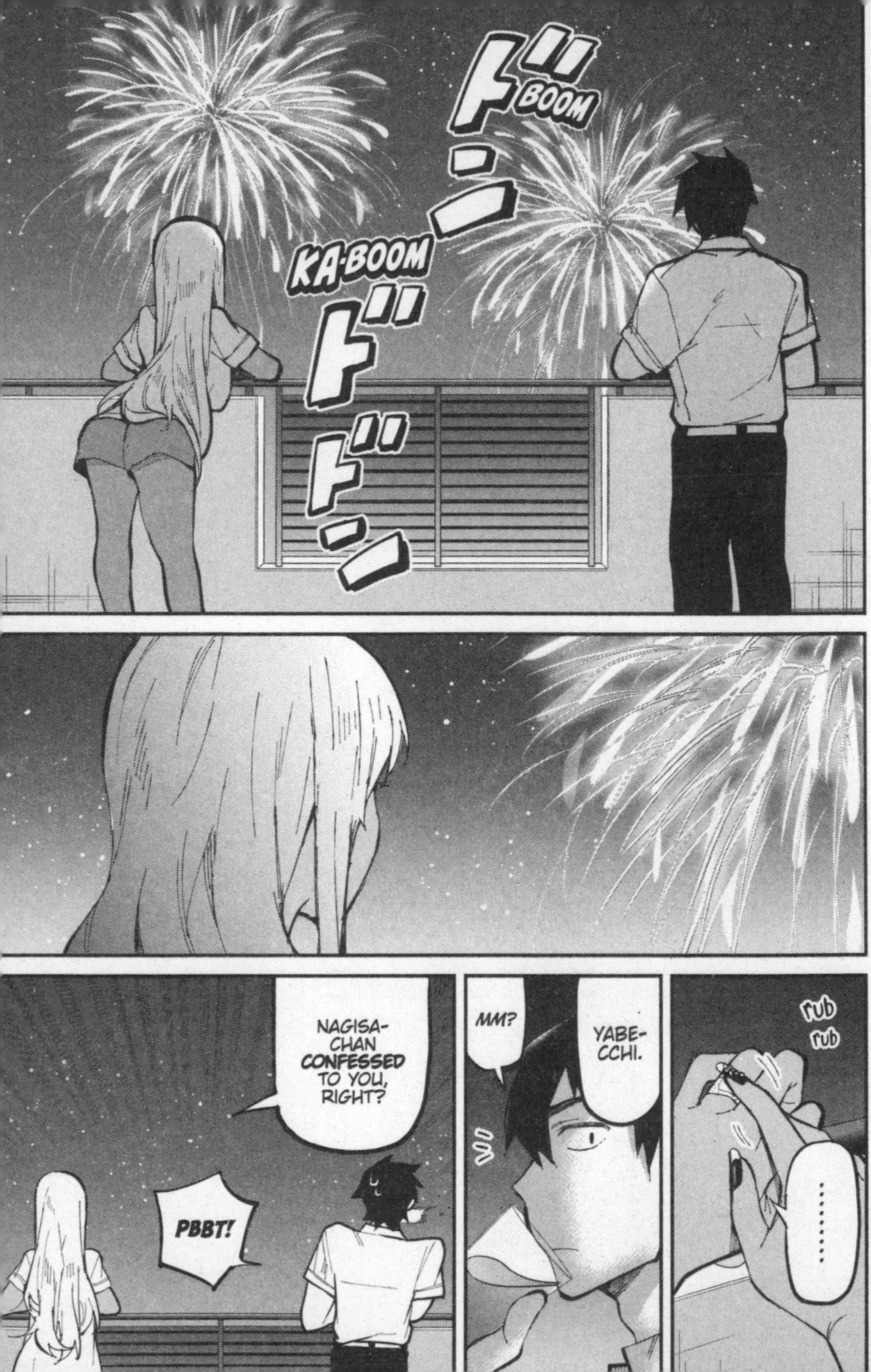
BOOM
KA-BOOM
rub rub
......
YABE-CCHI.
MM?
NAGISA-CHAN CONFESSED TO YOU, RIGHT?
PBBT!

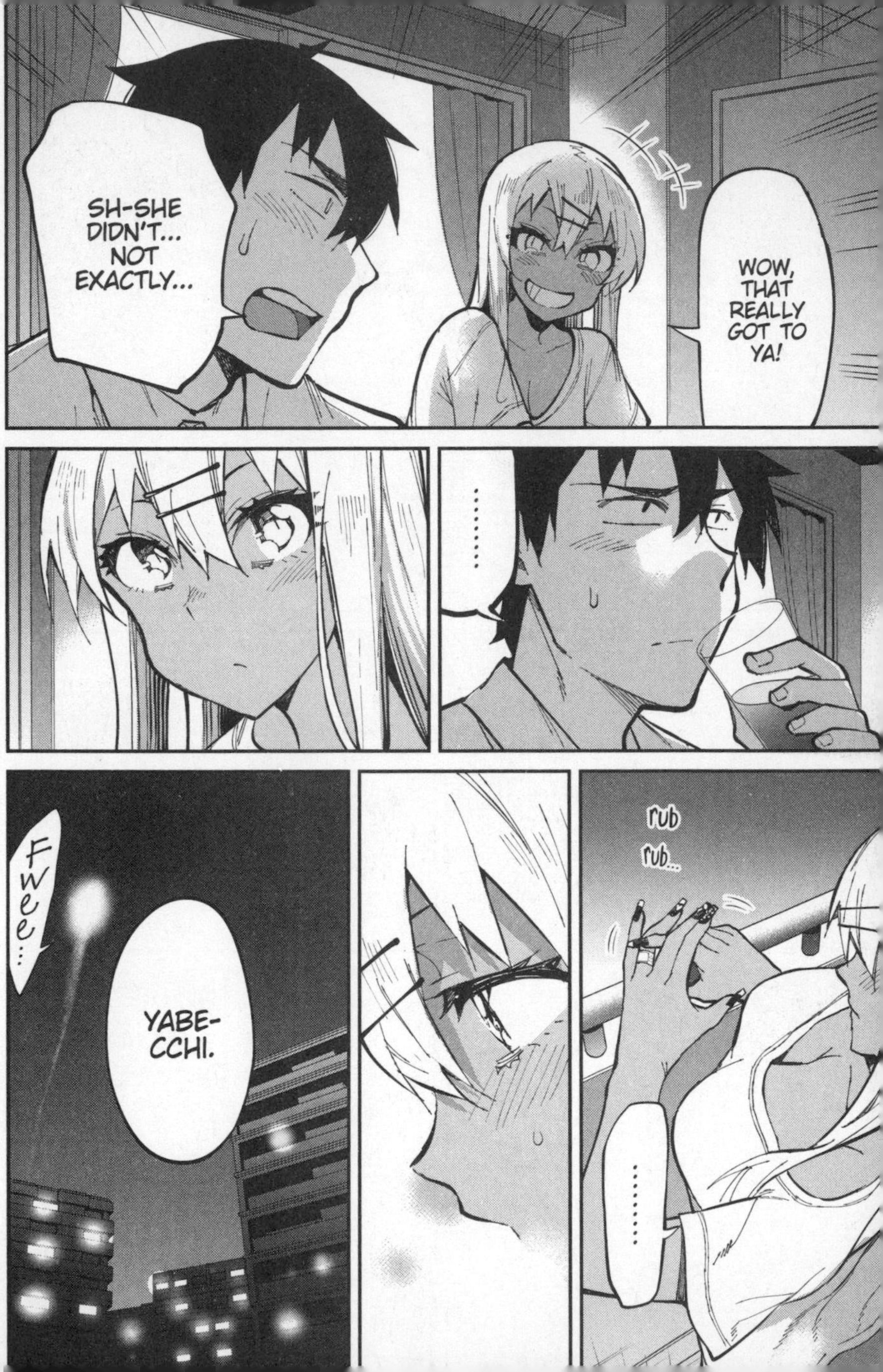
WOW, THAT REALLY GOT TO YA!
SH-SHE DIDN'T... NOT EXACTLY...
......
rub rub...
......
Fwee...
YABE-CCHI.

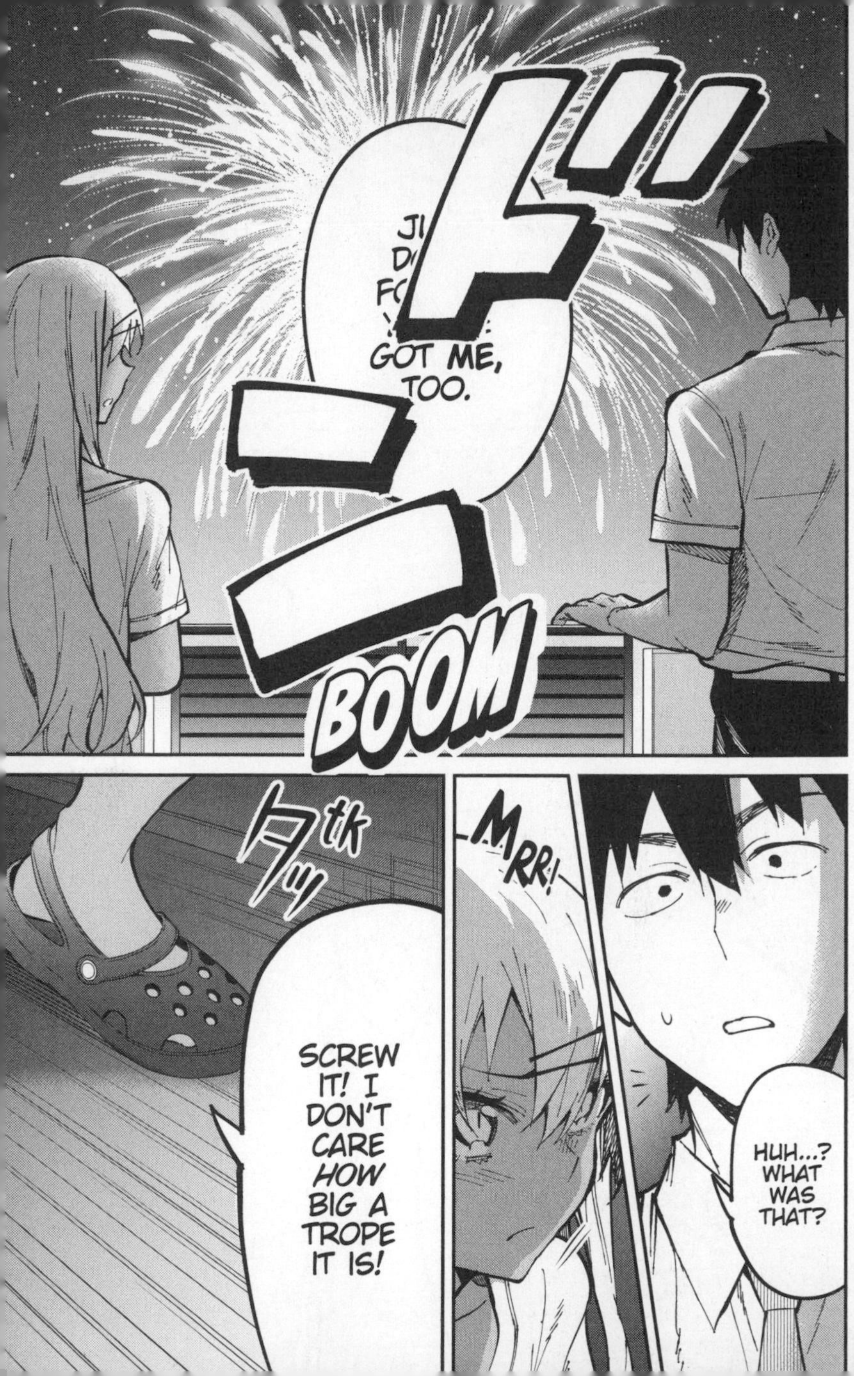
GOT ME, TOO.
BOOM
MRR!
HUH...? WHAT WAS THAT?
tk
SCREW IT! I DON'T CARE *HOW* BIG A TROPE IT IS!

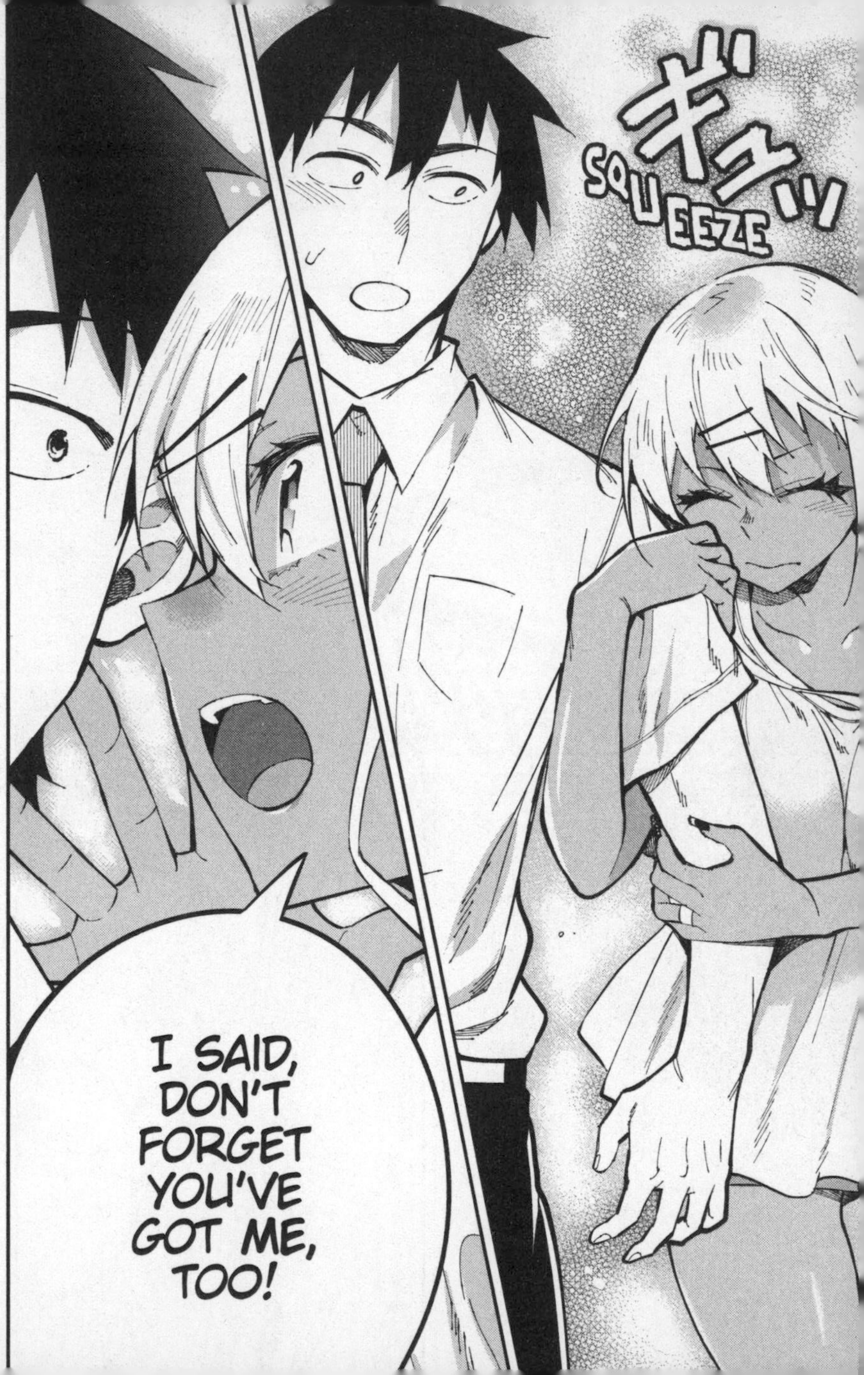
ギュッ SQUEEZE
I SAID, DON'T FORGET YOU'VE GOT ME, TOO!

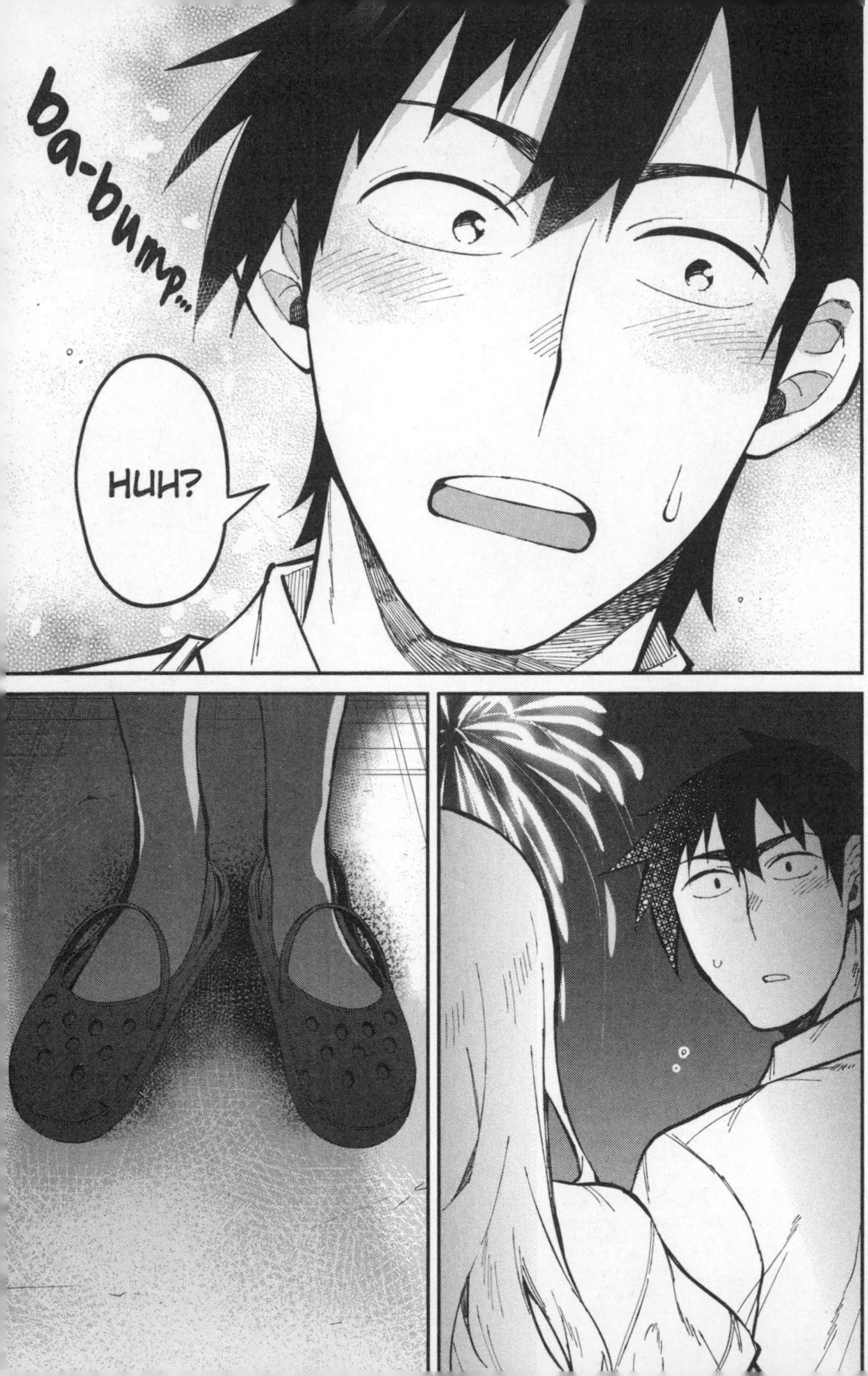
ba-bump...
HUH?

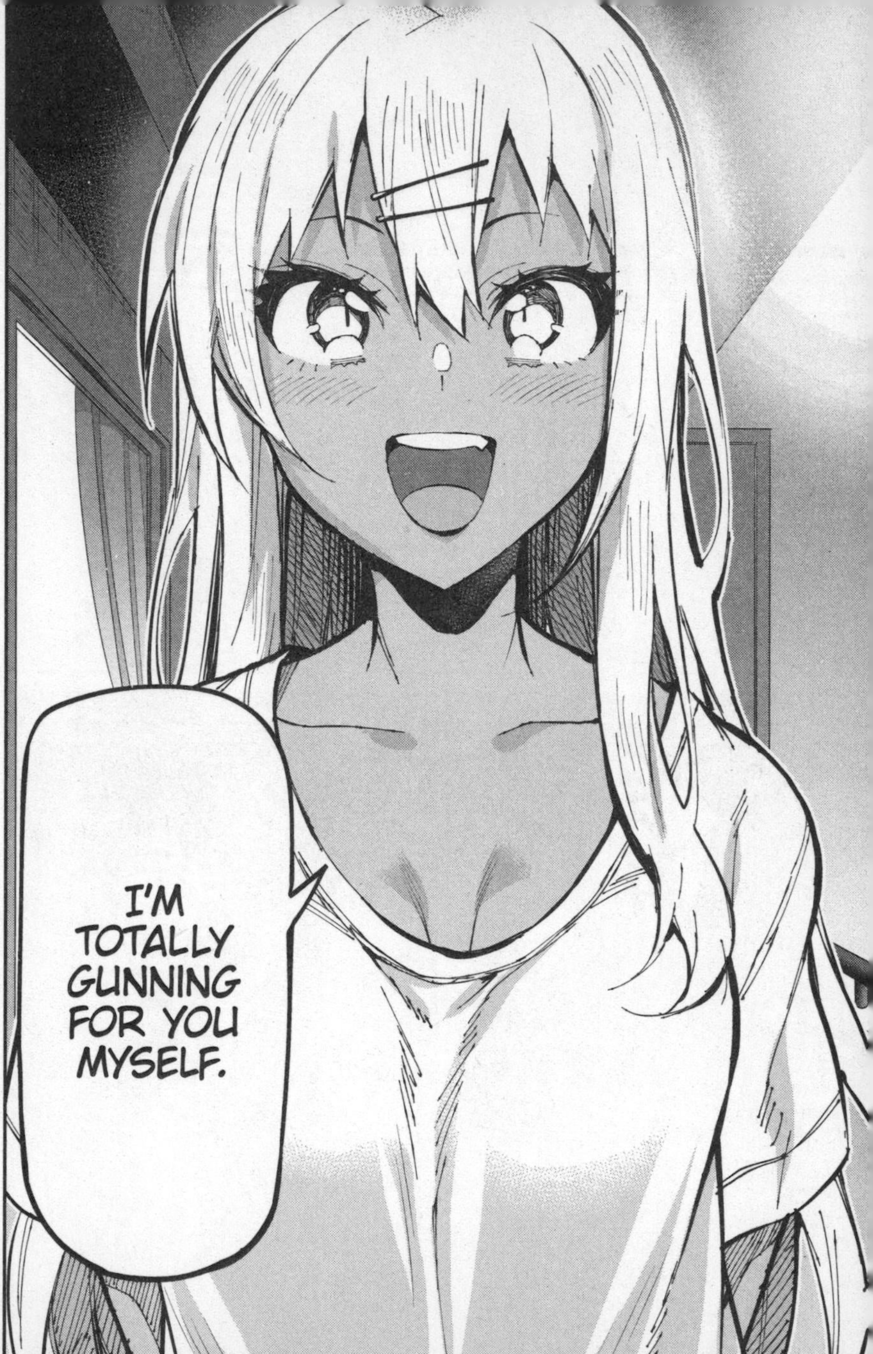
I'M TOTALLY GUNNING FOR YOU MYSELF.

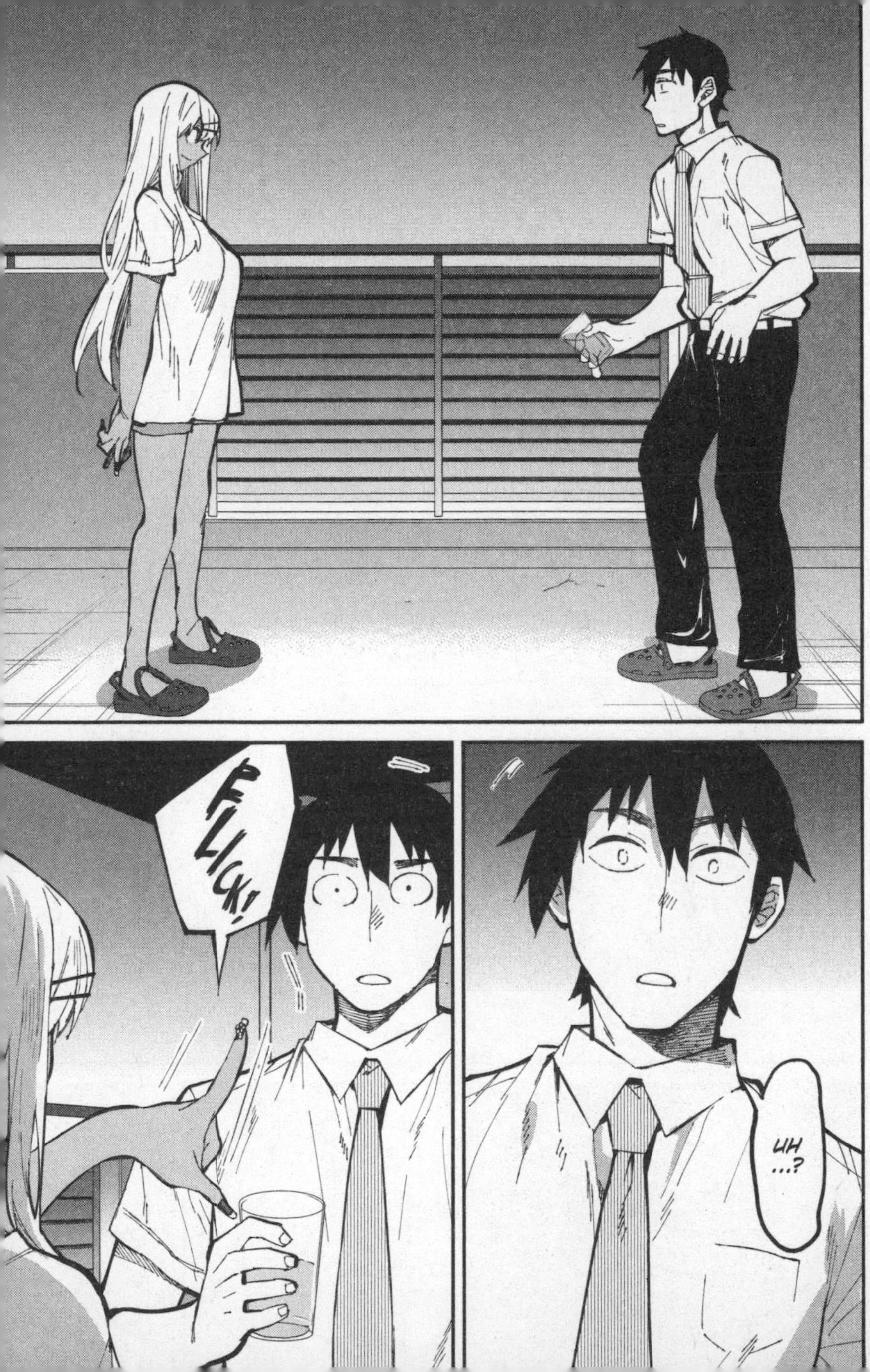
UH ...?
FLICK!

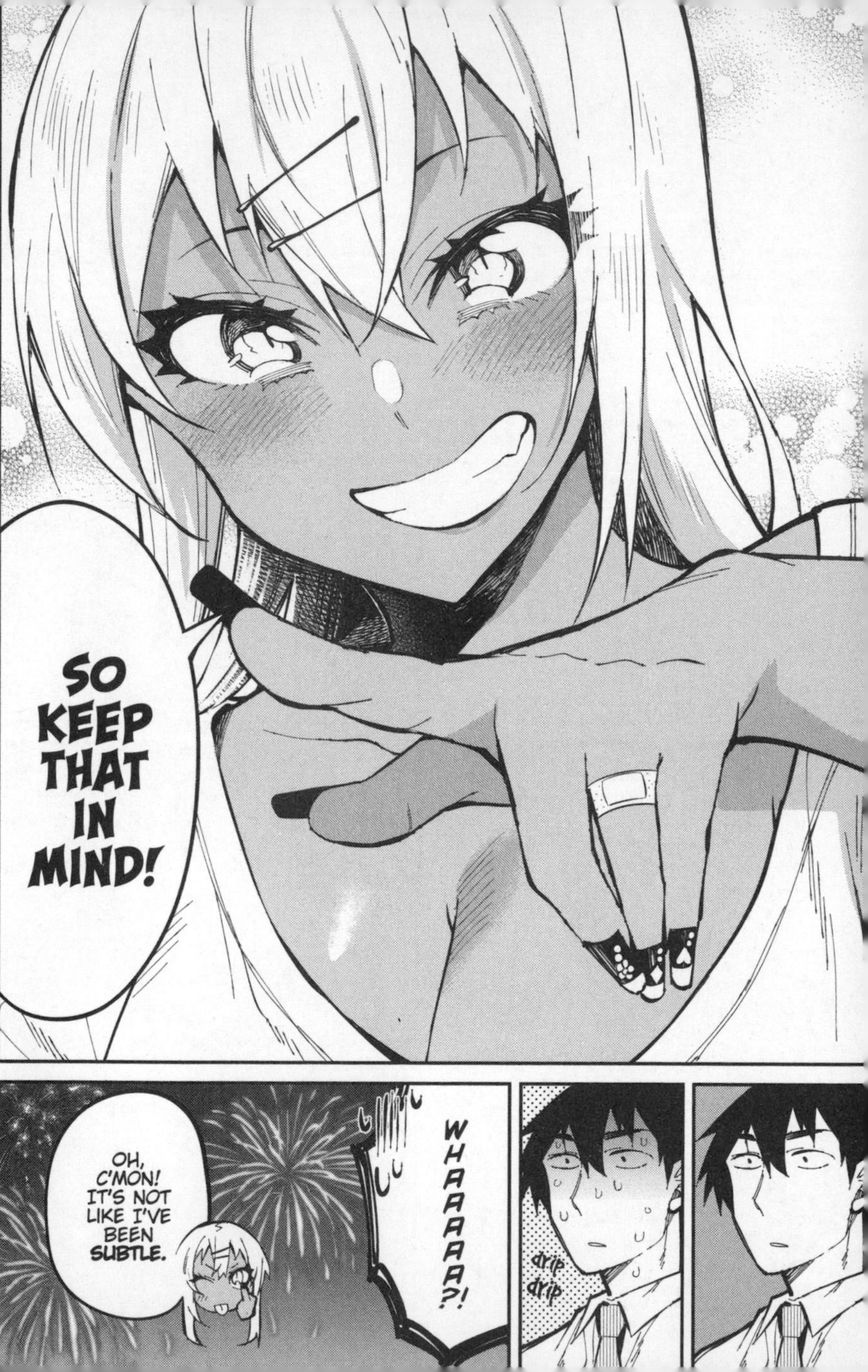
SO KEEP THAT IN MIND!
drip drip
WHAAAAA?!
OH, C'MON! IT'S NOT LIKE I'VE BEEN SUBTLE.

●FUJIWARA KOHARU●

BIRTHDAY: JANUARY 19TH
STAR SIGN: CAPRICORN
BLOOD TYPE: O

Gal
Gohan

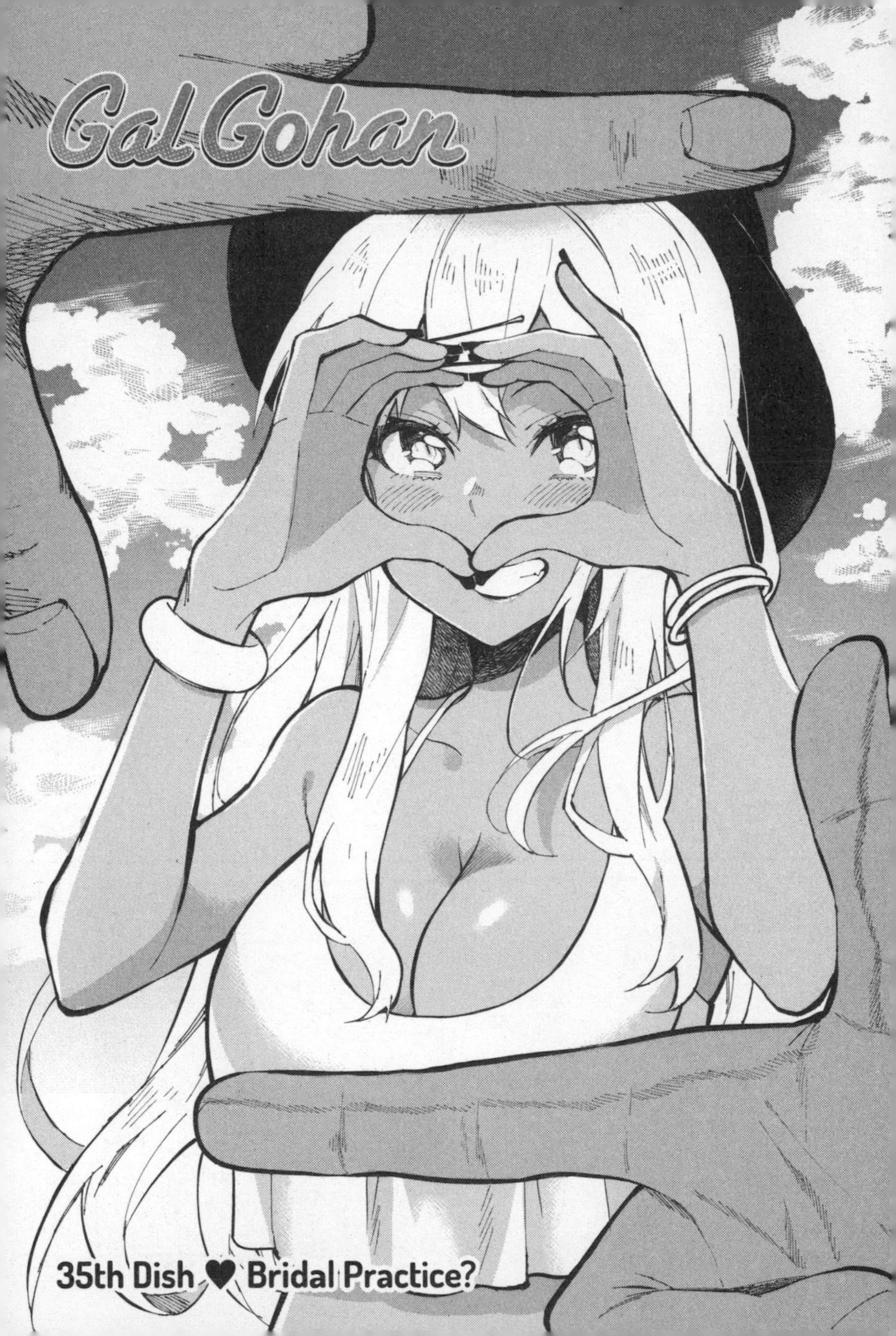
Gal Gohan
35th Dish ♥ Bridal Practice?

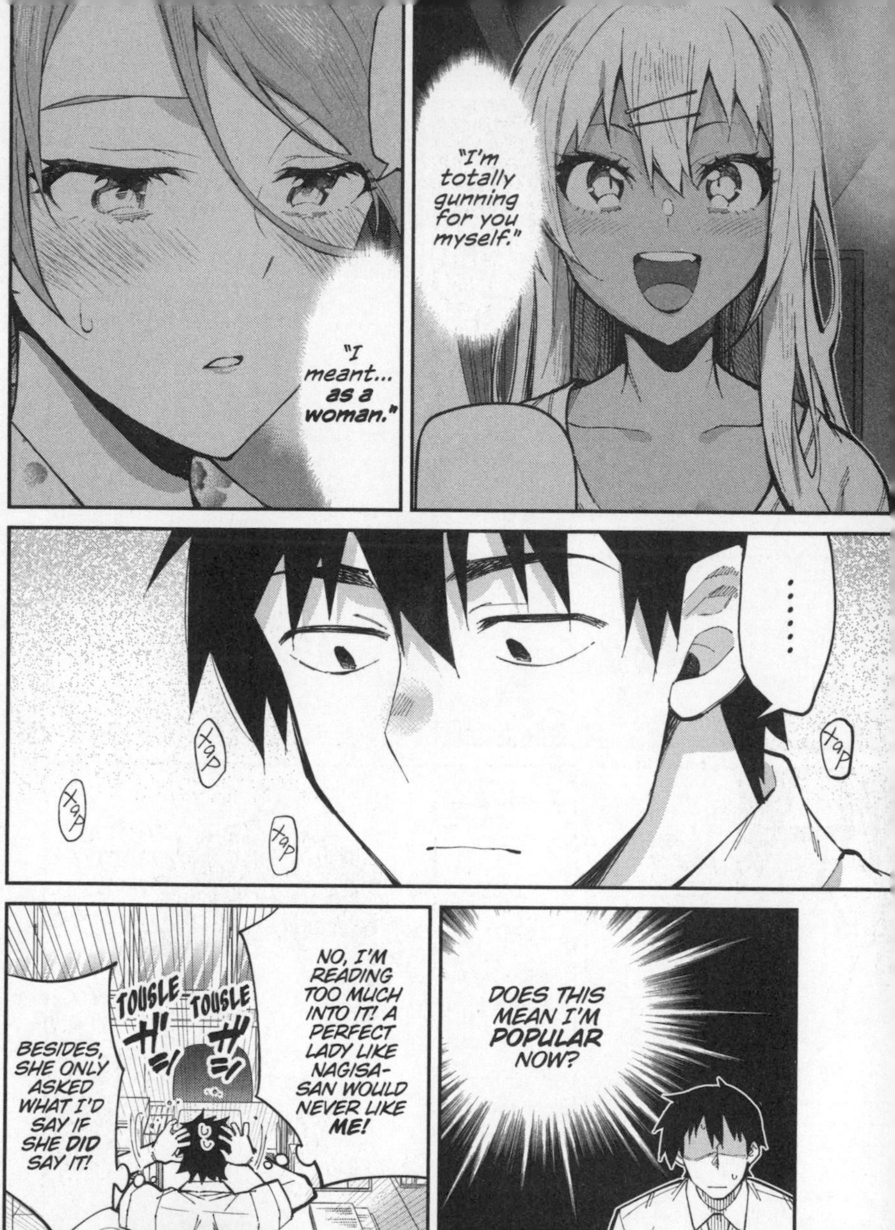
"I'm totally gunning for you myself."
"I meant... as a woman."
......
tap
tap
tap
tap
DOES THIS MEAN I'M POPULAR NOW?
NO, I'M READING TOO MUCH INTO IT! A PERFECT LADY LIKE NAGISA-SAN WOULD NEVER LIKE ME!
TOUSLE
TOUSLE
BESIDES, SHE ONLY ASKED WHAT I'D SAY IF SHE DID SAY IT!

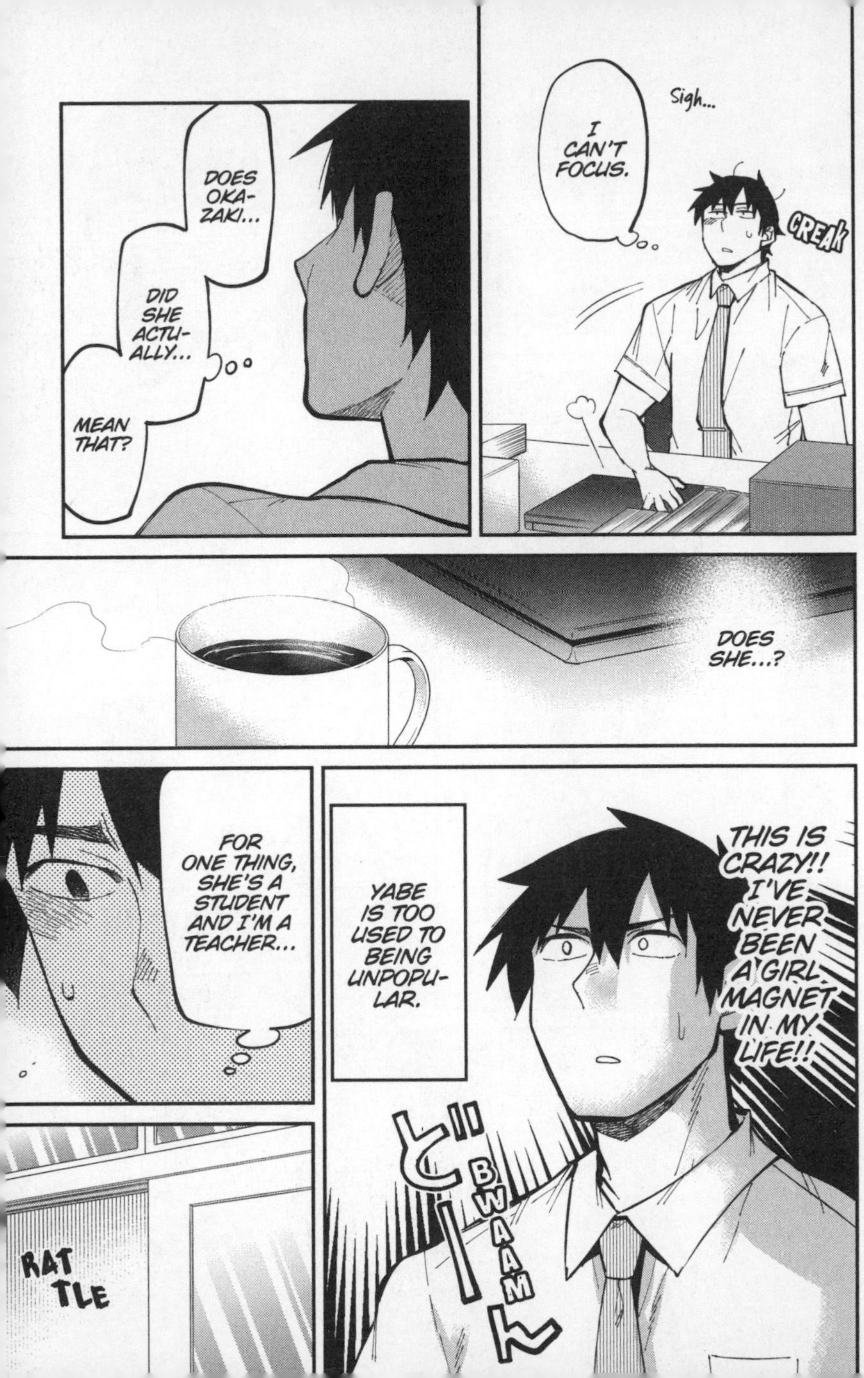
Sigh...
I CAN'T FOCUS.
CREAK
DOES OKAZAKI...
DID SHE ACTUALLY...
MEAN THAT?
DOES SHE...?
THIS IS CRAZY!! I'VE NEVER BEEN A GIRL MAGNET IN MY LIFE!!
YABE IS TOO USED TO BEING UNPOPULAR.
BWAAAM
FOR ONE THING, SHE'S A STUDENT AND I'M A TEACHER...
RATTLE

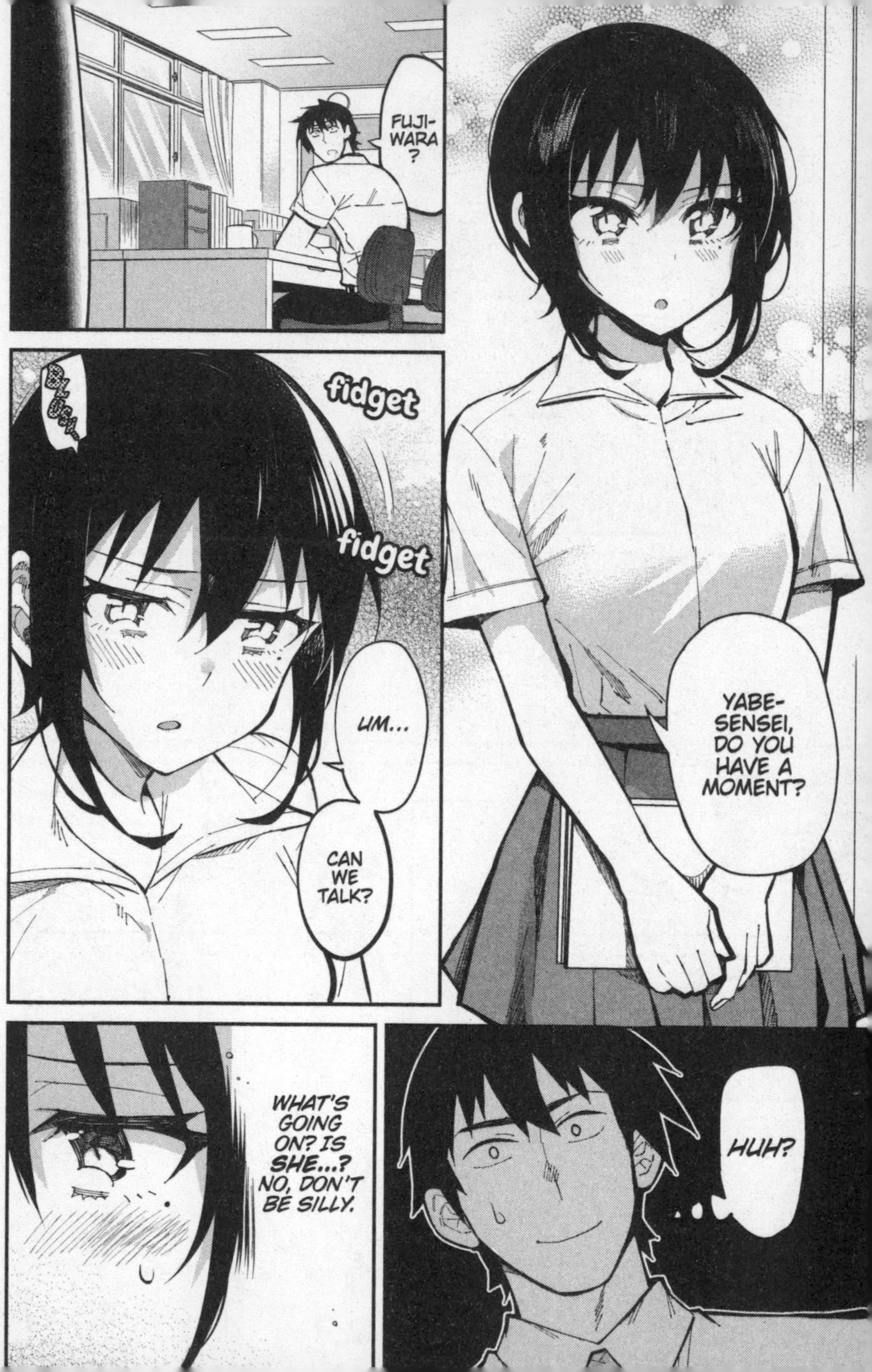
YABE-SENSEI, DO YOU HAVE A MOMENT?
FUJI-WARA?
fidget
fidget
UM...
CAN WE TALK?
HUH?
...
WHAT'S GOING ON? IS SHE...? NO, DON'T BE SILLY.

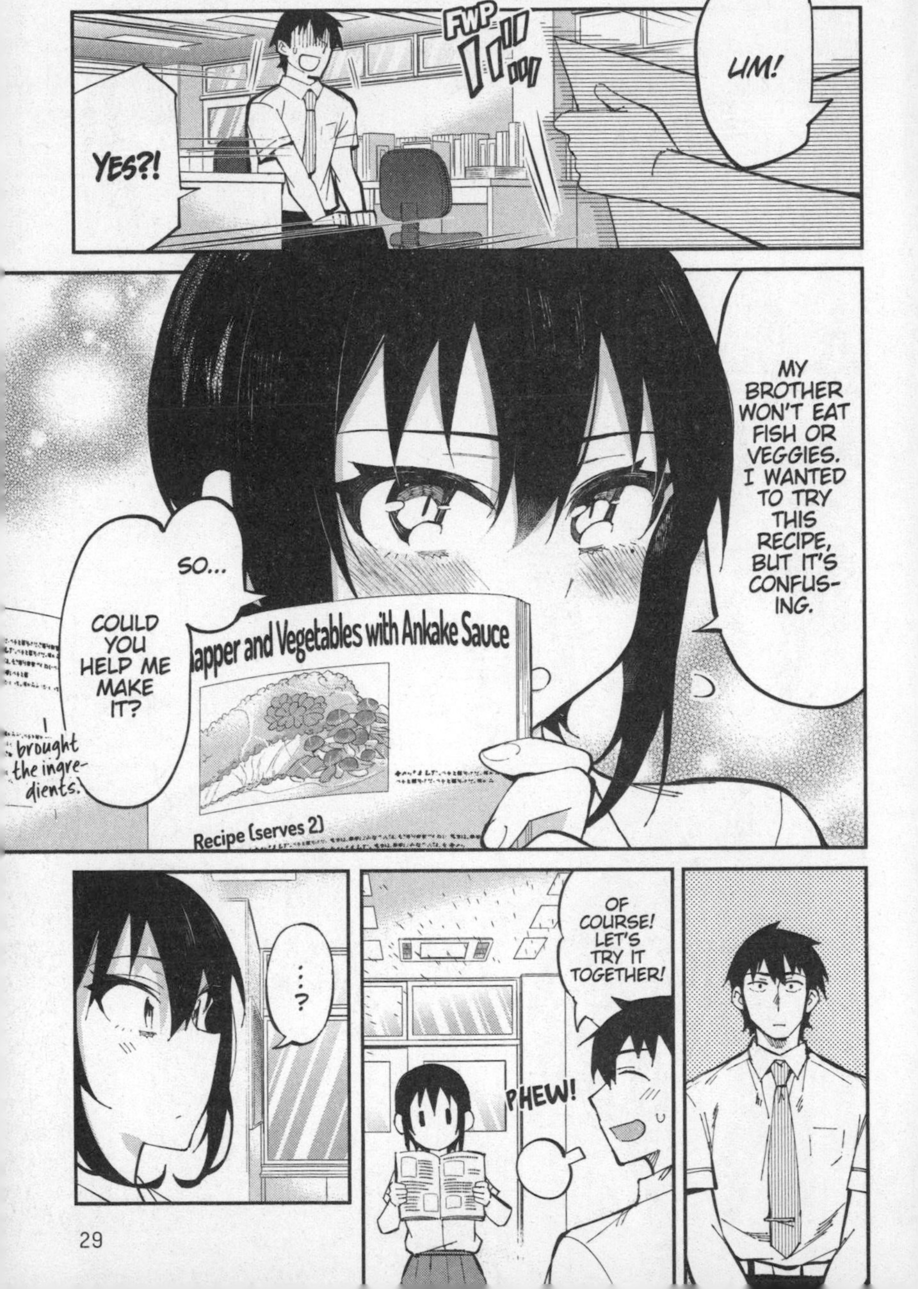
UM!
FWP
YES?!
MY BROTHER WON'T EAT FISH OR VEGGIES. I WANTED TO TRY THIS RECIPE, BUT IT'S CONFUSING.
SO...
COULD YOU HELP ME MAKE IT?
I brought the ingredients.
apper and Vegetables with Ankake Sauce
Recipe (serves 2)
OF COURSE! LET'S TRY IT TOGETHER!
PHEW!
...?

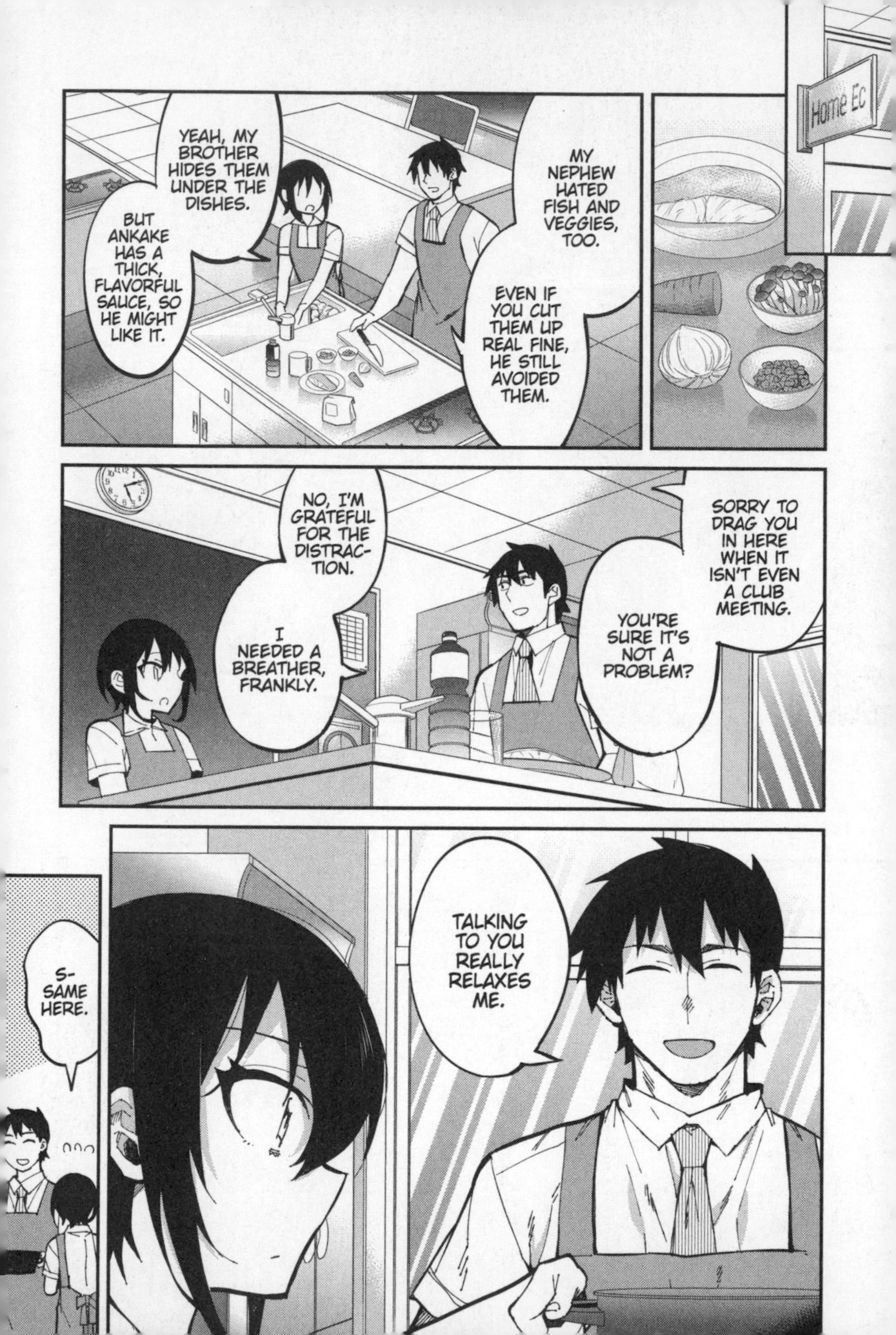
Home Ec
MY NEPHEW HATED FISH AND VEGGIES, TOO.
EVEN IF YOU CUT THEM UP REAL FINE, HE STILL AVOIDED THEM.
YEAH, MY BROTHER HIDES THEM UNDER THE DISHES.
BUT ANKAKE HAS A THICK, FLAVORFUL SAUCE, SO HE MIGHT LIKE IT.
SORRY TO DRAG YOU IN HERE WHEN IT ISN'T EVEN A CLUB MEETING.
YOU'RE SURE IT'S NOT A PROBLEM?
NO, I'M GRATEFUL FOR THE DISTRAC-TION.
I NEEDED A BREATHER, FRANKLY.
TALKING TO YOU REALLY RELAXES ME.
S-SAME HERE.

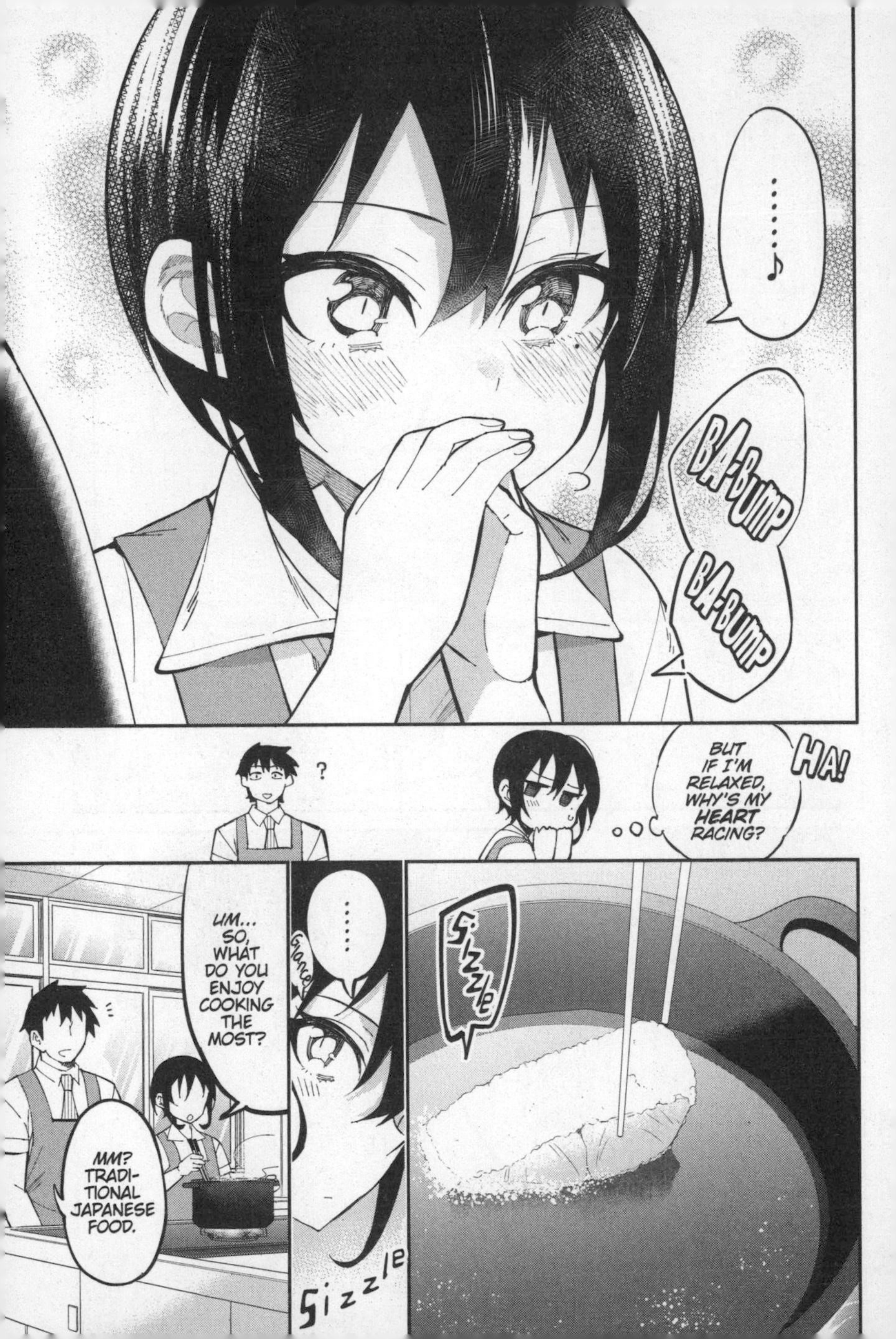
......♪
BA-BUMP
BA-BUMP
HA!
BUT IF I'M RELAXED, WHY'S MY HEART RACING?
?
Sizzle
Glance
......
UM... SO, WHAT DO YOU ENJOY COOKING THE MOST?
MM? TRADI-TIONAL JAPANESE FOOD.
Sizzle

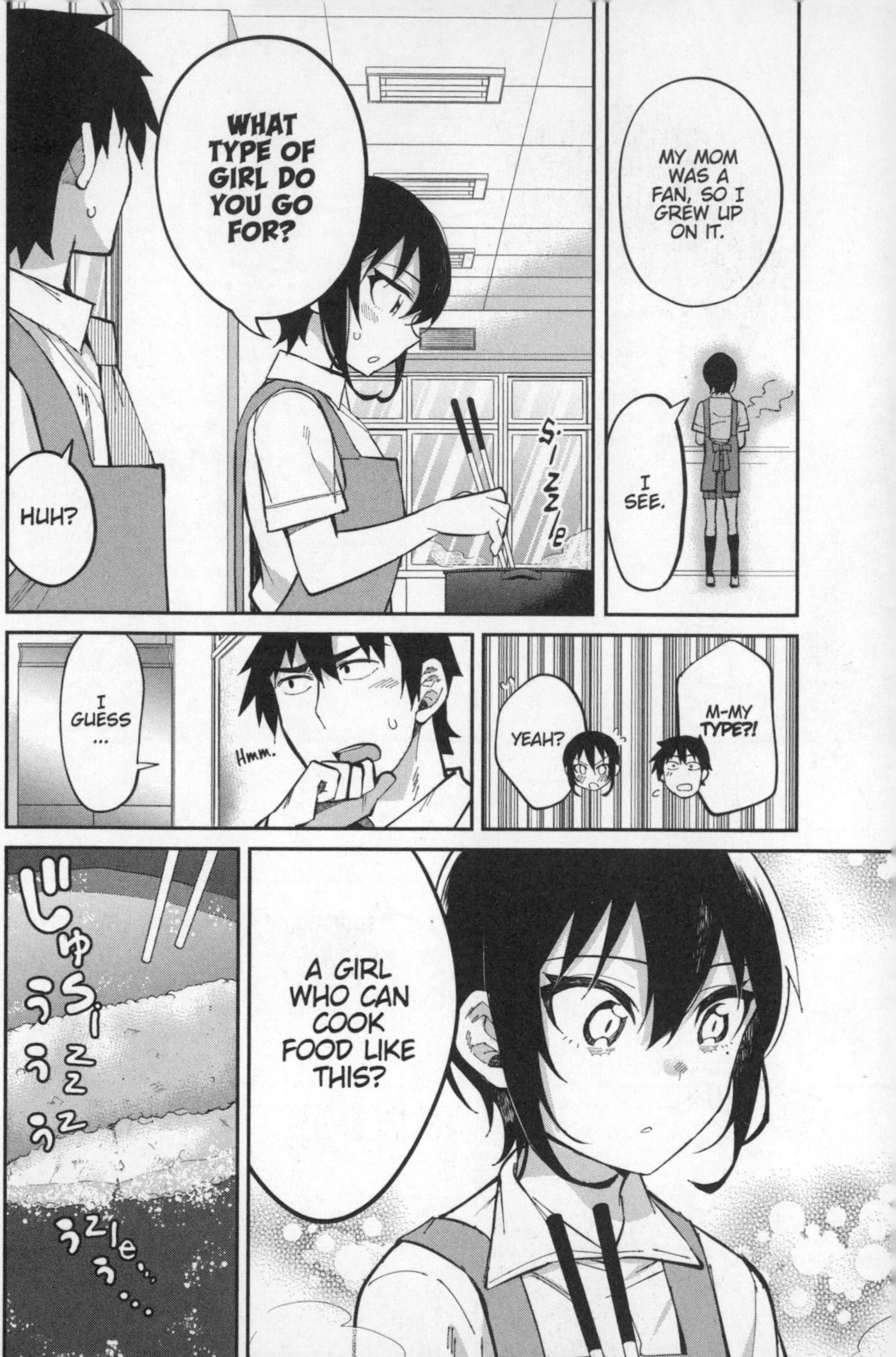
MY MOM WAS A FAN, SO I GREW UP ON IT.
I SEE.
WHAT TYPE OF GIRL DO YOU GO FOR?
SIZZLE
HUH?
M-MY TYPE?!
YEAH?
I GUESS ...
Hmm.
A GIRL WHO CAN COOK FOOD LIKE THIS?
Sizzzle...

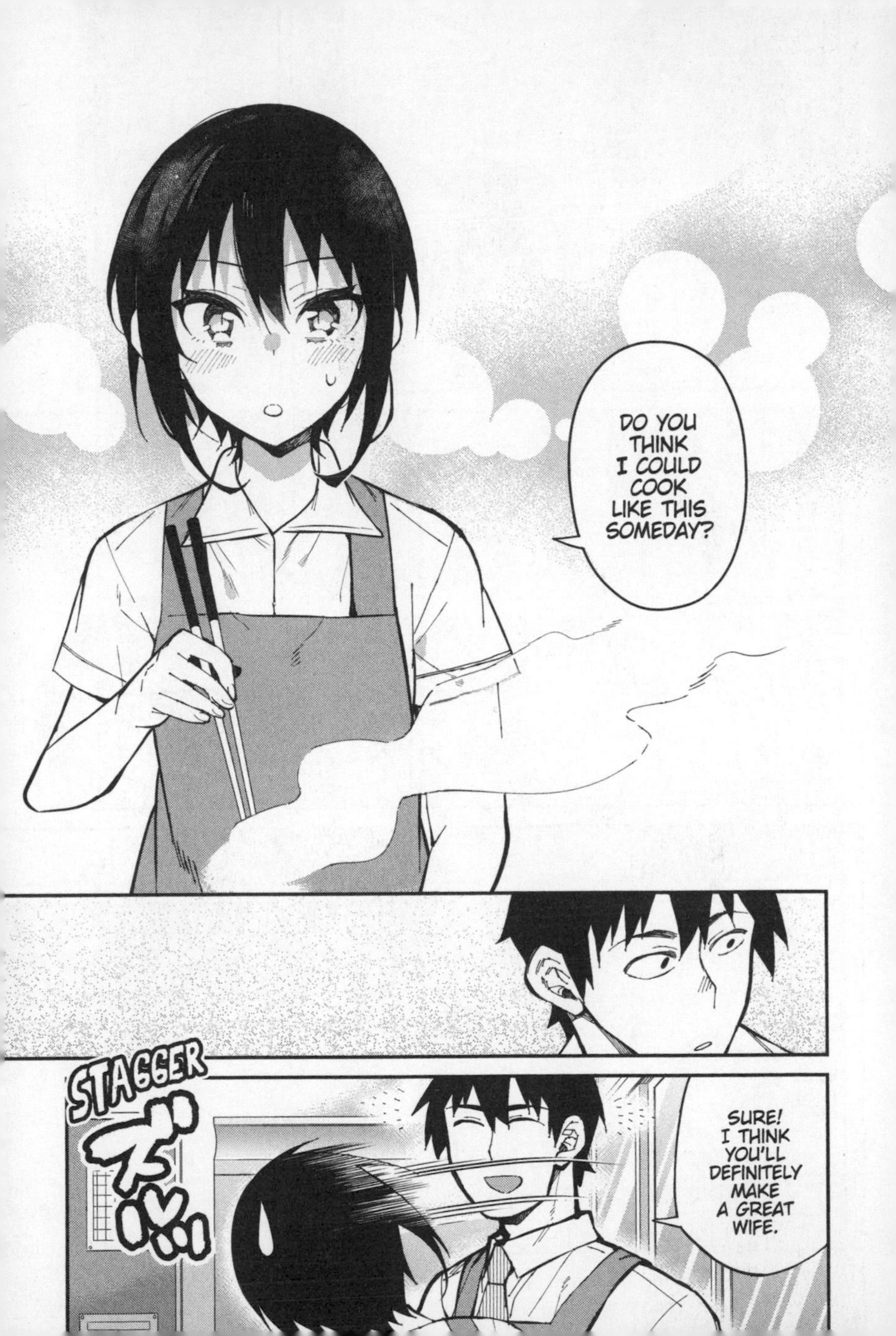
DO YOU THINK I COULD COOK LIKE THIS SOMEDAY?
SURE! I THINK YOU'LL DEFINITELY MAKE A GREAT WIFE.
STAGGER

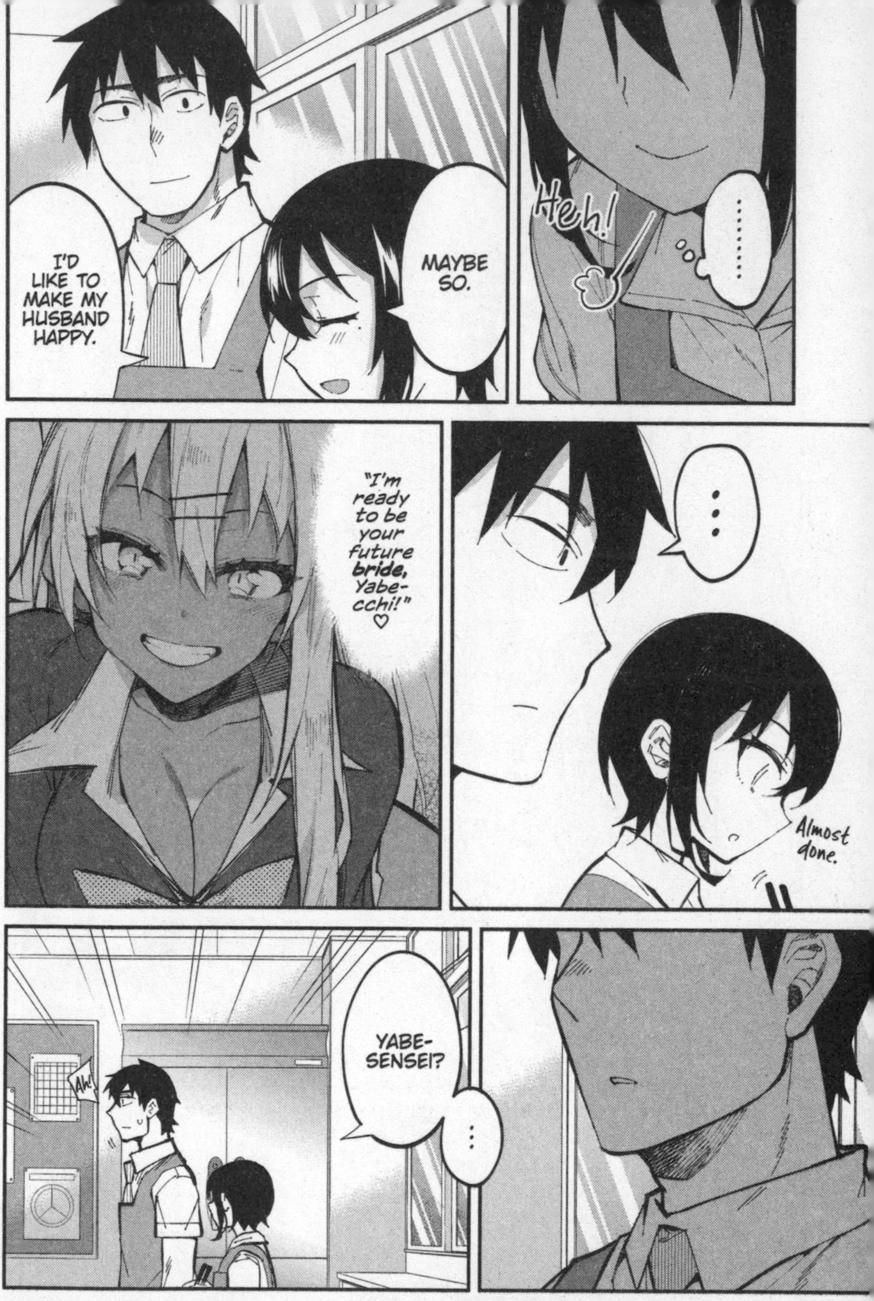

Heh!
......
MAYBE SO.
I'D LIKE TO MAKE MY HUSBAND HAPPY.
...
Almost done.
"I'm ready to be your future bride, Yabe-cchi!" ♡
YABE-SENSEI?
...
AW!

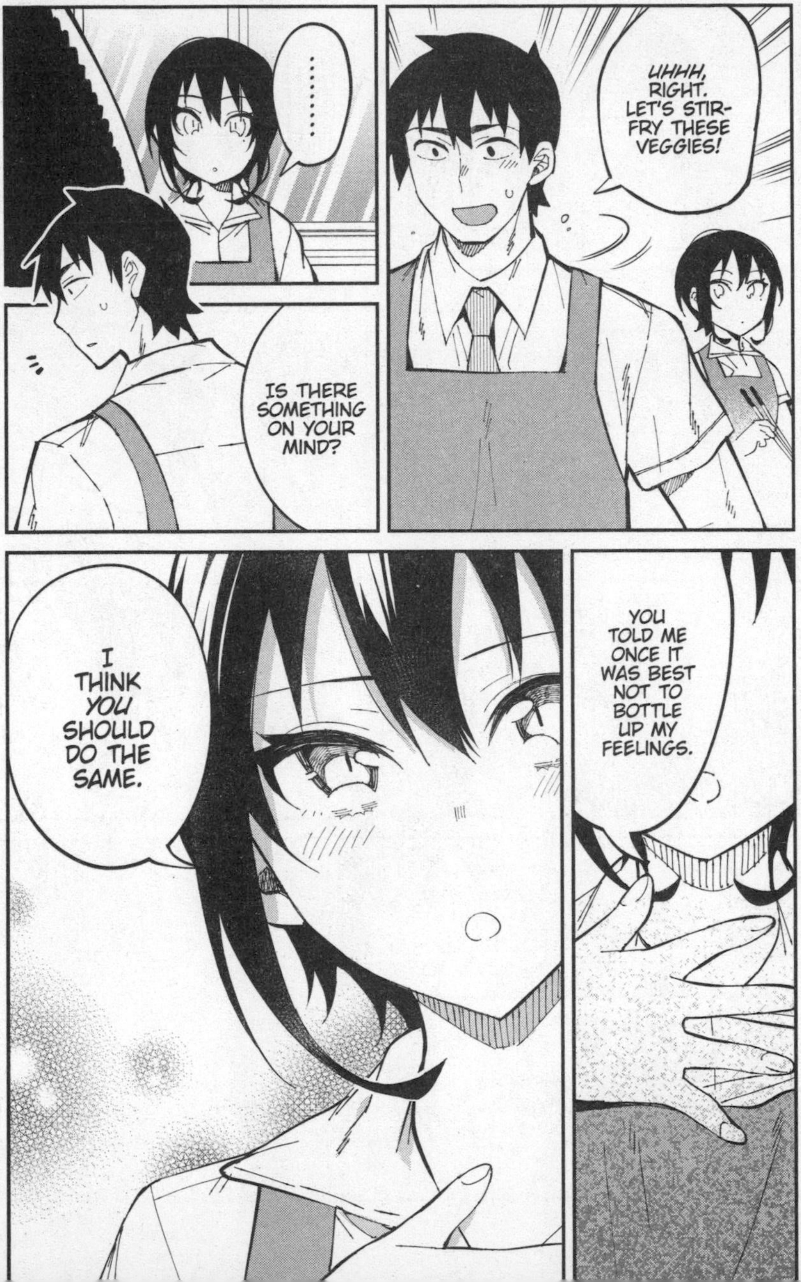
UHHH, RIGHT. LET'S STIR-FRY THESE VEGGIES!
......
IS THERE SOMETHING ON YOUR MIND?
YOU TOLD ME ONCE IT WAS BEST NOT TO BOTTLE UP MY FEELINGS.
I THINK *YOU* SHOULD DO THE SAME.

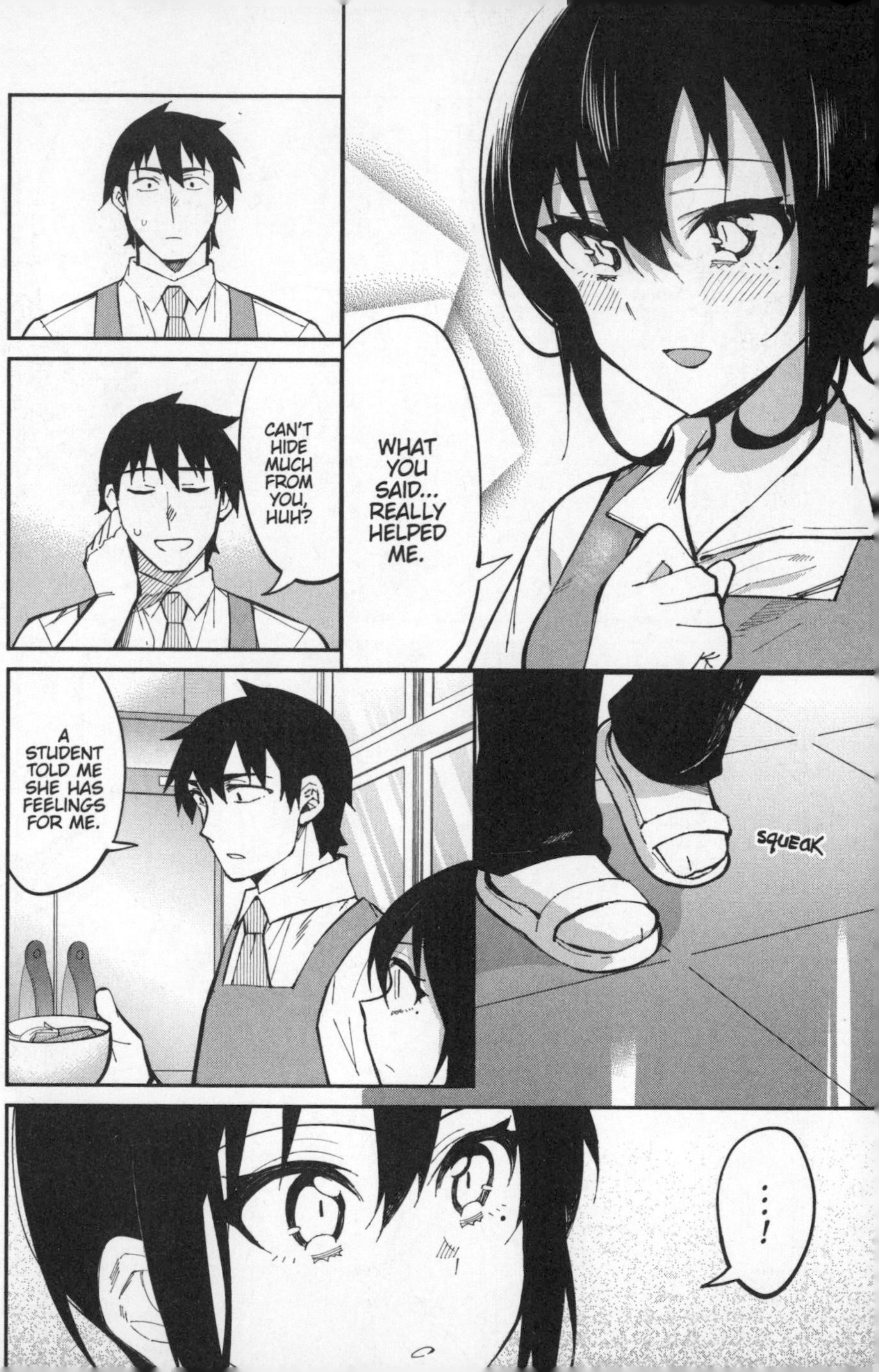
WHAT YOU SAID... REALLY HELPED ME.
CAN'T HIDE MUCH FROM YOU, HUH?
squeak
A STUDENT TOLD ME SHE HAS FEELINGS FOR ME.
...!

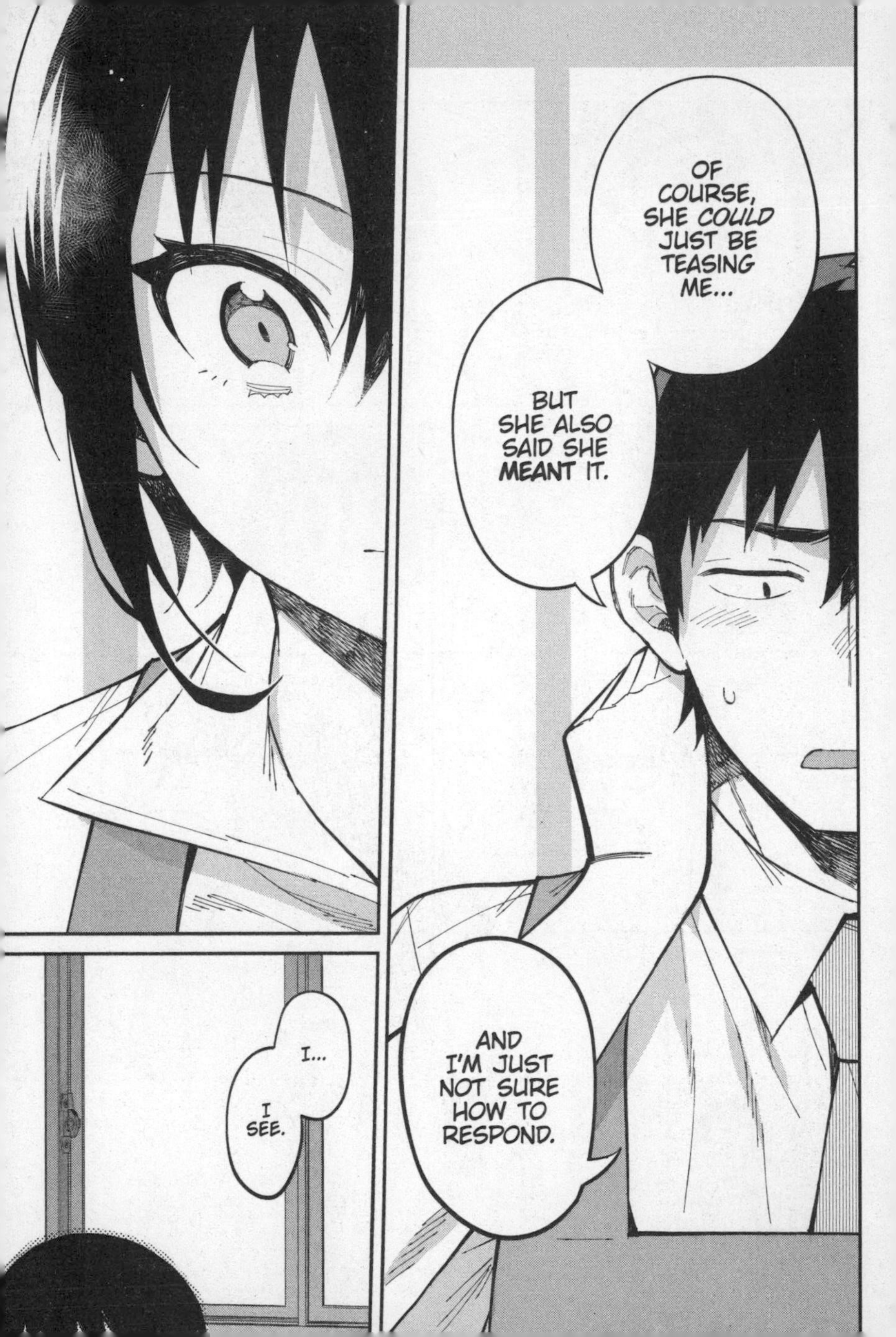
OF COURSE, SHE COULD JUST BE TEASING ME...
BUT SHE ALSO SAID SHE MEANT IT.
AND I'M JUST NOT SURE HOW TO RESPOND.
I...
I SEE.

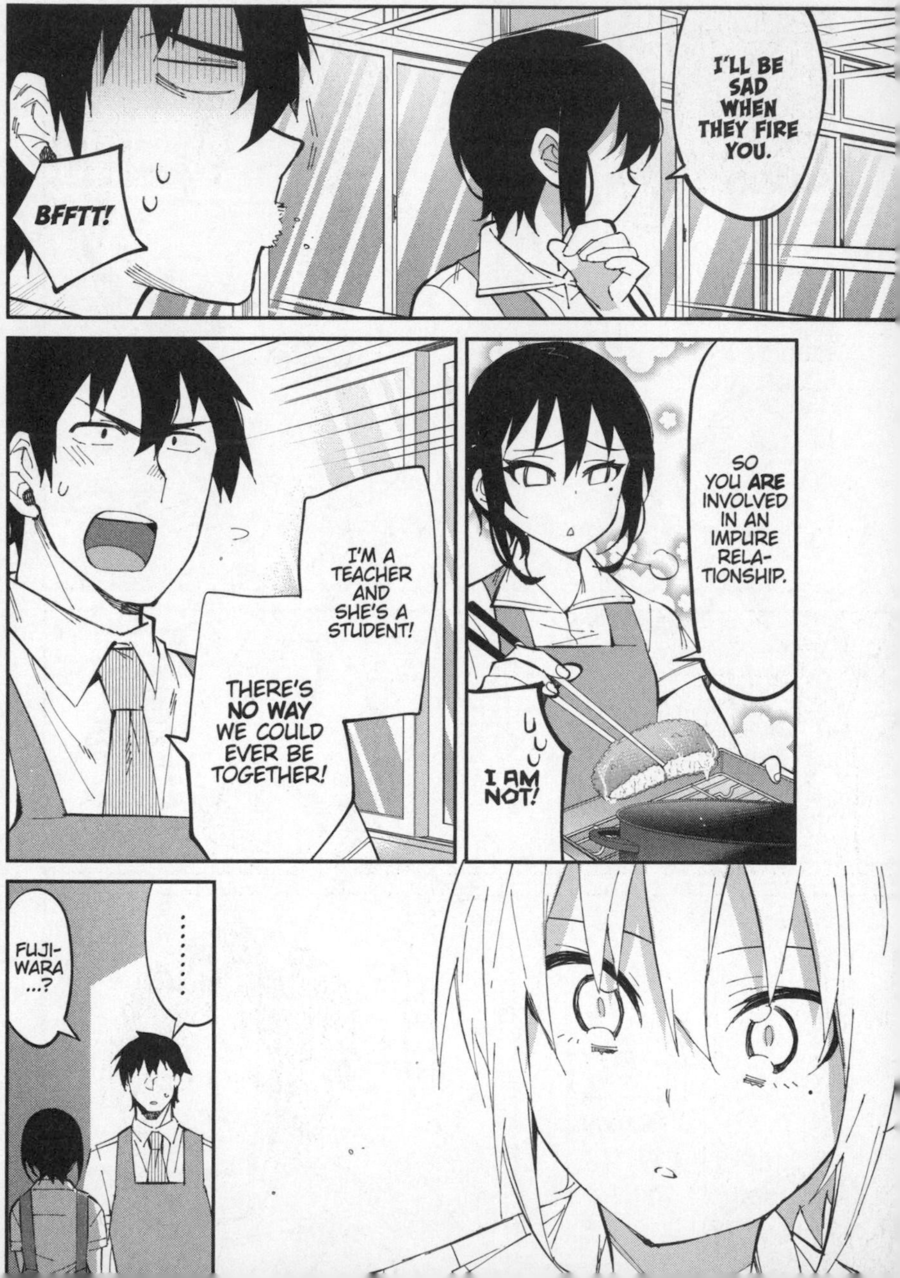
I'LL BE SAD WHEN THEY FIRE YOU.
BFFTT!
SO YOU ARE INVOLVED IN AN IMPURE RELA-TIONSHIP.
I AM NOT!
I'M A TEACHER AND SHE'S A STUDENT!
THERE'S NO WAY WE COULD EVER BE TOGETHER!
......
FUJI-WARA ...?

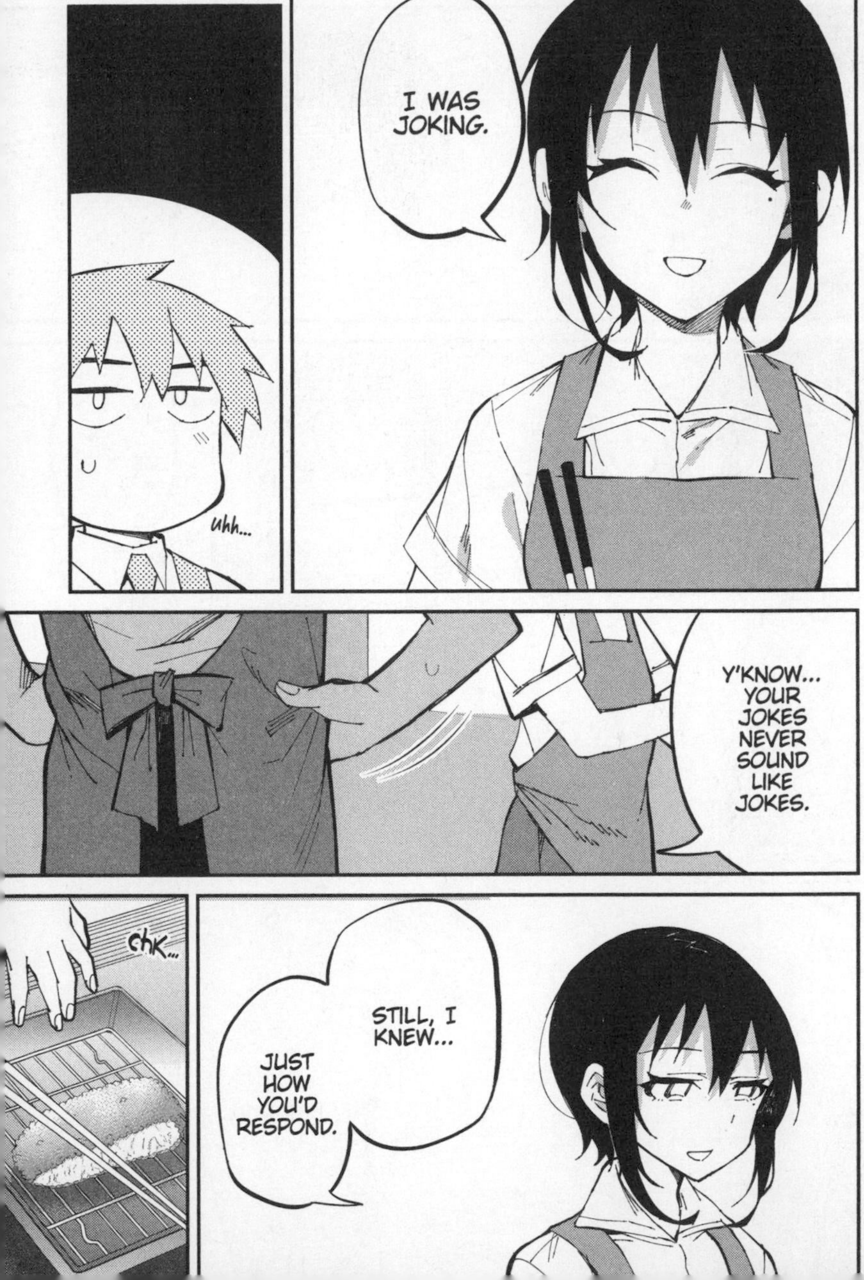
I WAS JOKING.
uhh...
Y'KNOW... YOUR JOKES NEVER SOUND LIKE JOKES.
STILL, I KNEW...
JUST HOW YOU'D RESPOND.
chk...

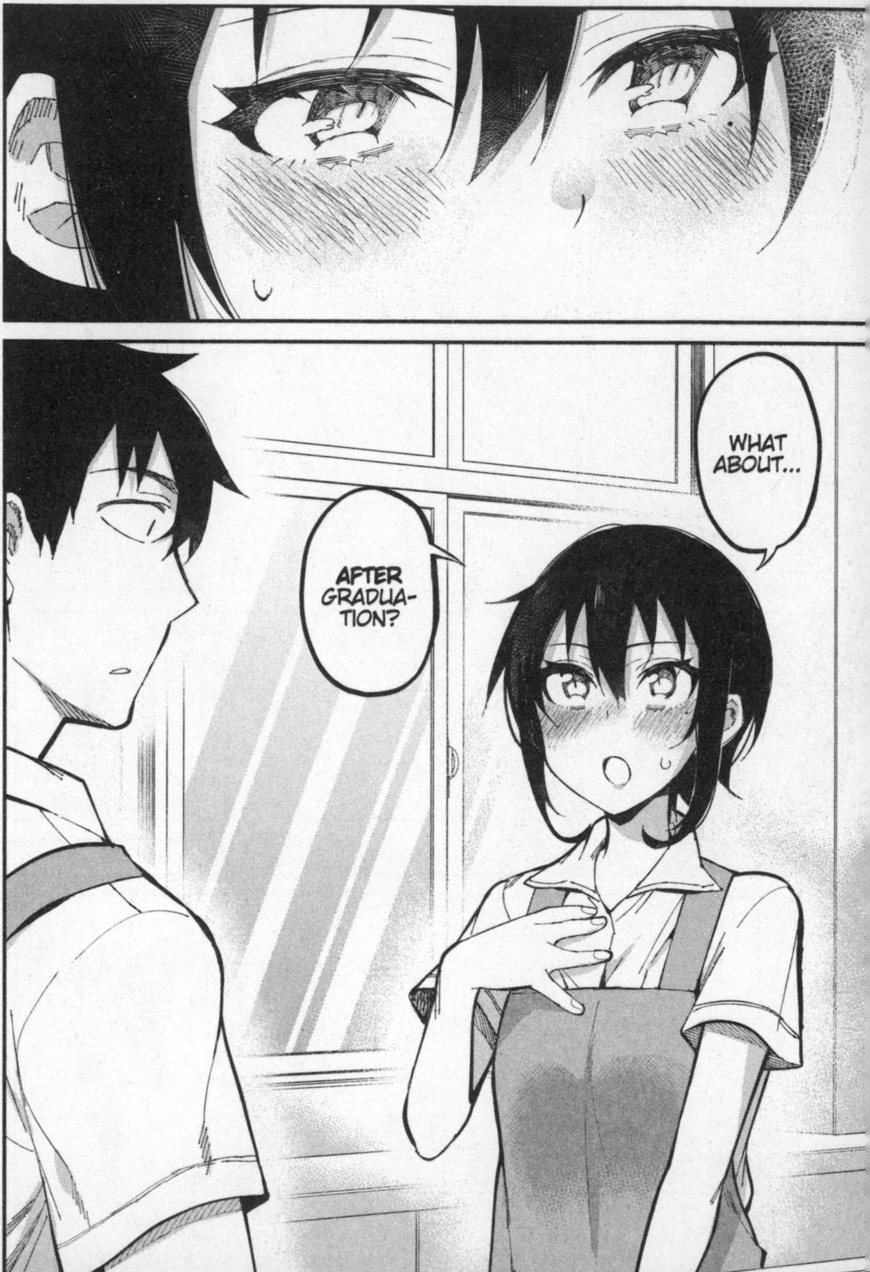
WHAT ABOUT...
AFTER GRADUA-TION?

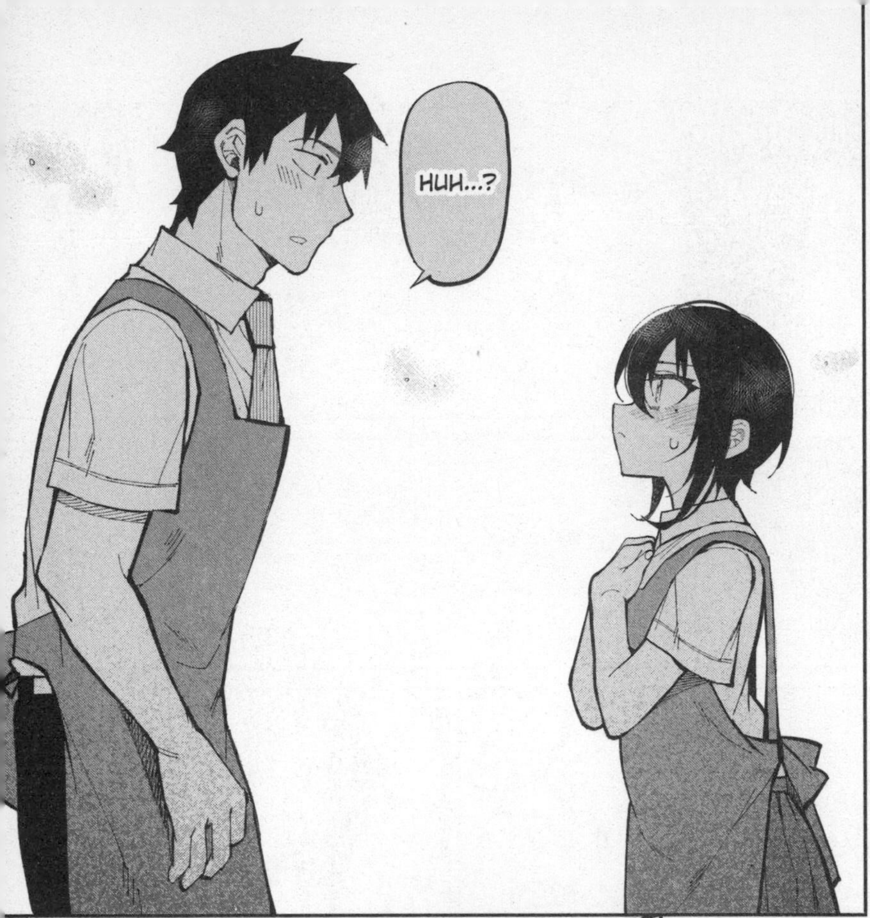
HUH...?

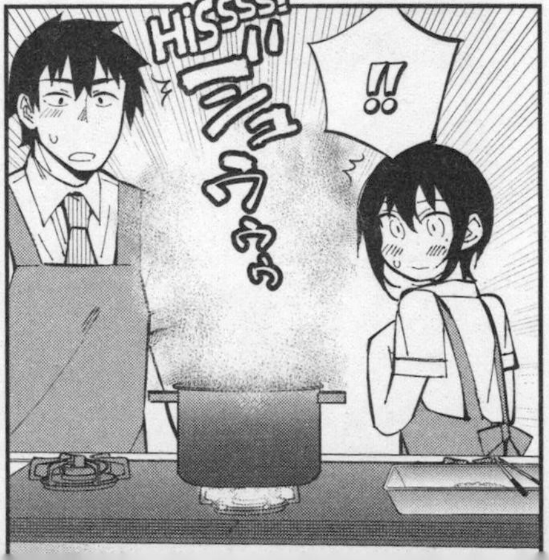
HiSSSS!
!!

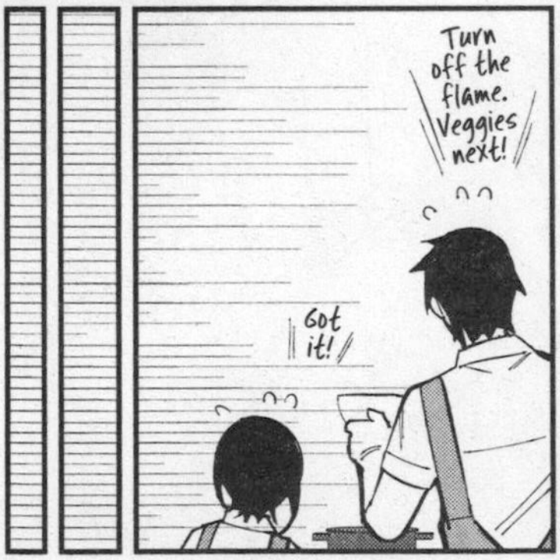
Turn off the flame. Veggies next!
Got it!

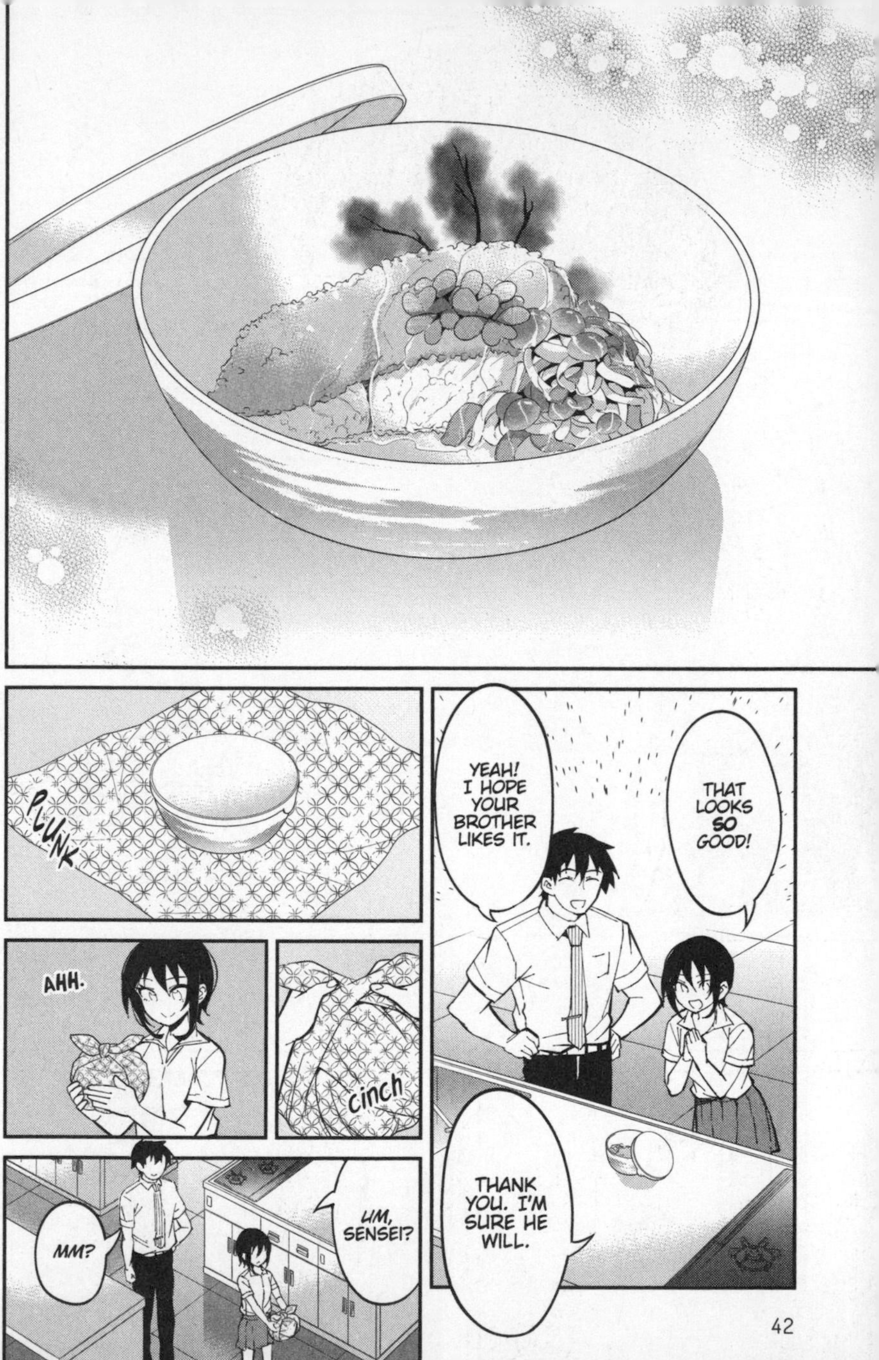
THAT LOOKS SO GOOD!
YEAH! I HOPE YOUR BROTHER LIKES IT.
THANK YOU. I'M SURE HE WILL.
PLUNK
cinch
AHH.
UM, SENSEI?
MM?

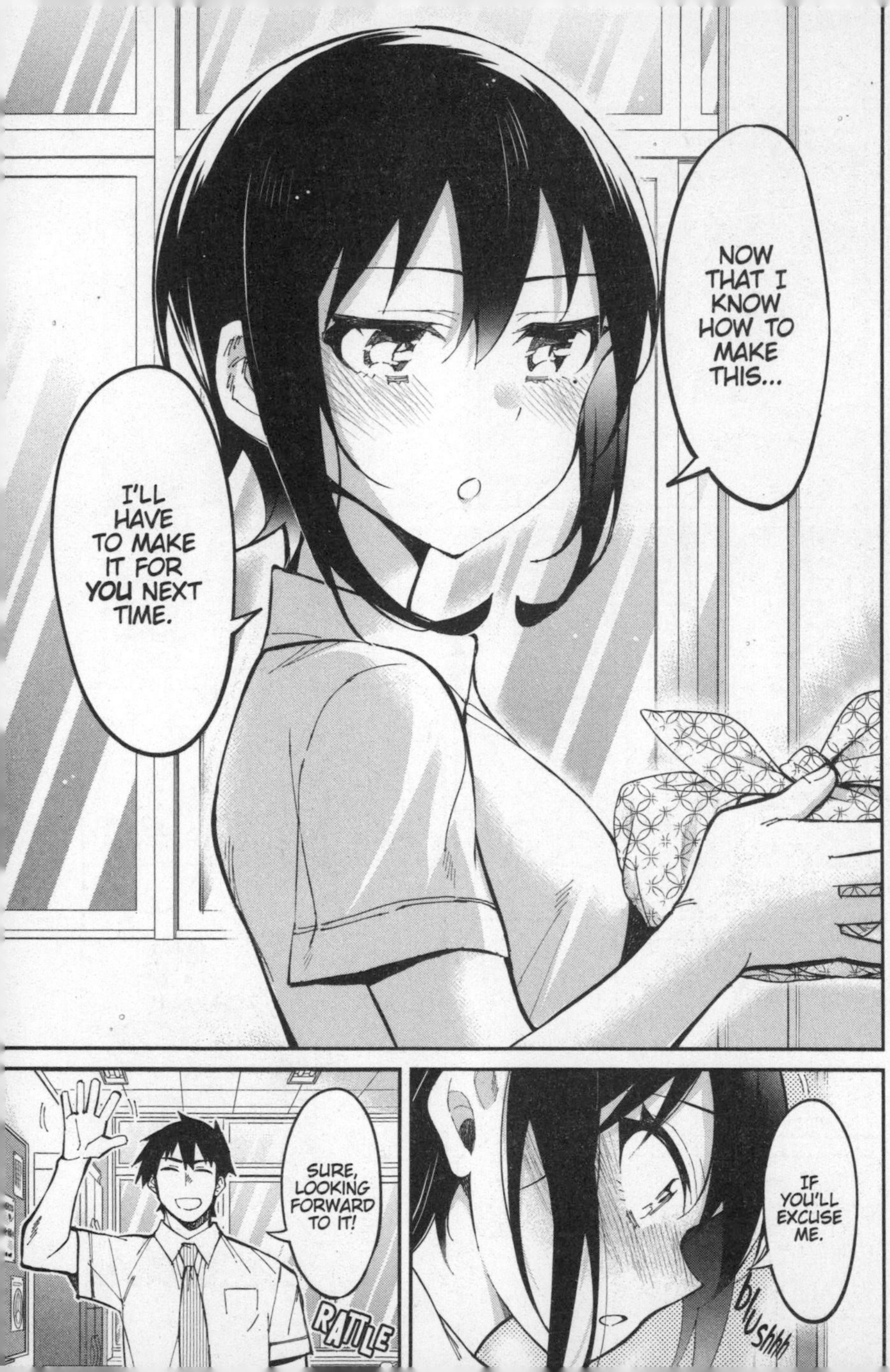
NOW THAT I KNOW HOW TO MAKE THIS...
I'LL HAVE TO MAKE IT FOR YOU NEXT TIME.
IF YOU'LL EXCUSE ME.
BLUSHHH
SURE, LOOKING FORWARD TO IT!
RATTLE

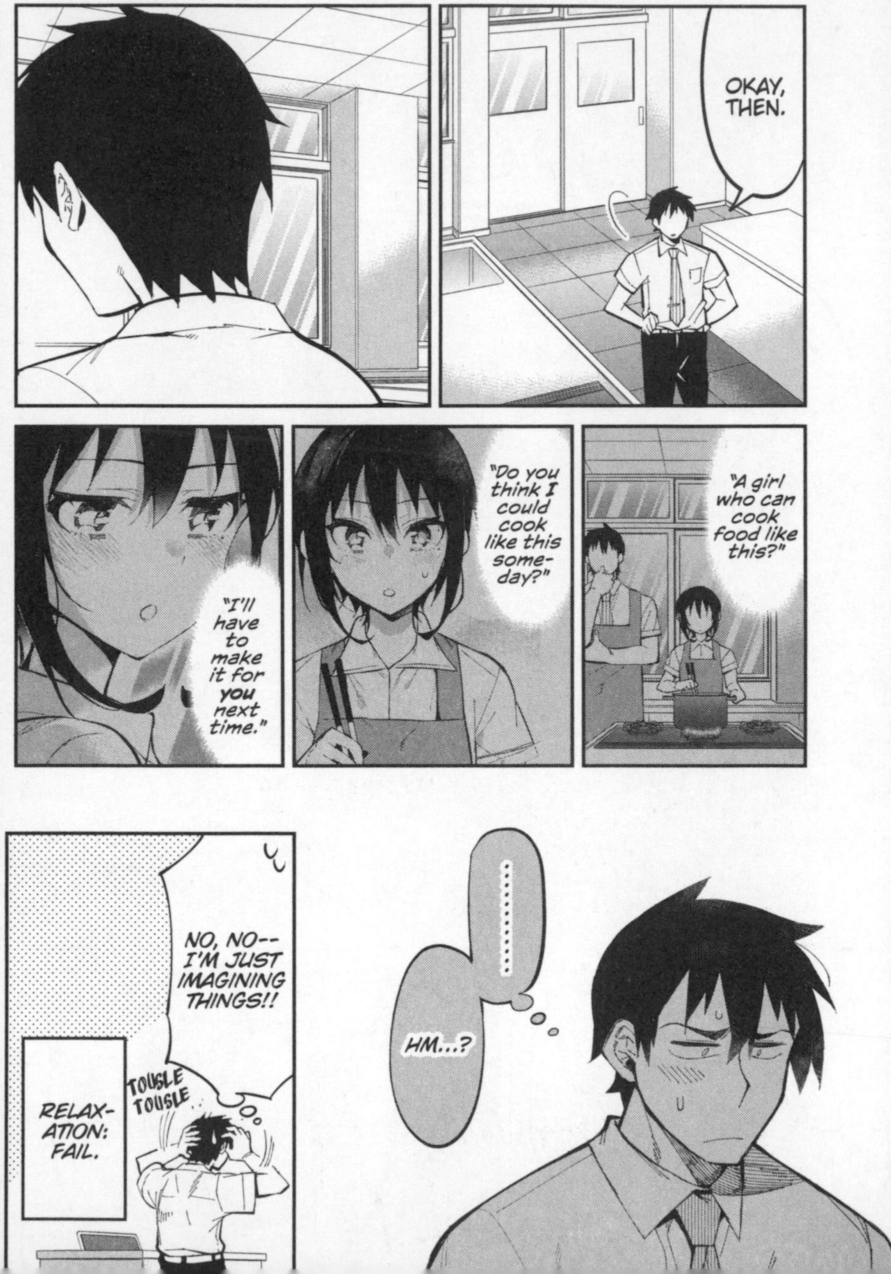
OKAY, THEN.
"A girl who can cook food like this?"
"Do you think I could cook like this someday?"
"I'll have to make it for you next time."
....
HM...?
NO, NO-- I'M JUST IMAGINING THINGS!!
TOUSLE TOUSLE
RELAXATION: FAIL.

●OKAZAKI MIKU●
BOOBS STILL GROWING.

Gal
Gohan

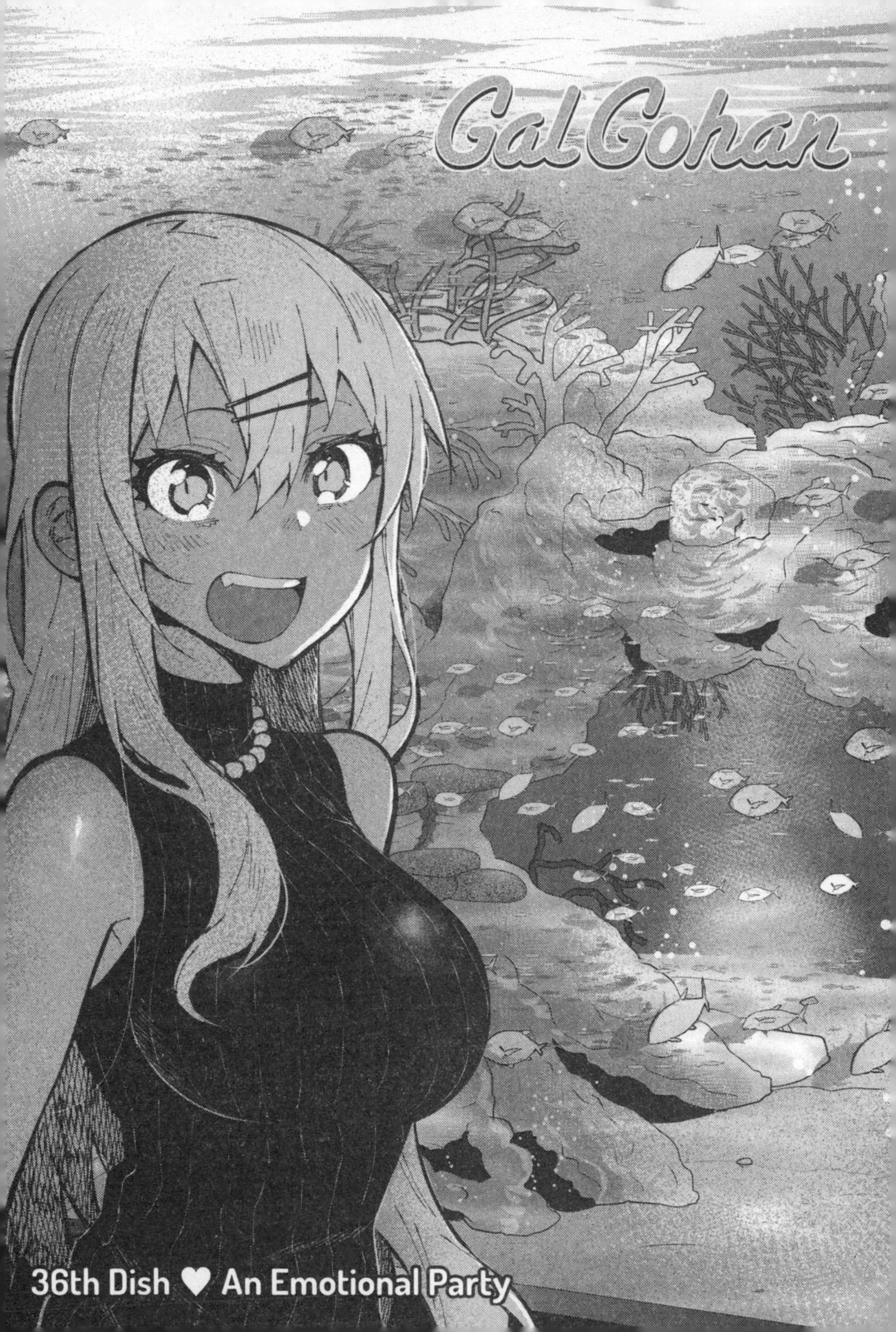
Gal Gohan
36th Dish ♥ An Emotional Party

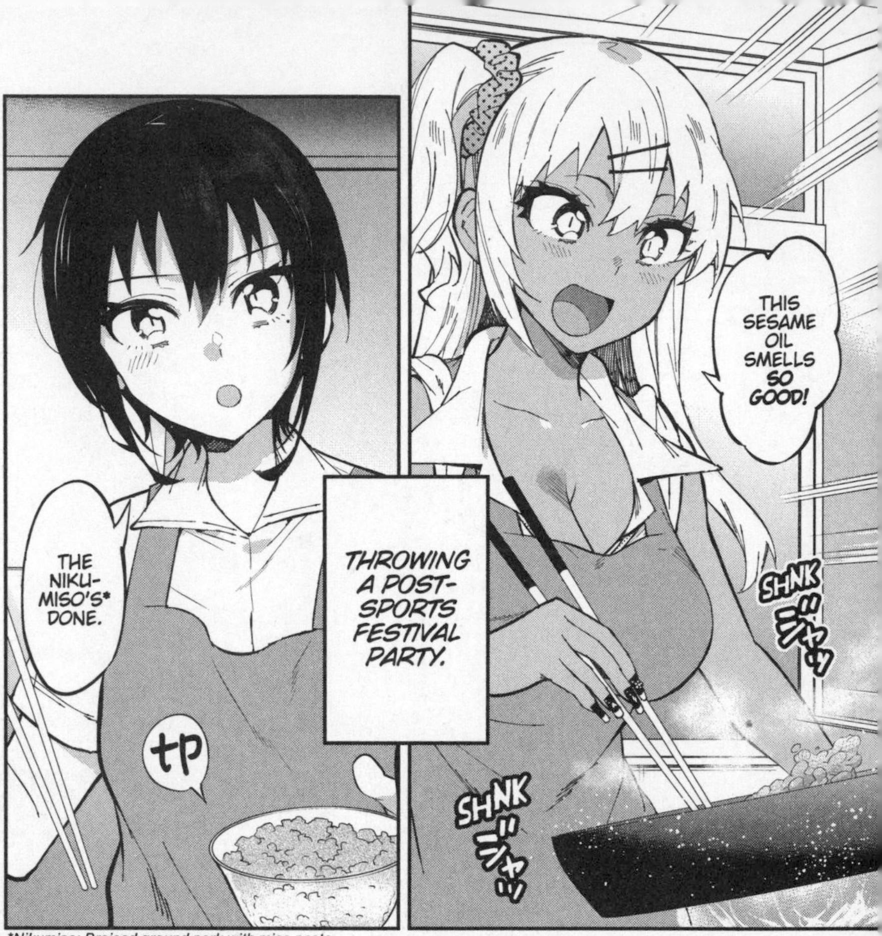
THIS SESAME OIL SMELLS SO GOOD!
SHNK
ジャッ
SHNK
ジャッ
THROWING A POST-SPORTS FESTIVAL PARTY.
THE NIKU-MISO'S* DONE.
tp

*Nikumiso: Braised ground pork with miso paste.

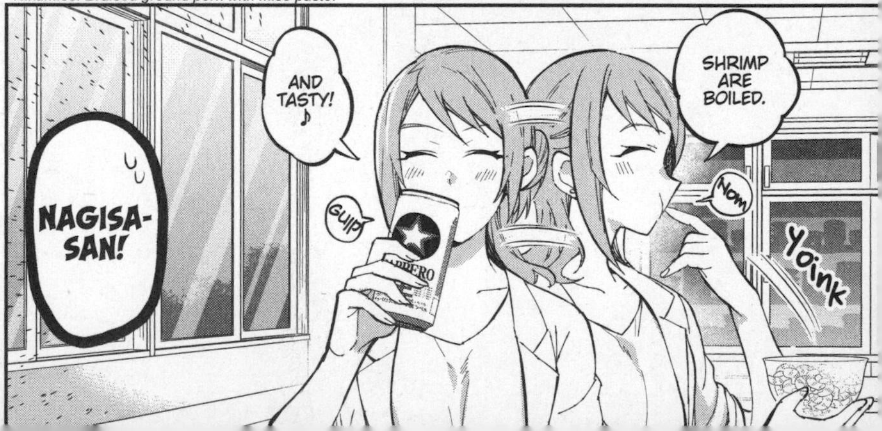
SHRIMP ARE BOILED.
Nom
Yoink
AND TASTY! ♪
Gulp
NAGISA-SAN!

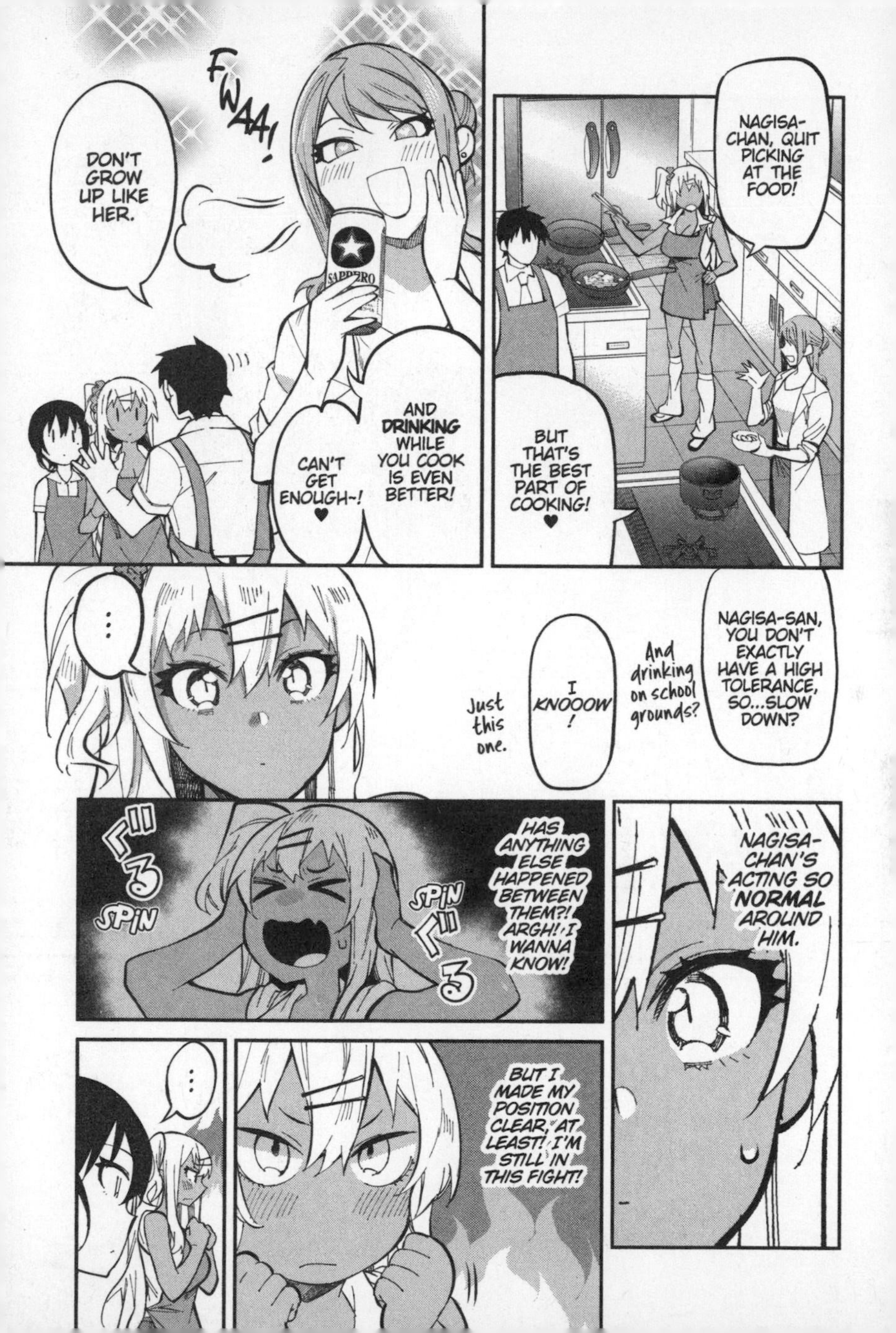
NAGISA-CHAN, QUIT PICKING AT THE FOOD!
BUT THAT'S THE BEST PART OF COOKING! ♥
FWAAA!
AND DRINKING WHILE YOU COOK IS EVEN BETTER!
CAN'T GET ENOUGH~! ♥
DON'T GROW UP LIKE HER.
NAGISA-SAN, YOU DON'T EXACTLY HAVE A HIGH TOLERANCE, SO...SLOW DOWN?
And drinking on school grounds?
I KNOOOW!
Just this one.
...
NAGISA-CHAN'S ACTING SO NORMAL AROUND HIM.
SPIN
HAS ANYTHING ELSE HAPPENED BETWEEN THEM?! ARGH! I WANNA KNOW!
SPIN
BUT I MADE MY POSITION CLEAR, AT LEAST! I'M STILL IN THIS FIGHT!
...

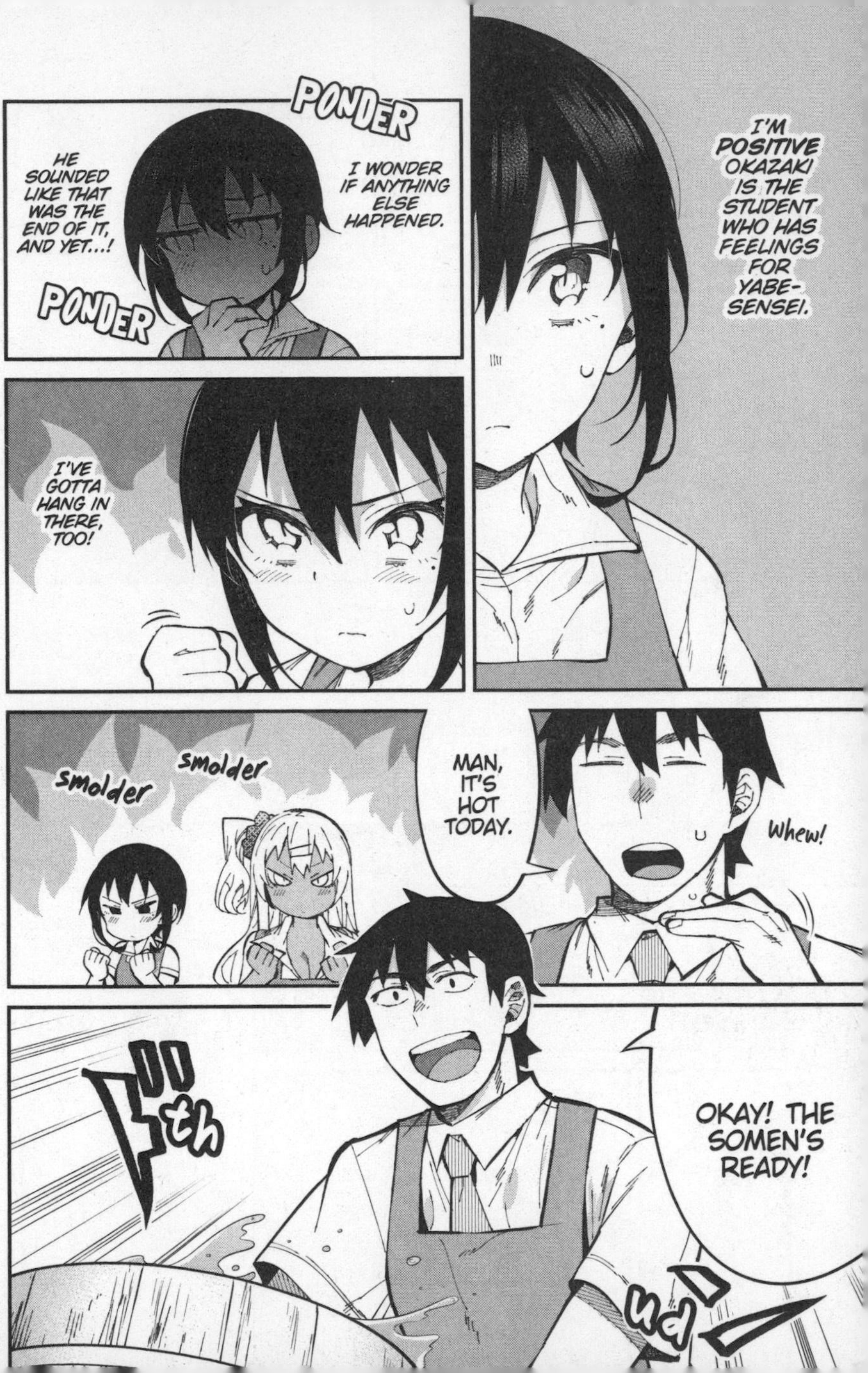
I'M POSITIVE OKAZAKI IS THE STUDENT WHO HAS FEELINGS FOR YABE-SENSEI.
PONDER
I WONDER IF ANYTHING ELSE HAPPENED.
HE SOUNDED LIKE THAT WAS THE END OF IT, AND YET...!
PONDER
I'VE GOTTA HANG IN THERE, TOO!
Whew!
MAN, IT'S HOT TODAY.
smolder
smolder
OKAY! THE SOMEN'S READY!

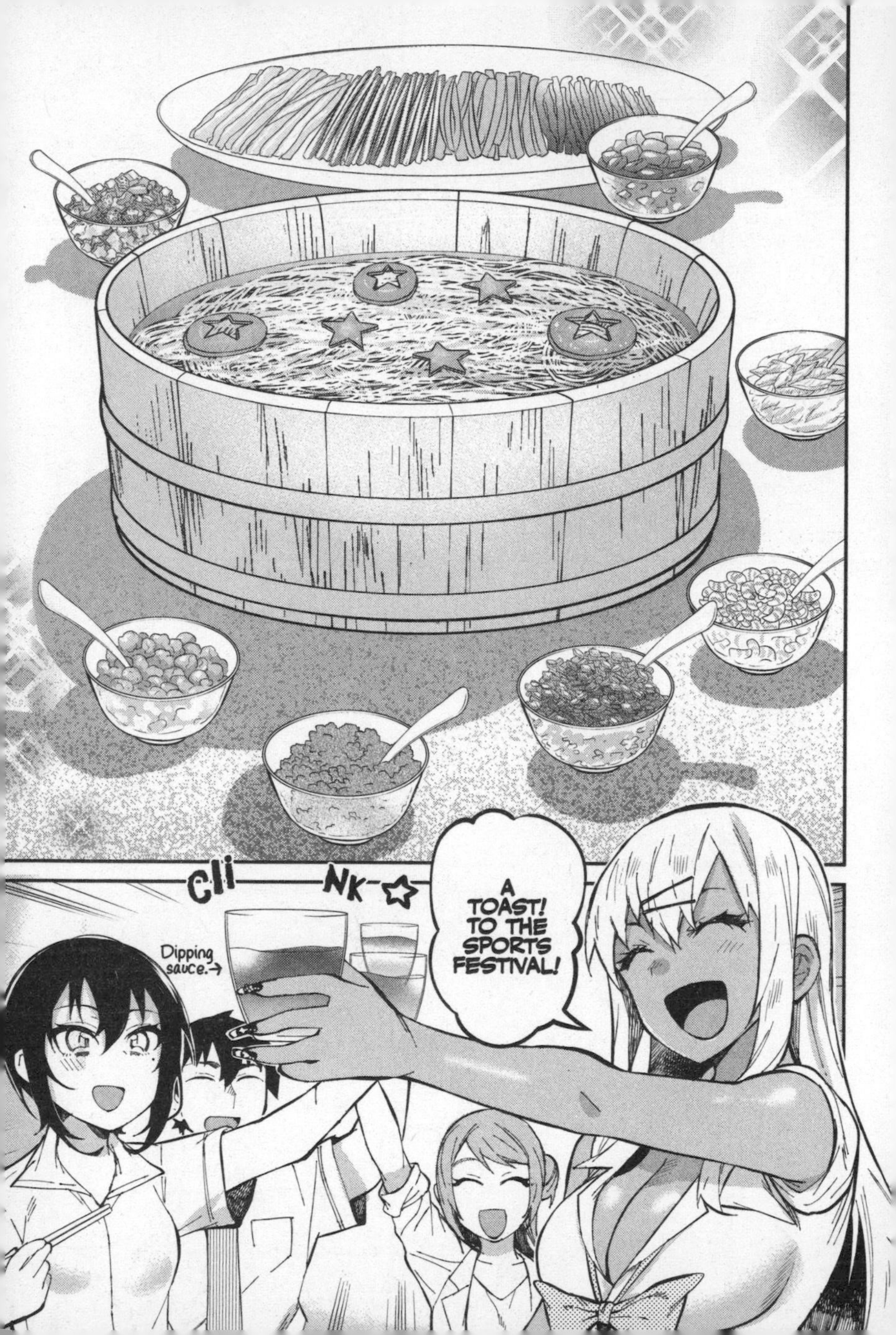
A TOAST! TO THE SPORTS FESTIVAL!
CLI NK ☆
Dipping sauce.→

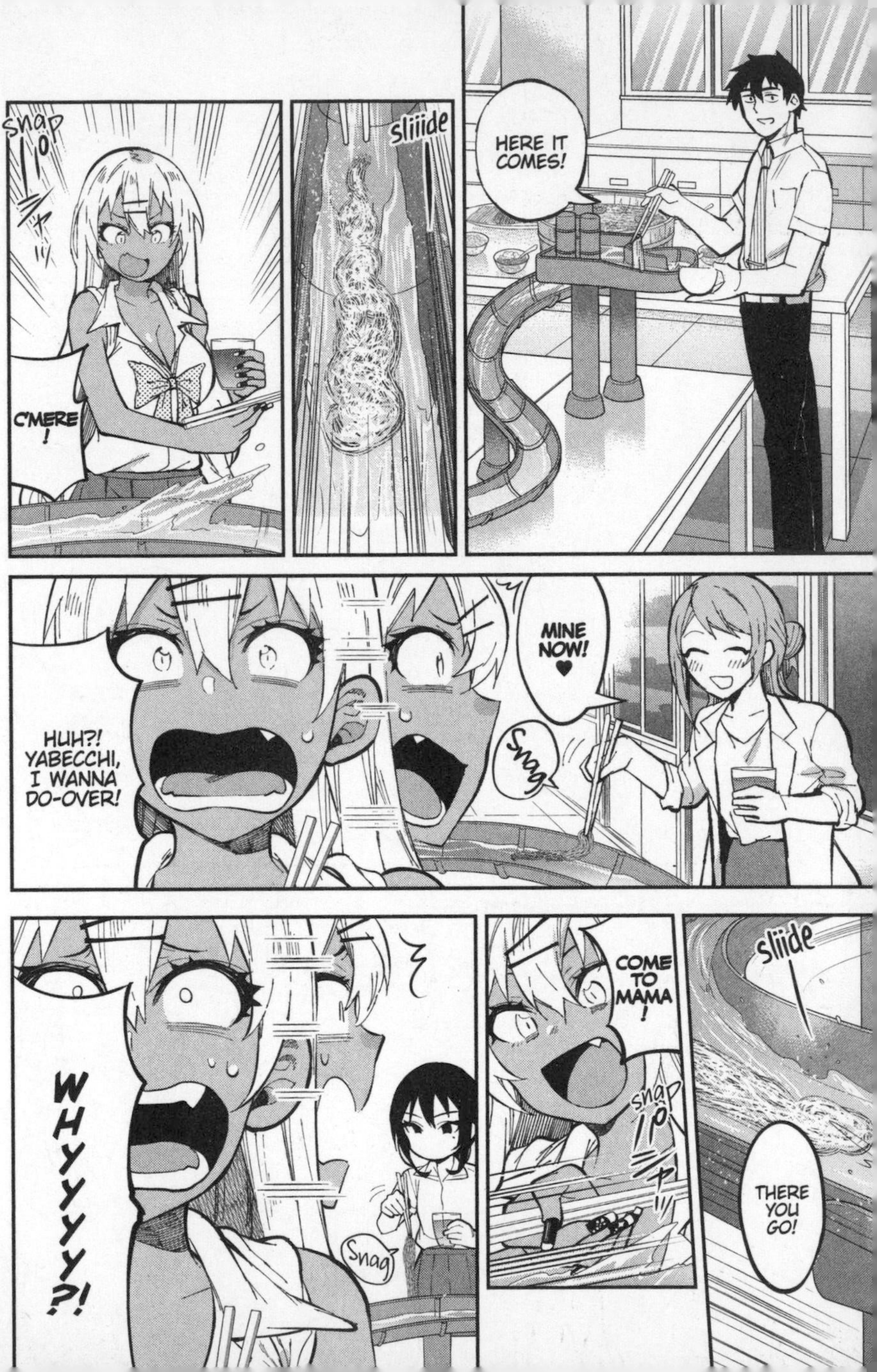
HERE IT COMES!
sliiide
snap
C'MERE!
MINE NOW! ♥
Snag
HUH?! YABECCHI, I WANNA DO-OVER!
sliiide
THERE YOU GO!
COME TO MAMA!
snap
WHYYYYY?!
Snag

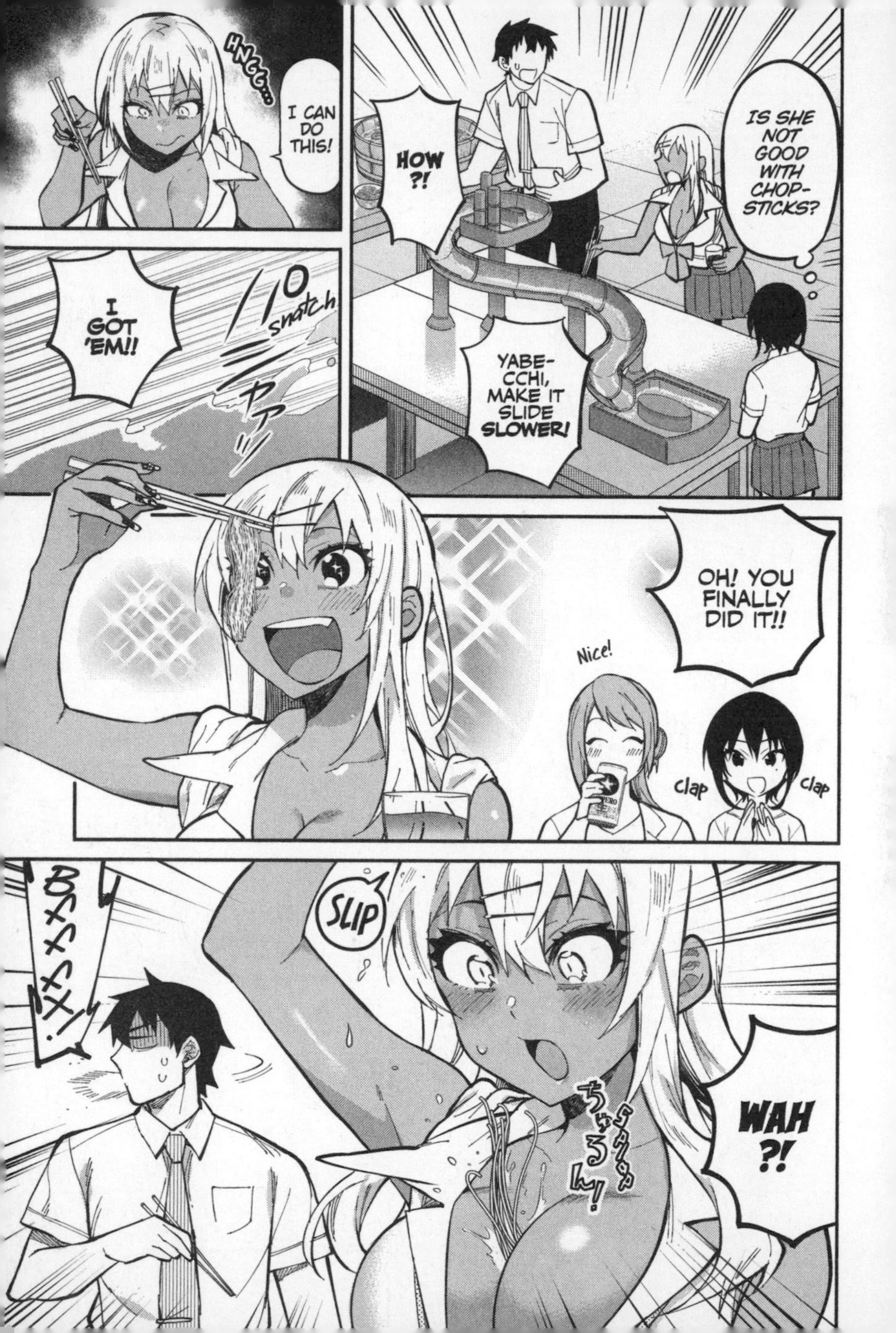
IS SHE NOT GOOD WITH CHOP-STICKS?
HOW?!
YABE-CCHI, MAKE IT SLIDE SLOWER!
HNGG...
I CAN DO THIS!
snatch
I GOT 'EM!!
OH! YOU FINALLY DID IT!!
Nice!
Clap
Clap
WAH?!
ちゅるん!
SLIP

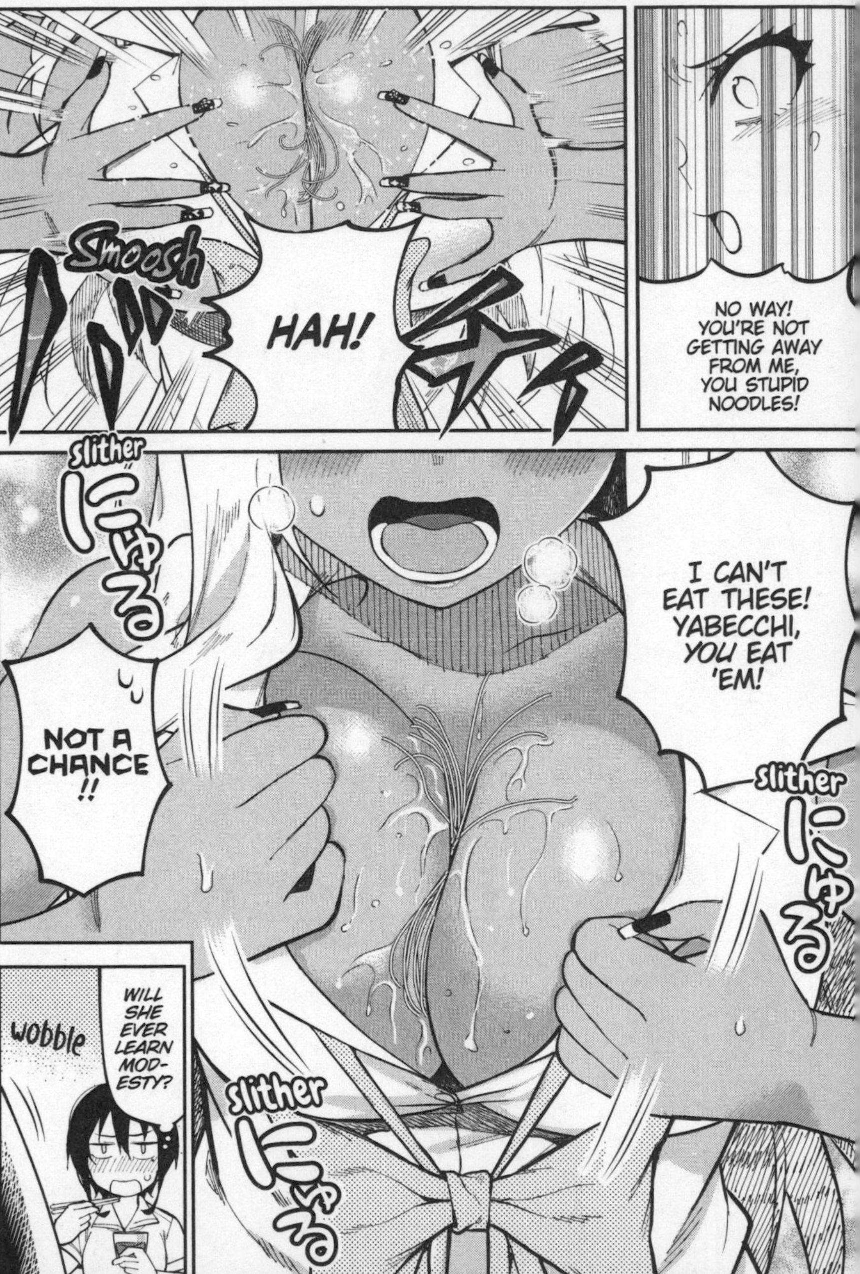
NO WAY! YOU'RE NOT GETTING AWAY FROM ME, YOU STUPID NOODLES!
Smoosh
HAH!
I CAN'T EAT THESE! YABECCHI, YOU EAT 'EM!
slither
にゅる
slither
にゅる
NOT A CHANCE!!
slither
にゅる
WILL SHE EVER LEARN MOD-ESTY?
wobble

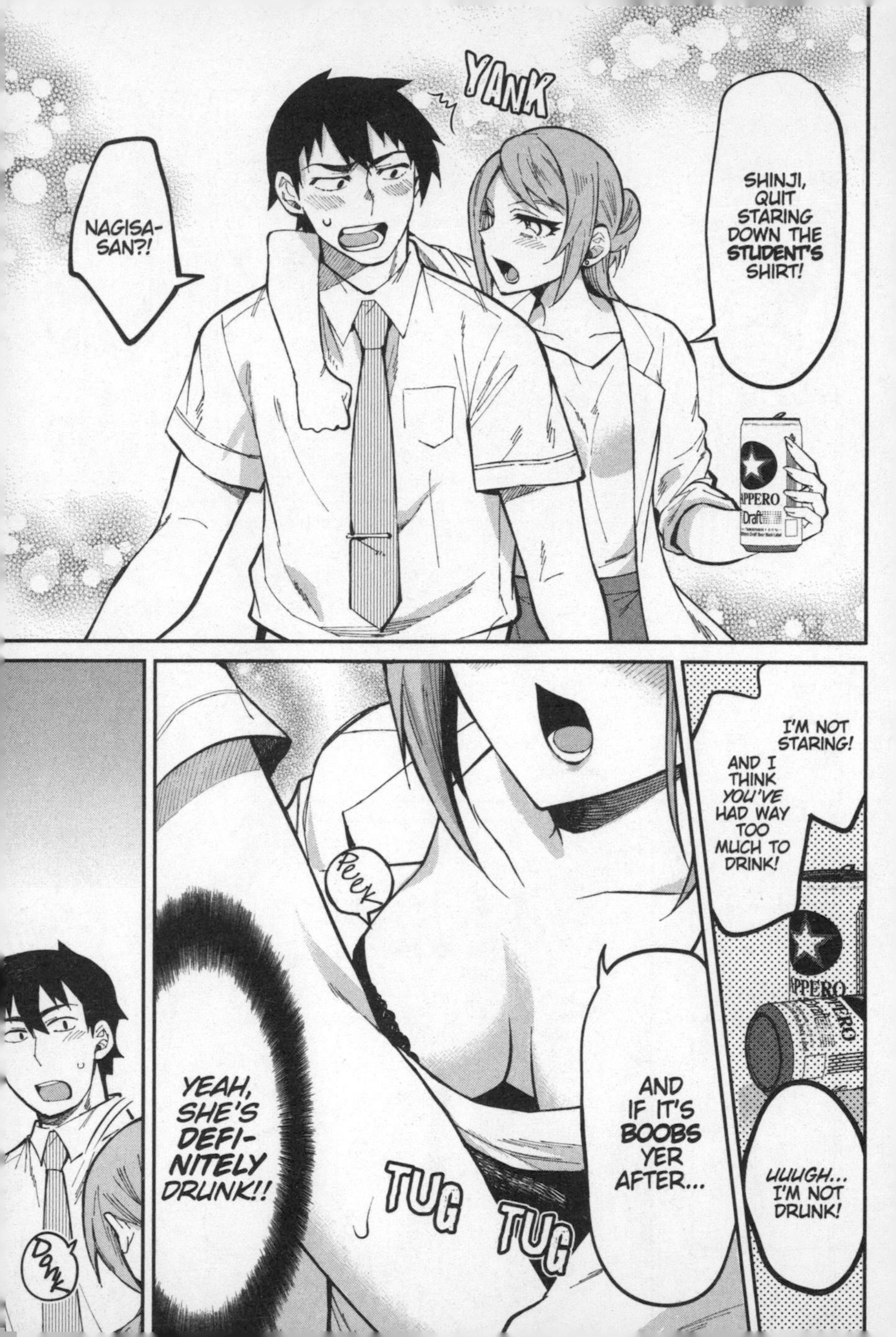
SHINJI, QUIT STARING DOWN THE STUDENT'S SHIRT!
YANK
NAGISA-SAN?!
I'M NOT STARING!
AND I THINK YOU'VE HAD WAY TOO MUCH TO DRINK!
UUUGH... I'M NOT DRUNK!
PEEK
AND IF IT'S BOOBS YER AFTER...
TUG TUG
YEAH, SHE'S DEFINITELY DRUNK!!
DONK

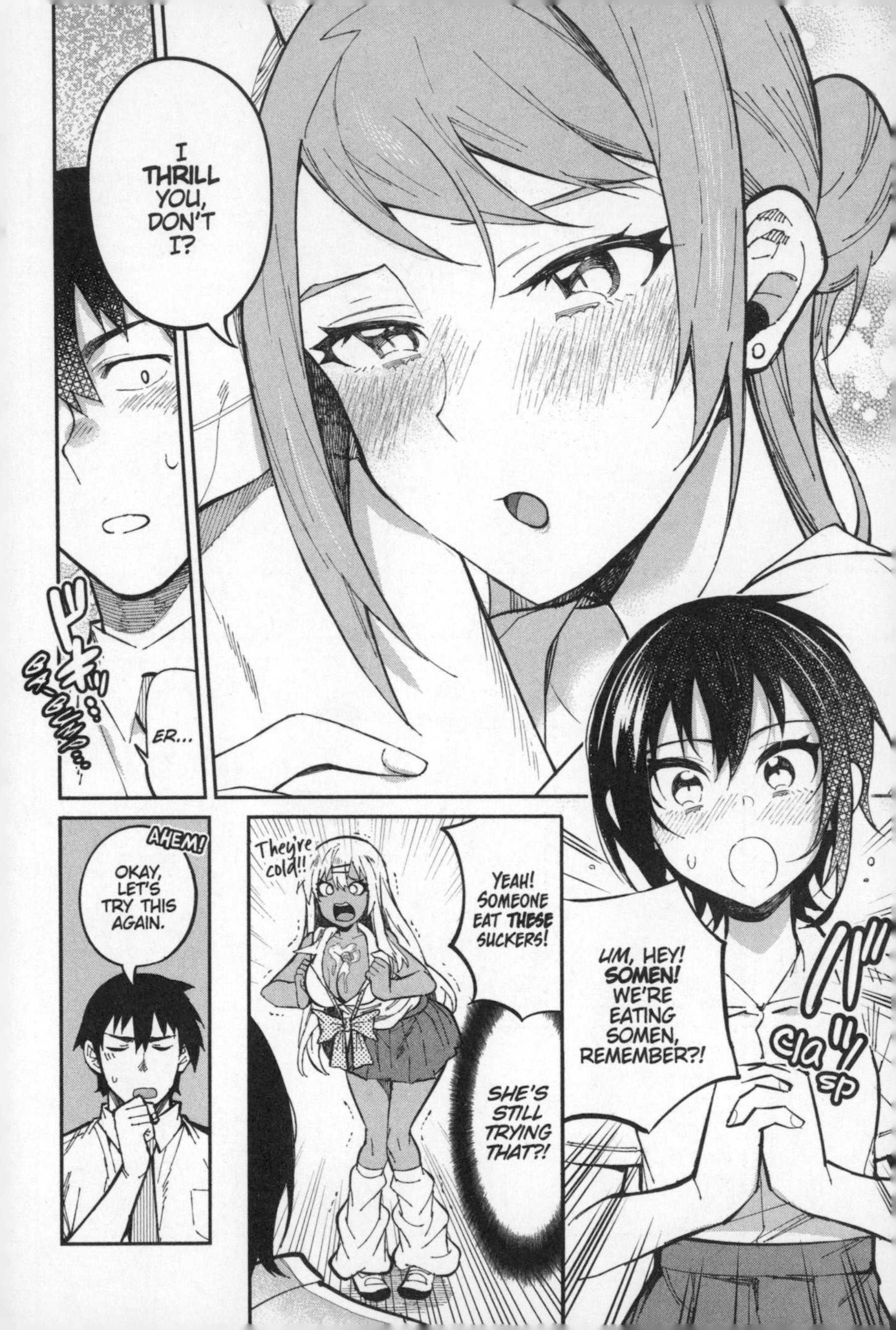
I THRILL YOU, DON'T I?
BA-BUMP...
ER...
UM, HEY! SOMEN! WE'RE EATING SOMEN, REMEMBER?!
clasp
YEAH! SOMEONE EAT THESE SUCKERS!
They're cold!!
SHE'S STILL TRYING THAT?!
AHEM!
OKAY, LET'S TRY THIS AGAIN.

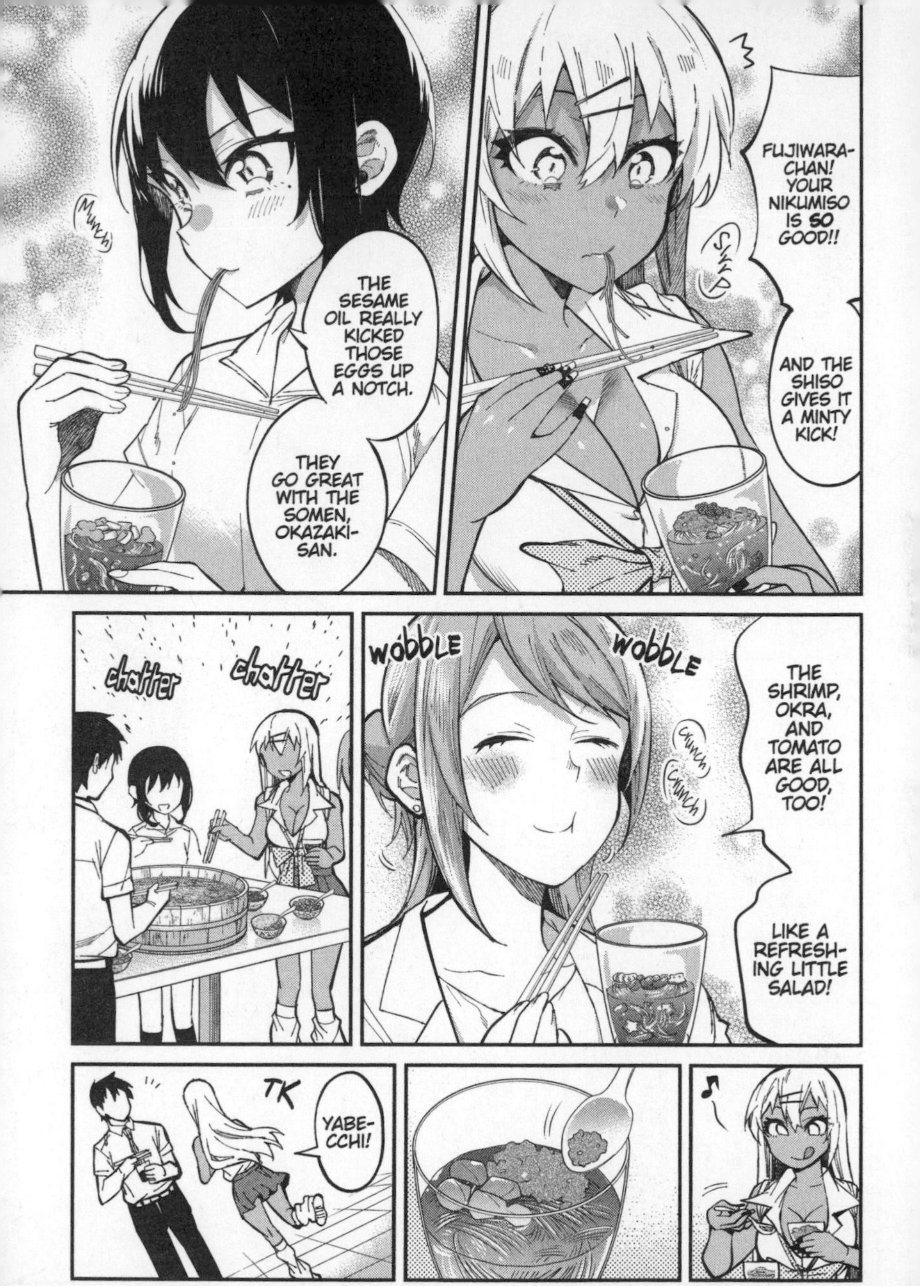
FUJIWARA-CHAN! YOUR NIKUMISO IS SO GOOD!!
AND THE SHISO GIVES IT A MINTY KICK!
Munch
THE SESAME OIL REALLY KICKED THOSE EGGS UP A NOTCH.
THEY GO GREAT WITH THE SOMEN, OKAZAKI-SAN.
wobble
wobble
THE SHRIMP, OKRA, AND TOMATO ARE ALL GOOD, TOO!
Crunch
Crunch
LIKE A REFRESHING LITTLE SALAD!
chatter
chatter
TK
YABE-CCHI!

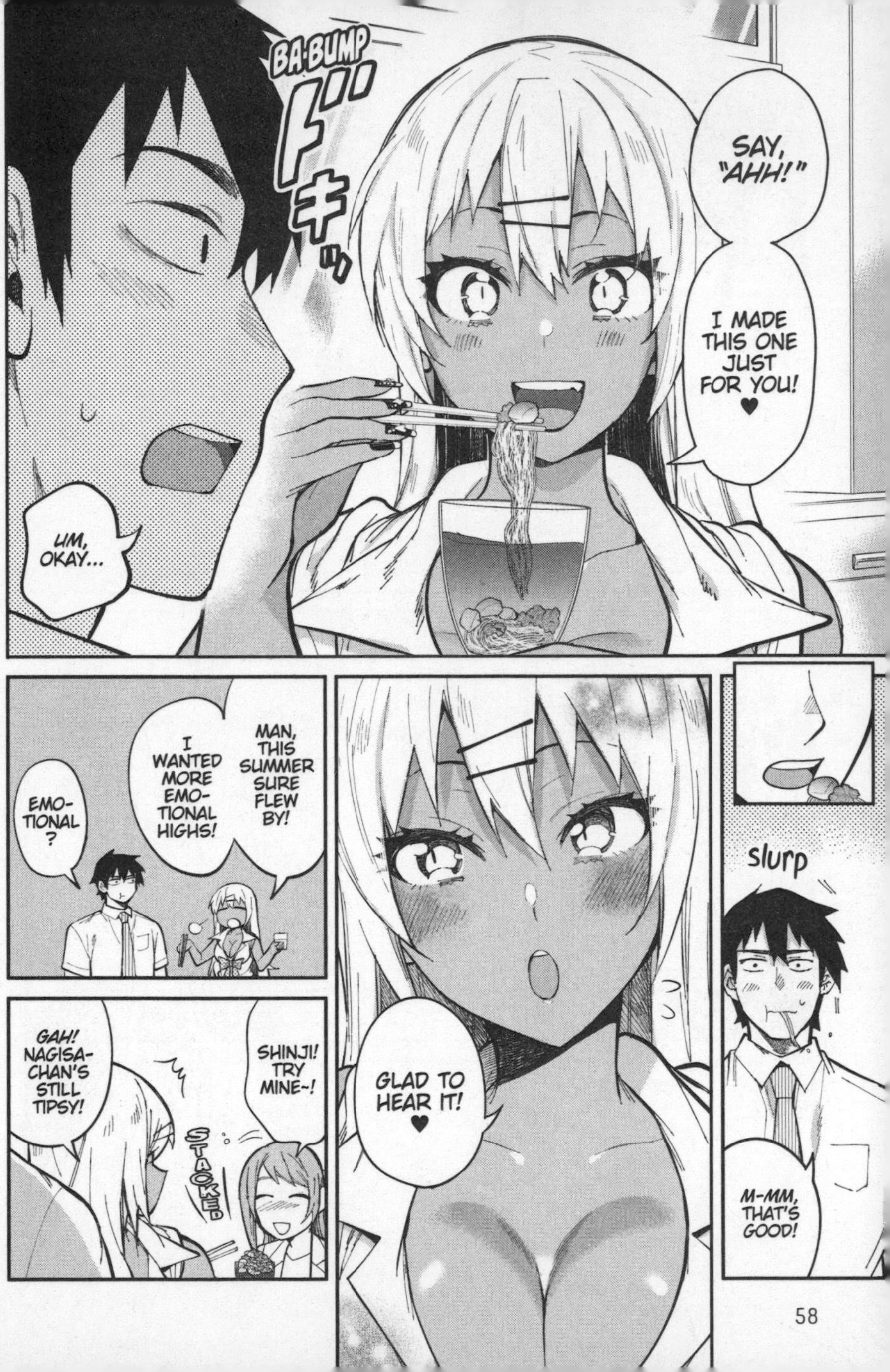
SAY, "AHH!"
I MADE THIS ONE JUST FOR YOU! ♥
BA-BUMP
ドキッ
UM, OKAY...
slurp
M-MM, THAT'S GOOD!
GLAD TO HEAR IT! ♥
MAN, THIS SUMMER SURE FLEW BY!
I WANTED MORE EMO-TIONAL HIGHS!
EMO-TIONAL?
SHINJI! TRY MINE~!
GAH! NAGISA-CHAN'S STILL TIPSY!
STACKED

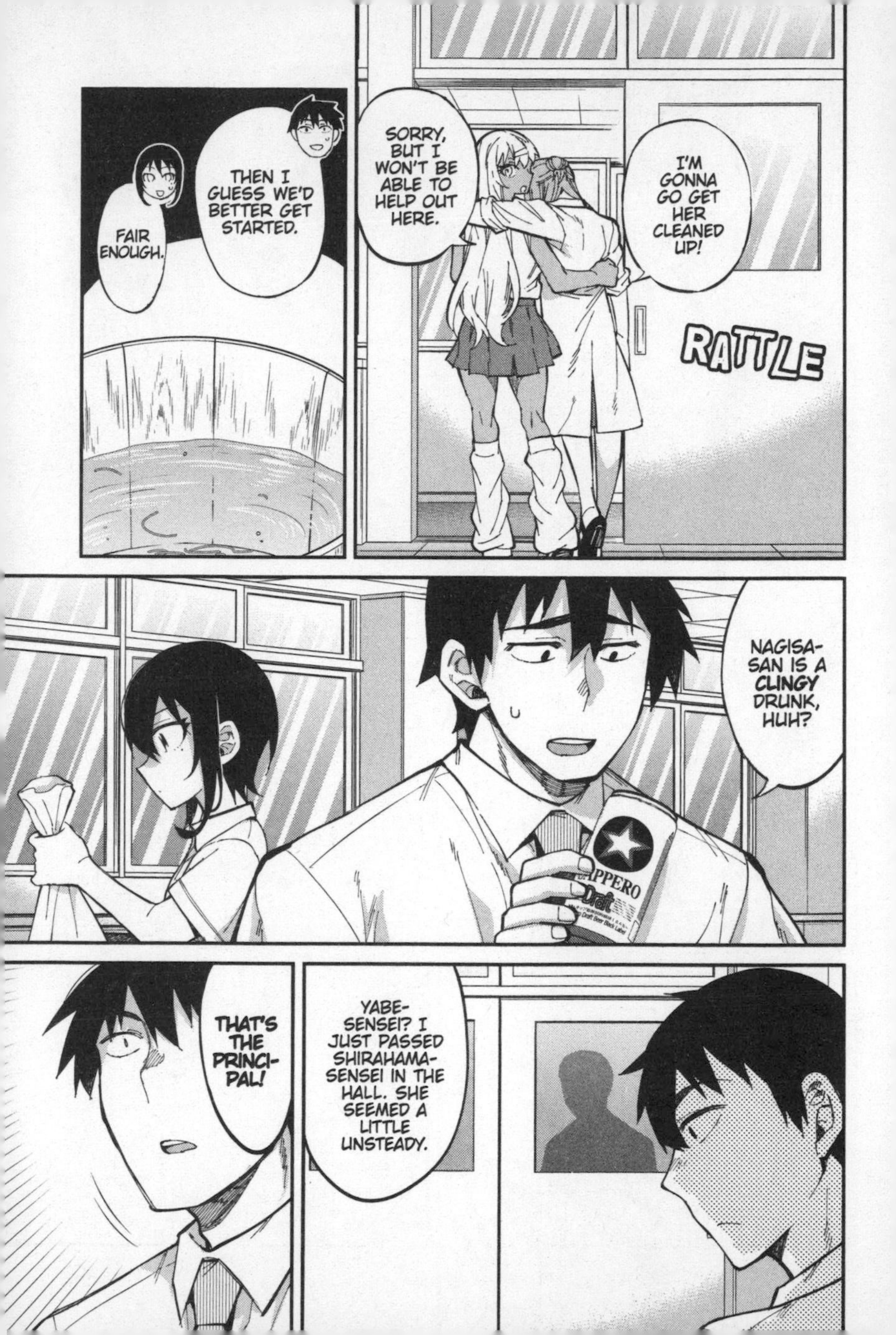
I'M GONNA GO GET HER CLEANED UP!
SORRY, BUT I WON'T BE ABLE TO HELP OUT HERE.
RATTLE
THEN I GUESS WE'D BETTER GET STARTED.
FAIR ENOUGH.
NAGISA-SAN IS A CLINGY DRUNK, HUH?
YABE-SENSEI? I JUST PASSED SHIRAHAMA-SENSEI IN THE HALL. SHE SEEMED A LITTLE UNSTEADY.
THAT'S THE PRINCIPAL!

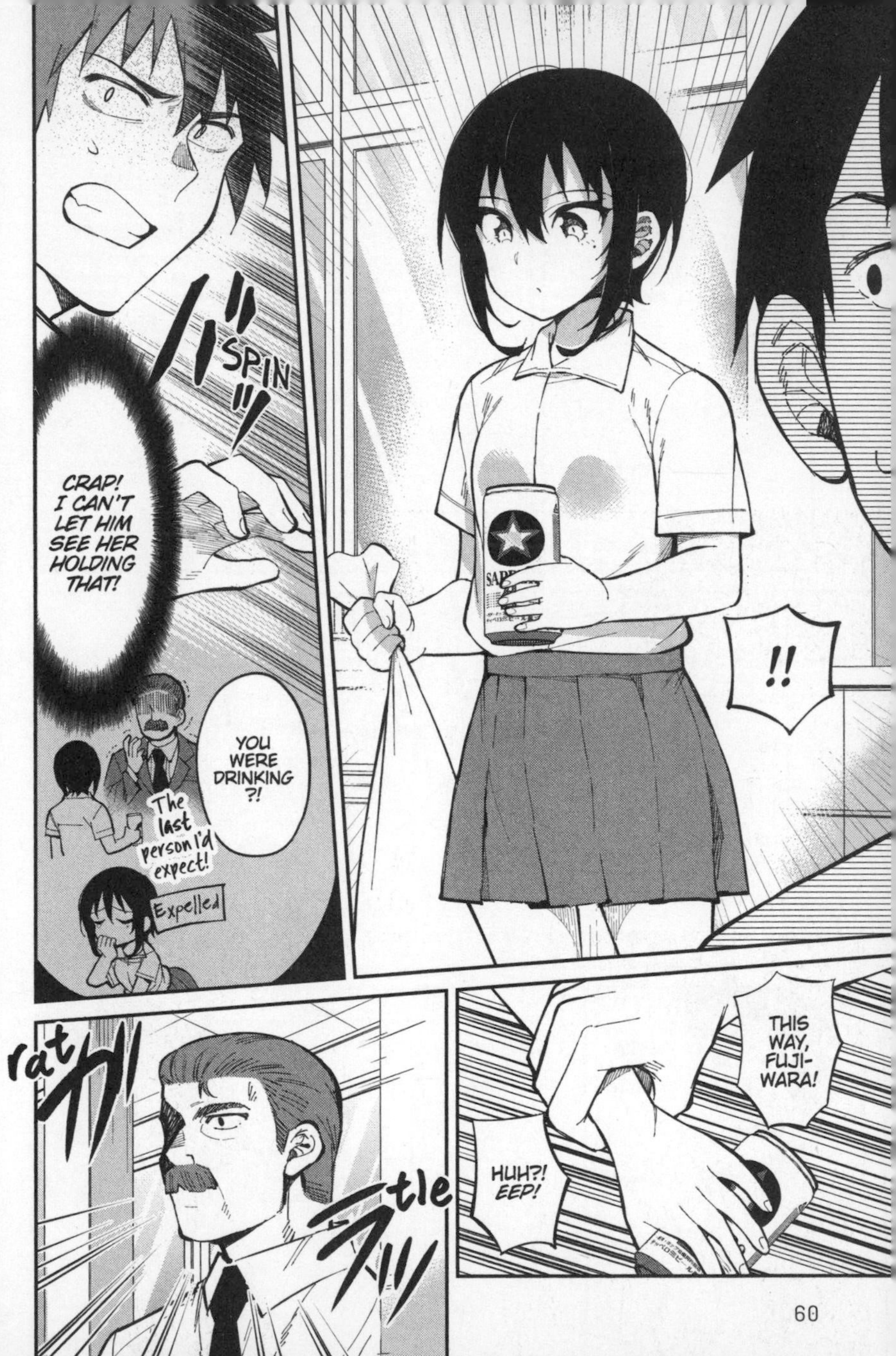

!!
SPIN
CRAP! I CAN'T LET HIM SEE HER HOLDING THAT!
YOU WERE DRINKING?!
The last person I'd expect!
Expelled
THIS WAY, FUJI-WARA!
HUH?! EEP!
rat
tle

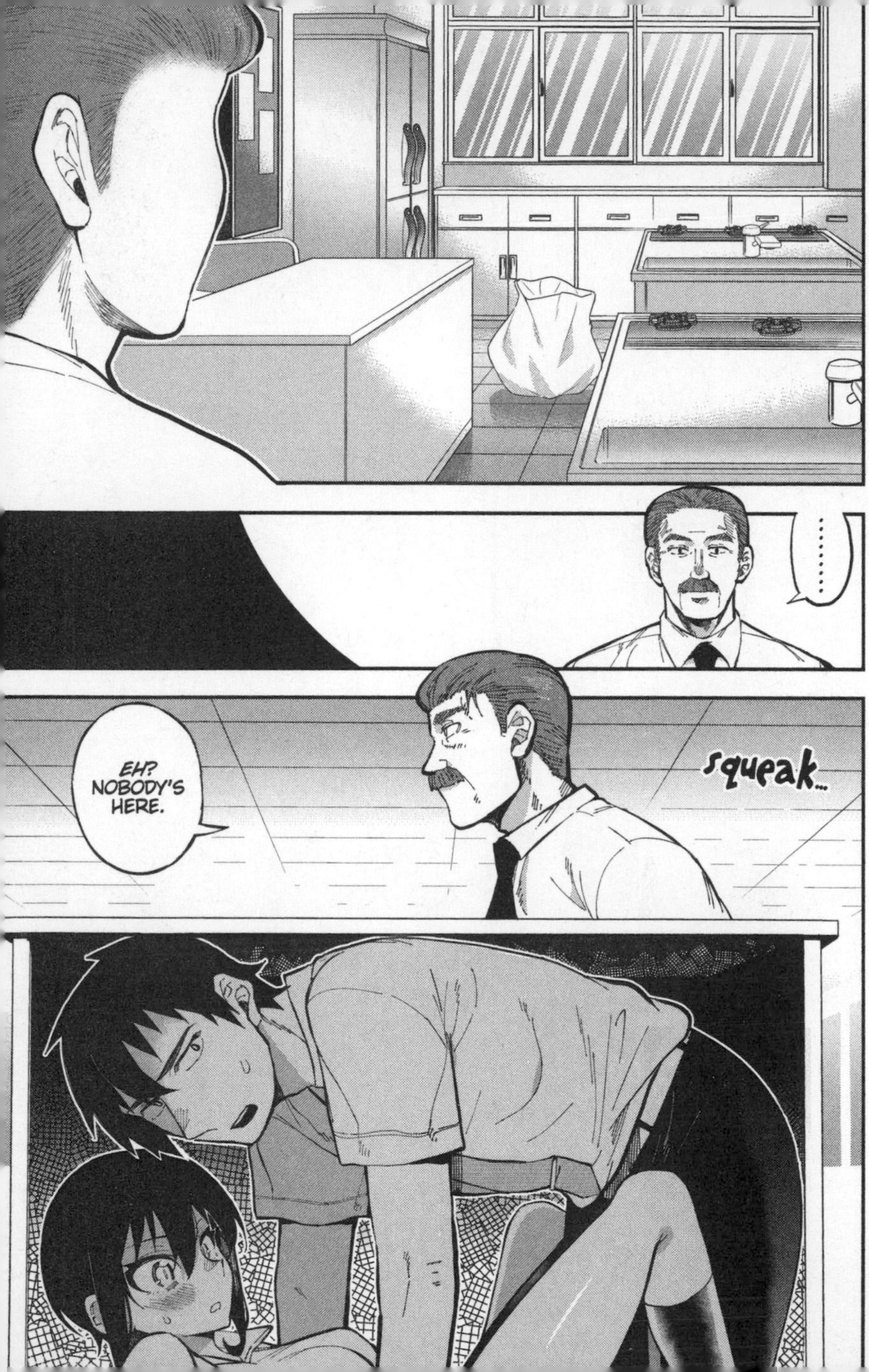
......
squeak...
EH? NOBODY'S HERE.

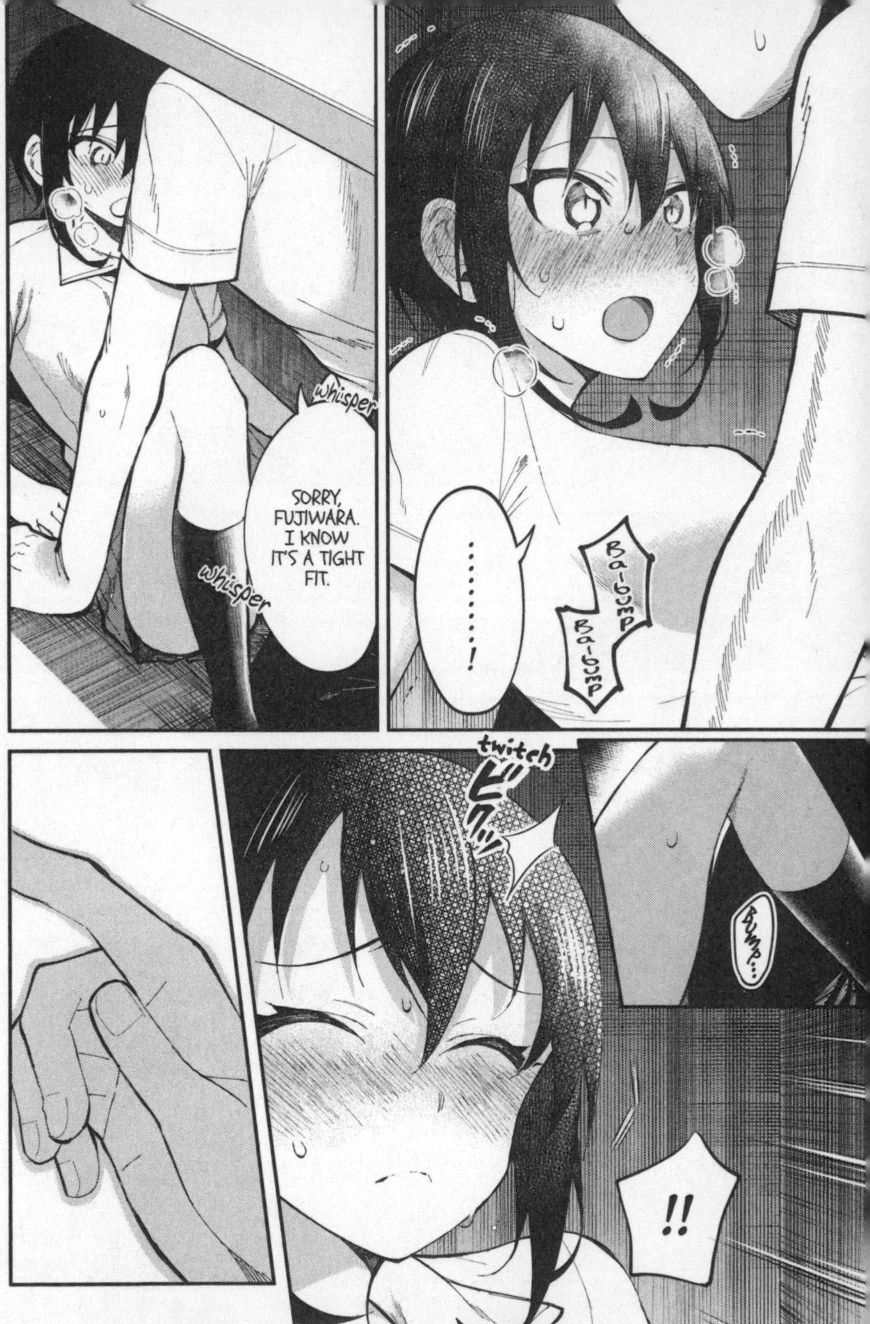
......!
Ba-bump
Ba-bump
whisper
SORRY, FUJIWARA. I KNOW IT'S A TIGHT FIT.
whisper
BUMP...
twitch
!!

SHH...
QUIET.

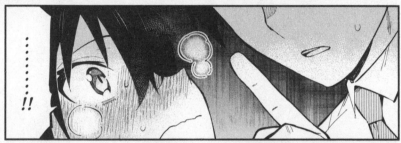

・・・・・・

!!

Squeak

Squeak...

Squeak

Squeak

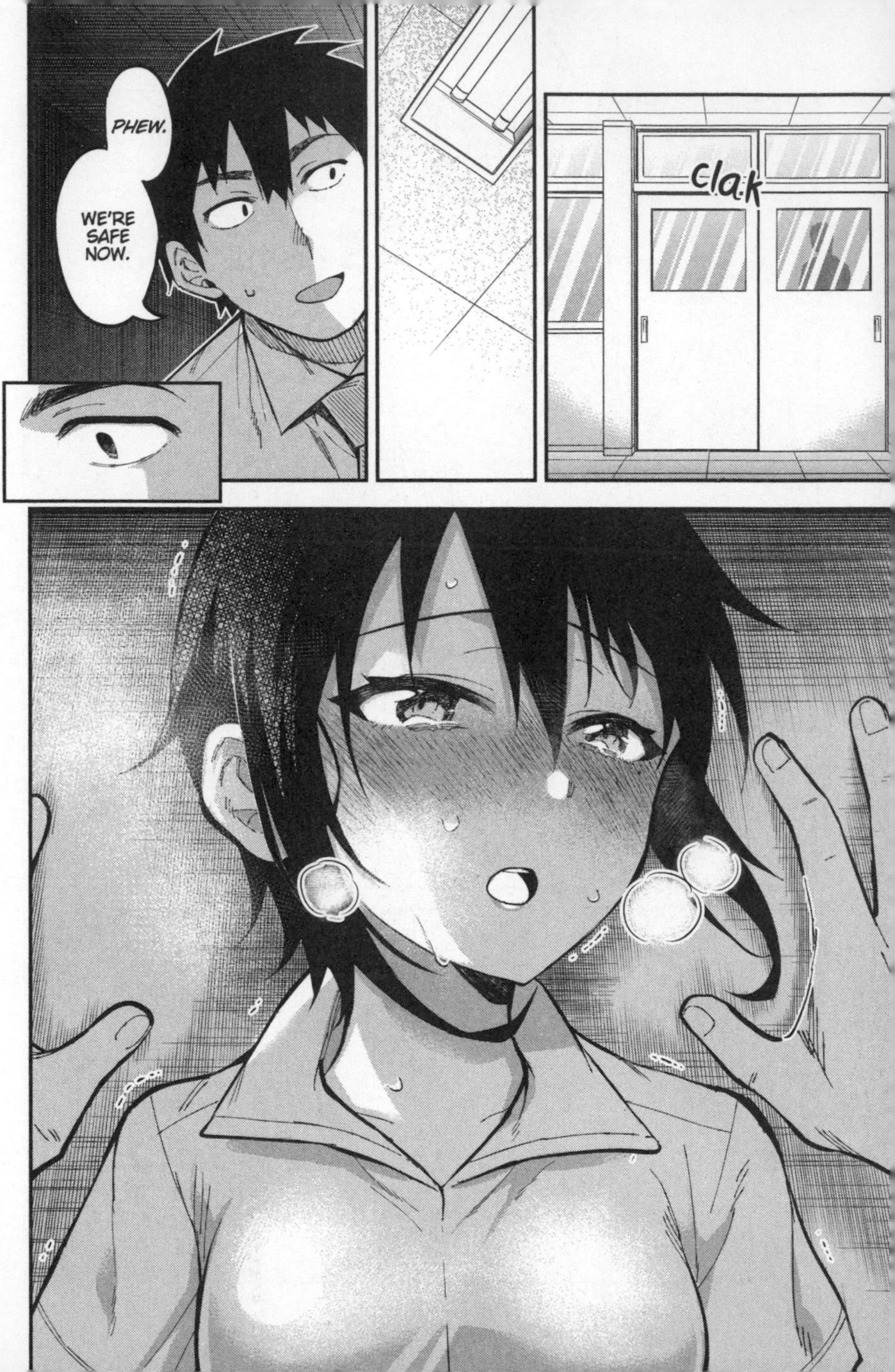
clak
PHEW.
WE'RE SAFE NOW.

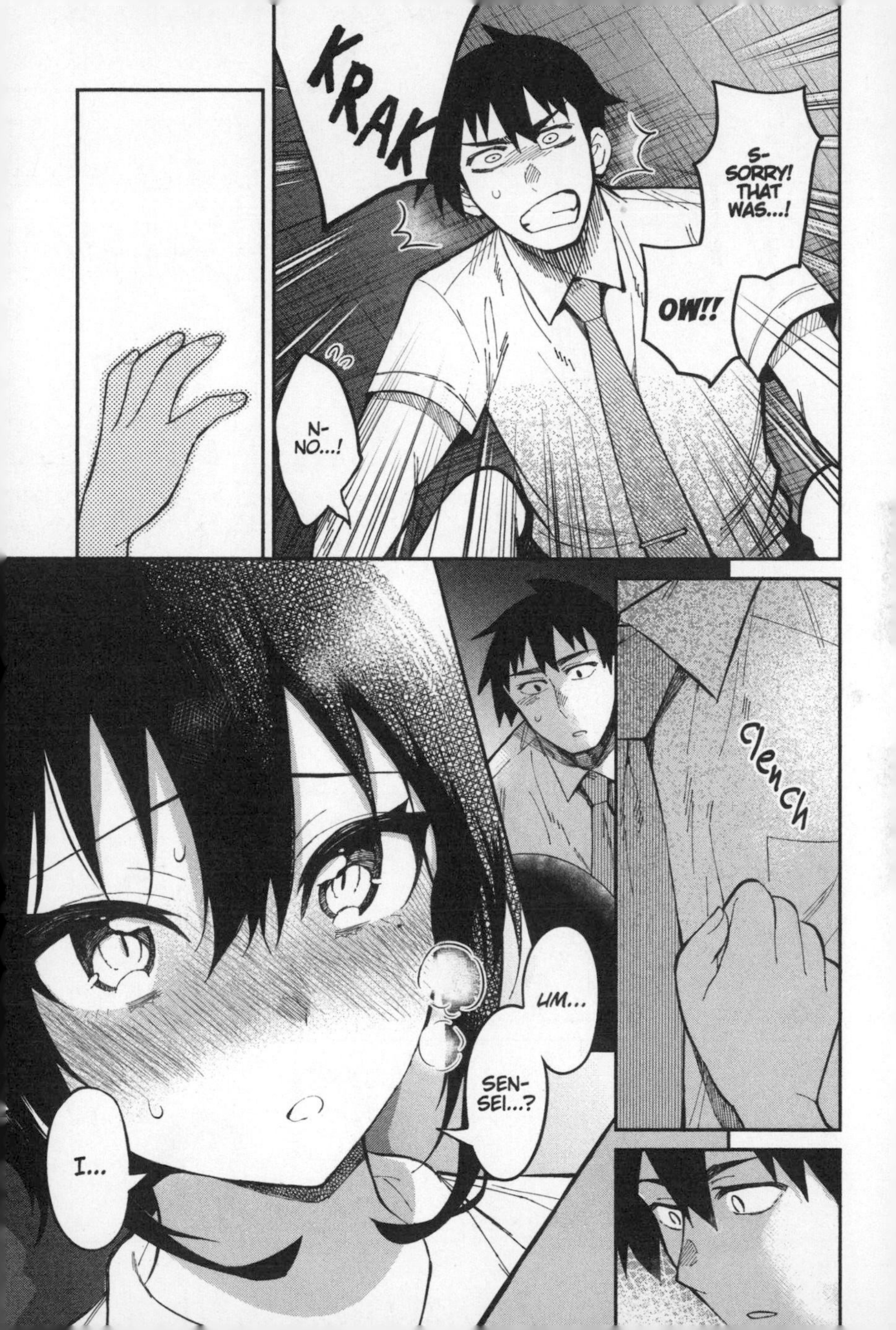
KRAK
S-SORRY! THAT WAS...!
OW!!
N-NO...!
clench
UM...
SEN-SEI...?
I...

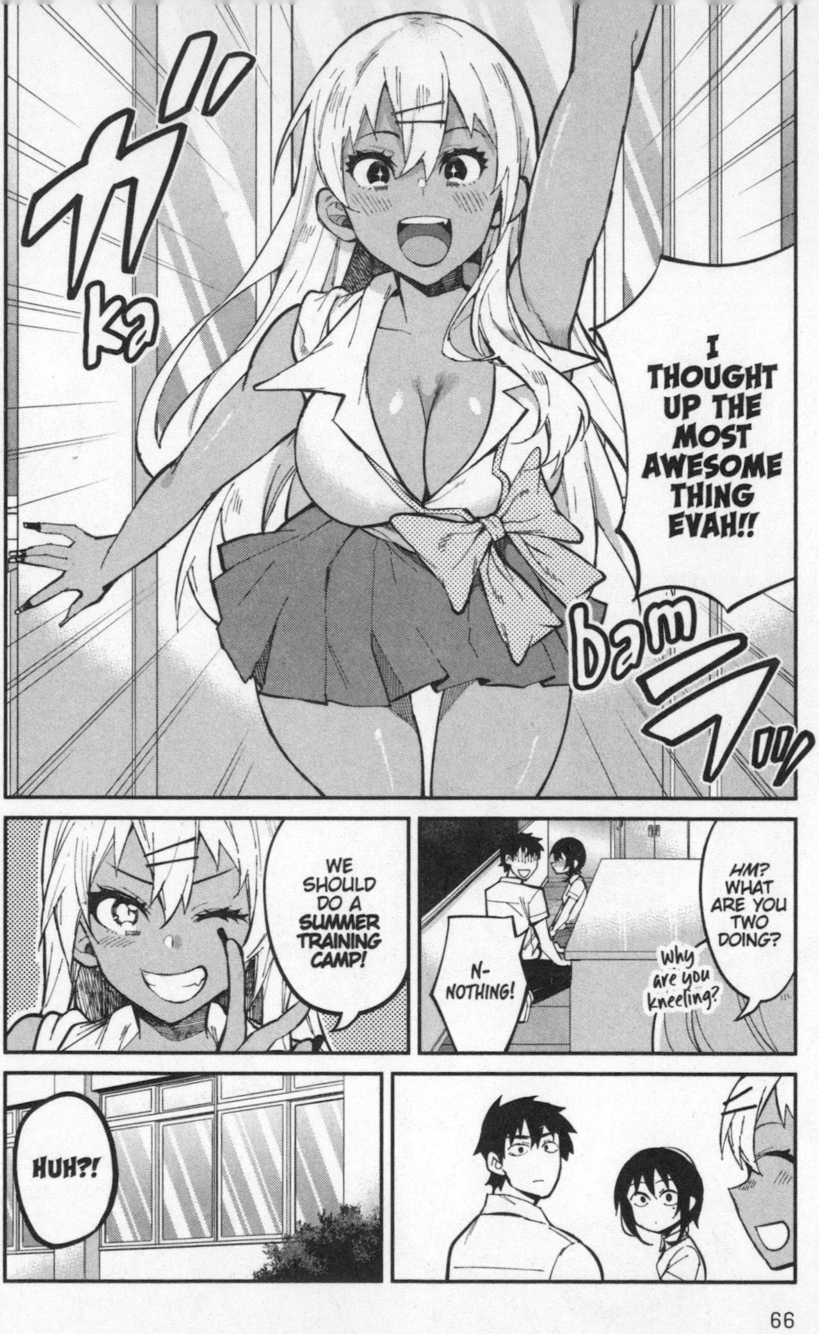
I THOUGHT UP THE MOST AWESOME THING EVAH!!
ka
bam
HM? WHAT ARE YOU TWO DOING?
why are you kneeling?
N-NOTHING!
WE SHOULD DO A SUMMER TRAINING CAMP!
HUH?!

Gal Gohan

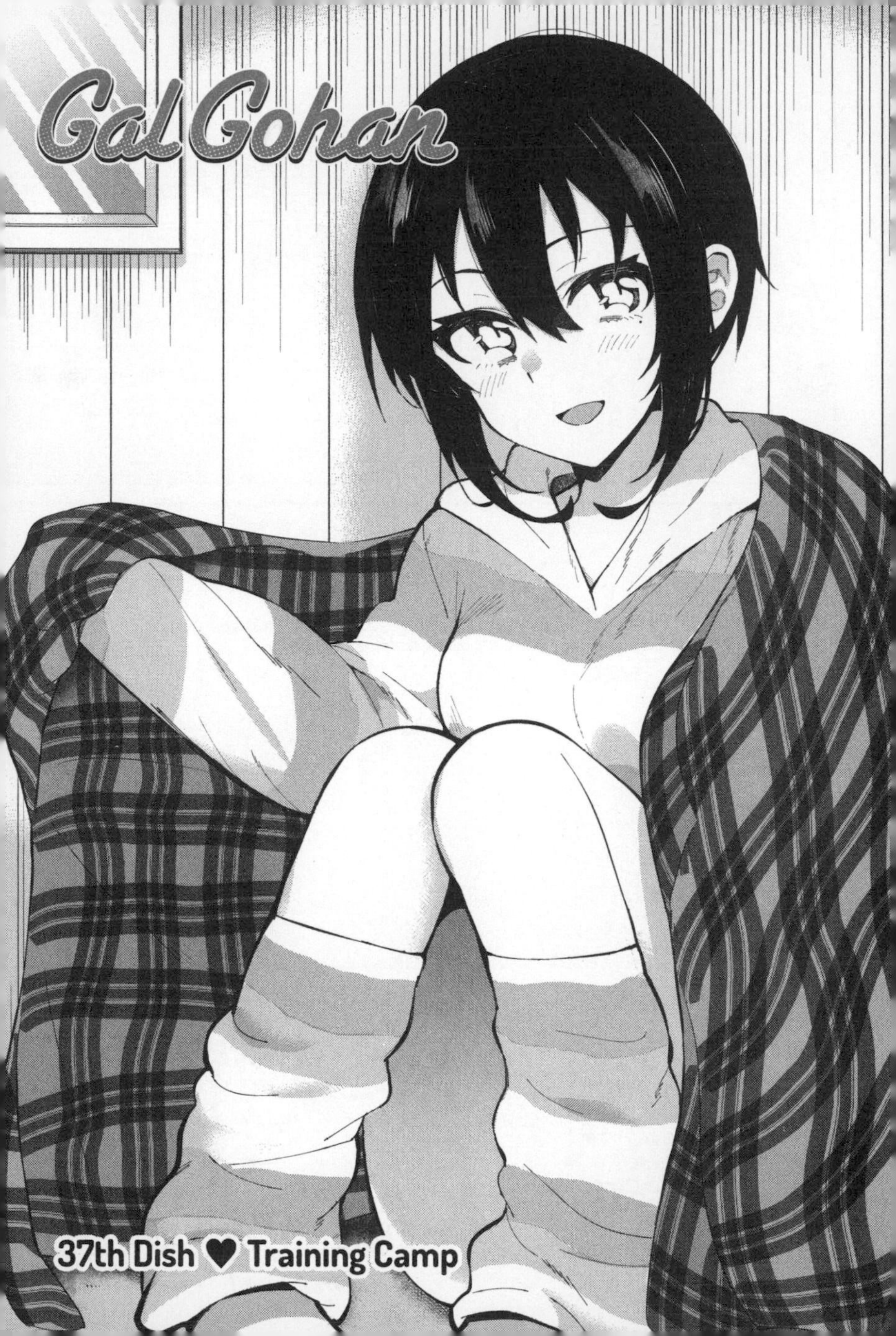
Gal Gohan
37th Dish ♥ Training Camp

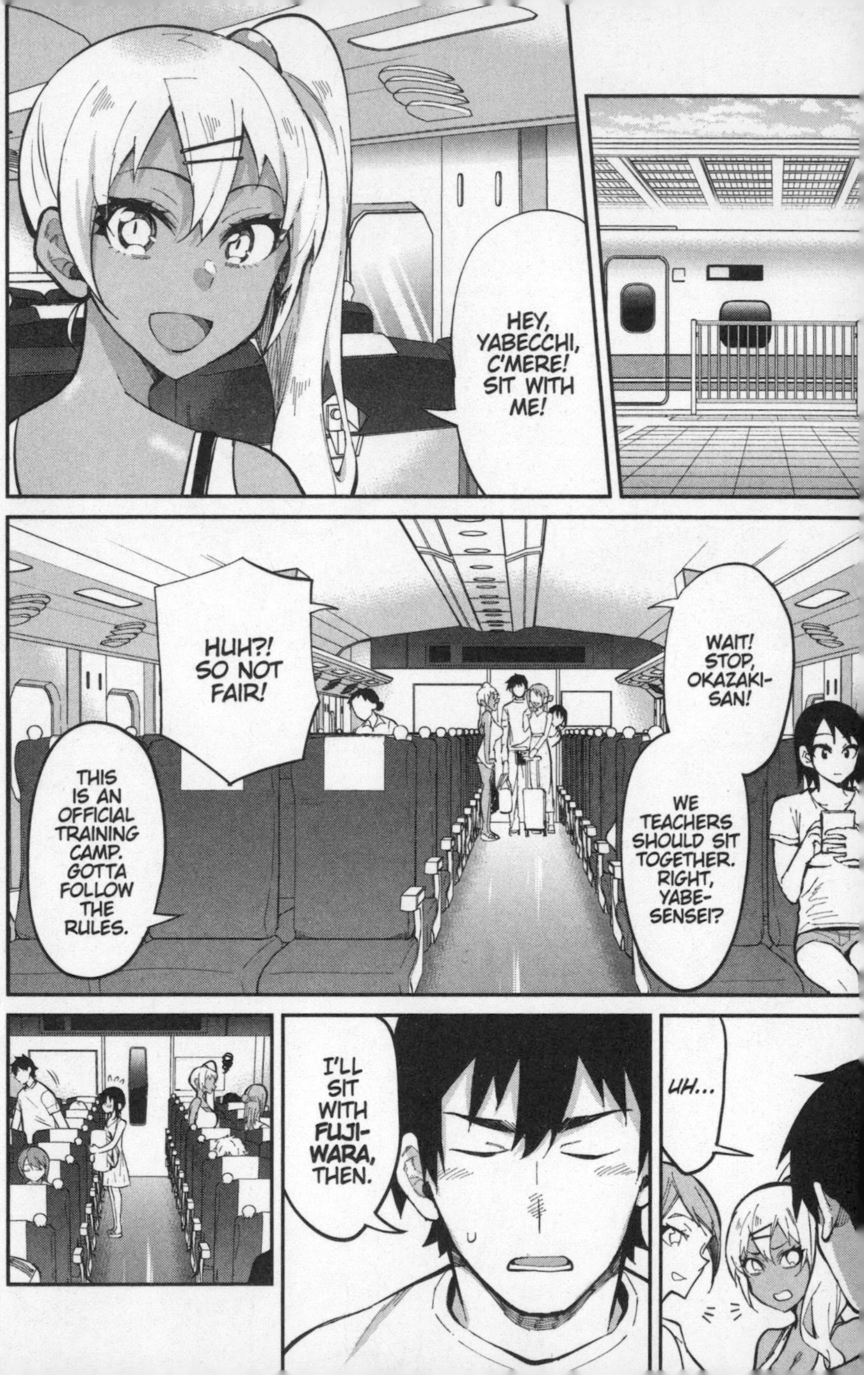
HEY, YABECCHI, C'MERE! SIT WITH ME!
WAIT! STOP, OKAZAKI-SAN!
WE TEACHERS SHOULD SIT TOGETHER. RIGHT, YABE-SENSEI?
HUH?! SO NOT FAIR!
THIS IS AN OFFICIAL TRAINING CAMP. GOTTA FOLLOW THE RULES.
UH...
I'LL SIT WITH FUJIWARA, THEN.

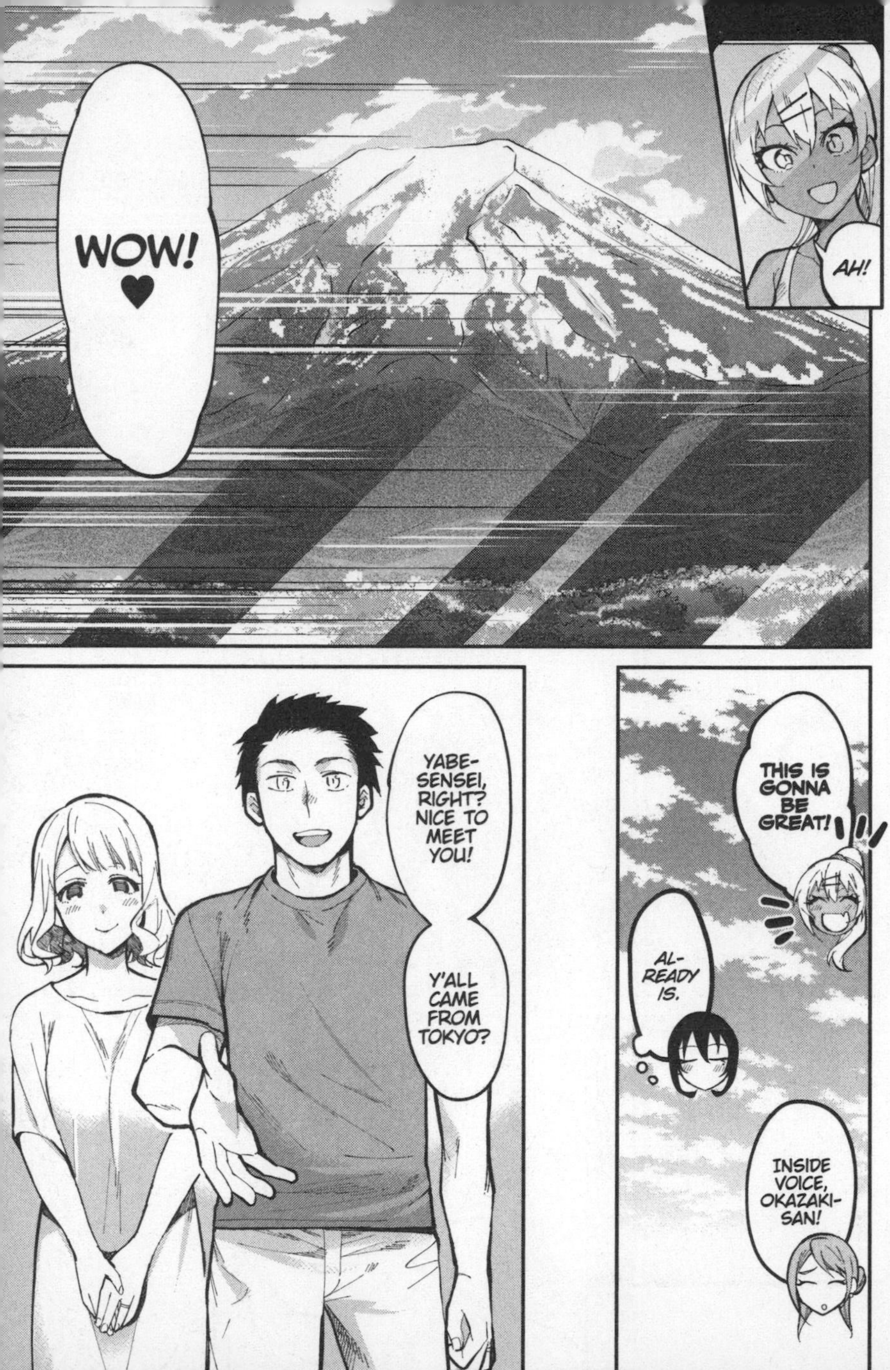
AH!
WOW! ♥
THIS IS GONNA BE GREAT!
AL-READY IS.
INSIDE VOICE, OKAZAKI-SAN!
YABE-SENSEI, RIGHT? NICE TO MEET YOU!
Y'ALL CAME FROM TOKYO?

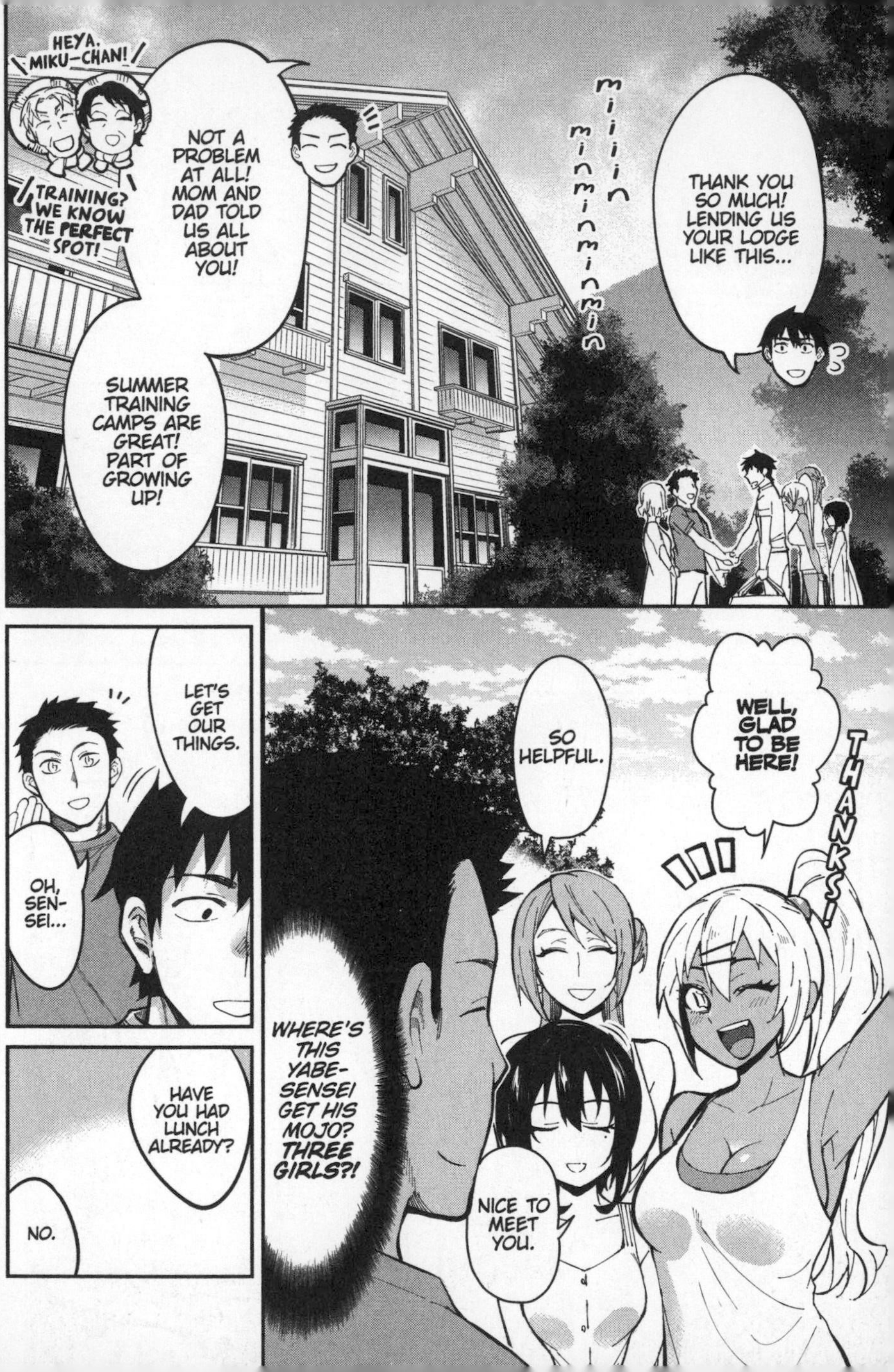
THANK YOU SO MUCH! LENDING US YOUR LODGE LIKE THIS...
miiiin minminminmin
NOT A PROBLEM AT ALL! MOM AND DAD TOLD US ALL ABOUT YOU!
SUMMER TRAINING CAMPS ARE GREAT! PART OF GROWING UP!
HEYA, MIKU-CHAN!
TRAINING? WE KNOW THE PERFECT SPOT!
WELL, GLAD TO BE HERE!
THANKS!
SO HELPFUL.
NICE TO MEET YOU.
WHERE'S THIS YABE-SENSEI GET HIS MOJO? THREE GIRLS?!
LET'S GET OUR THINGS.
OH, SEN-SEI...
HAVE YOU HAD LUNCH ALREADY?
NO.

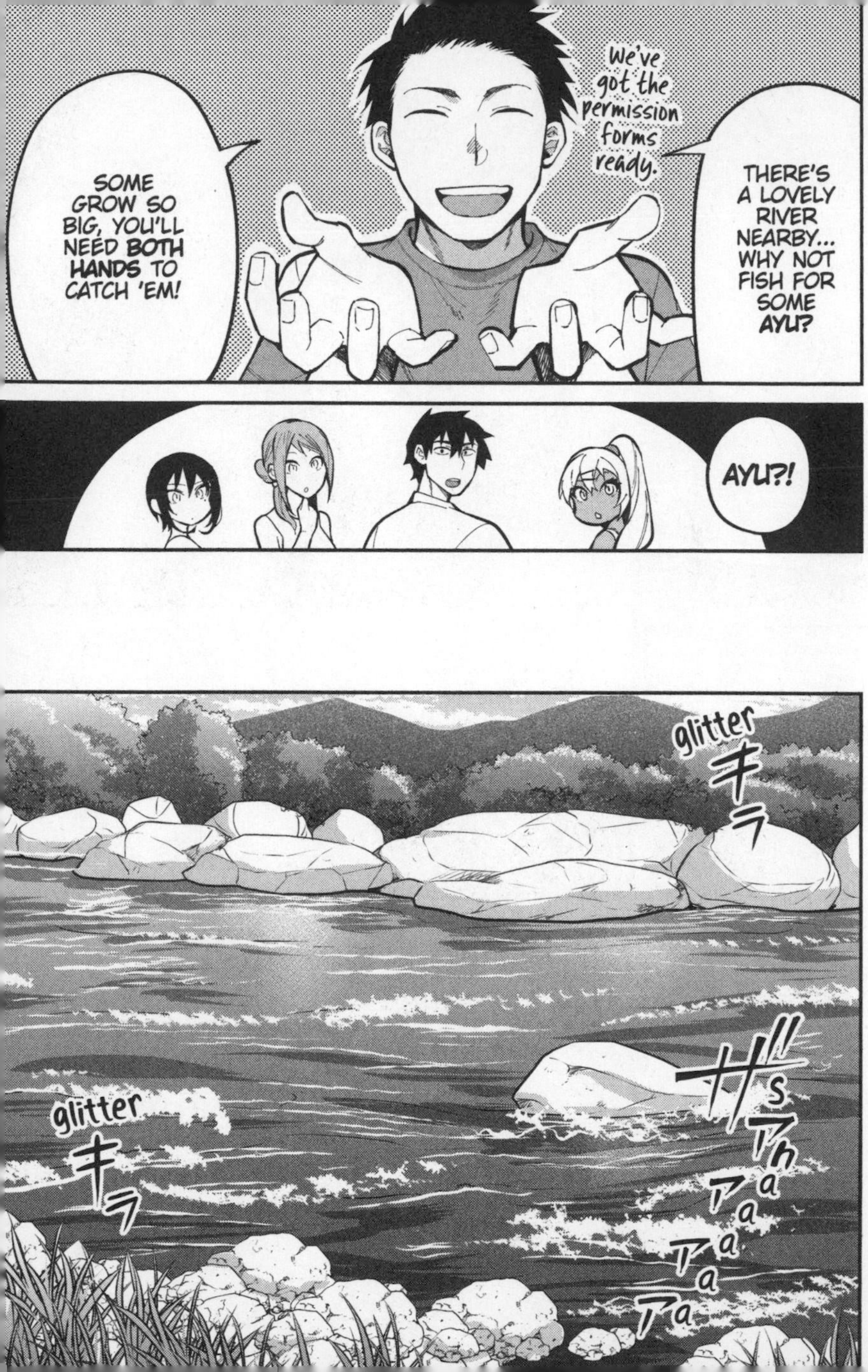
THERE'S A LOVELY RIVER NEARBY... WHY NOT FISH FOR SOME AYU?
We've got the permission forms ready.
SOME GROW SO BIG, YOU'LL NEED BOTH HANDS TO CATCH 'EM!
AYU?!
glitter キラ
ザァアアアア shaaaaa
glitter キラ

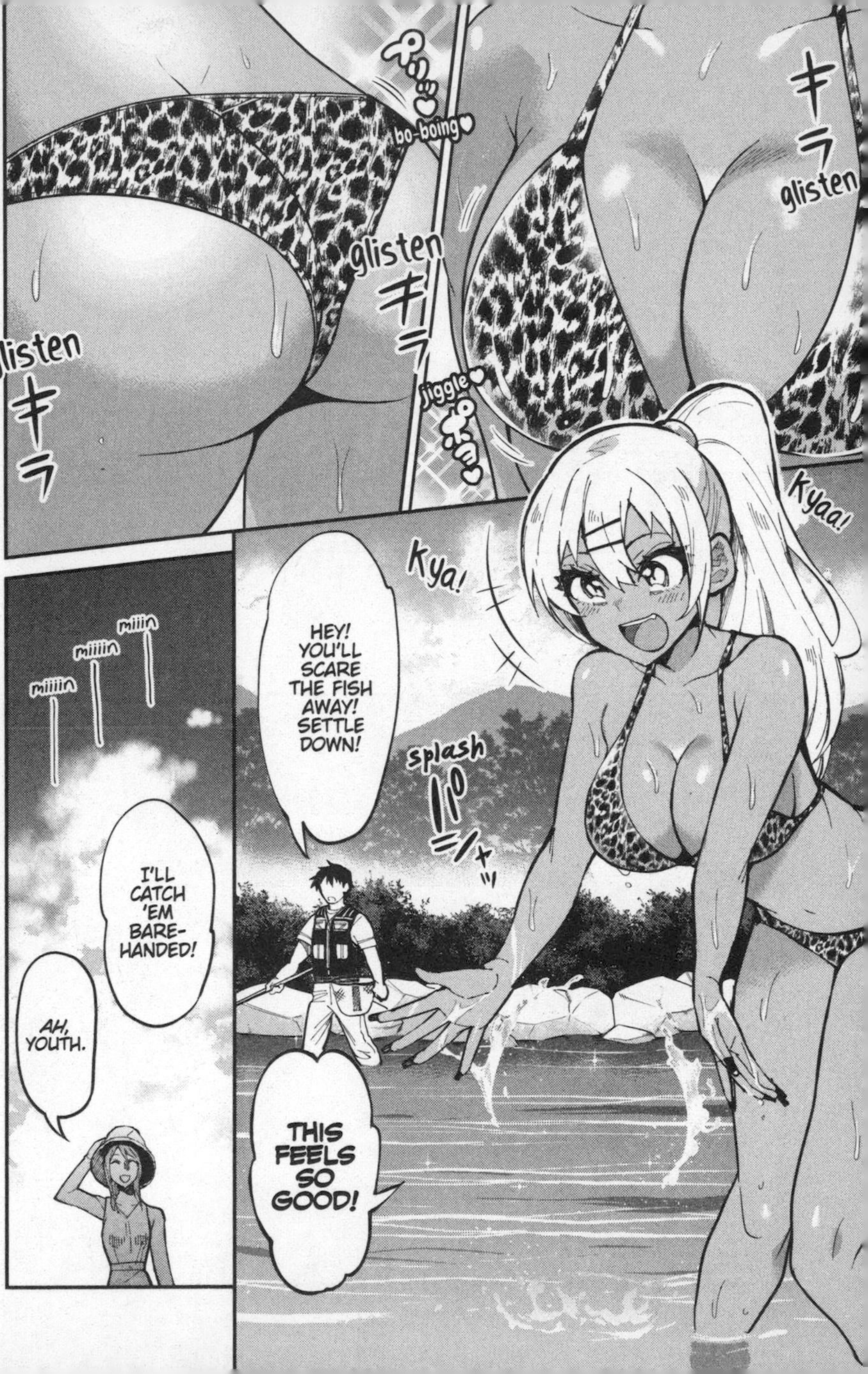
キラ
glisten
bo-boing♥
glisten
キラ
jiggle♥
glisten
キラ
Kyaa!
Kya!
splash
HEY! YOU'LL SCARE THE FISH AWAY! SETTLE DOWN!
THIS FEELS SO GOOD!
miiin
miiiin
miiiin
I'LL CATCH 'EM BARE-HANDED!
AH, YOUTH.

WHATCHA DOING THERE, FUJIWARA-CHAN? COME ON IN!

twitch

!

UH-HUH.

...

KA-CHUNK

I-I'M MONITORING YOUR ACTIVITIES ON BEHALF OF THE STUDENT COUNCIL.

EEP?! THAT'S COLD!

FsssHHH

GOTCHA!!

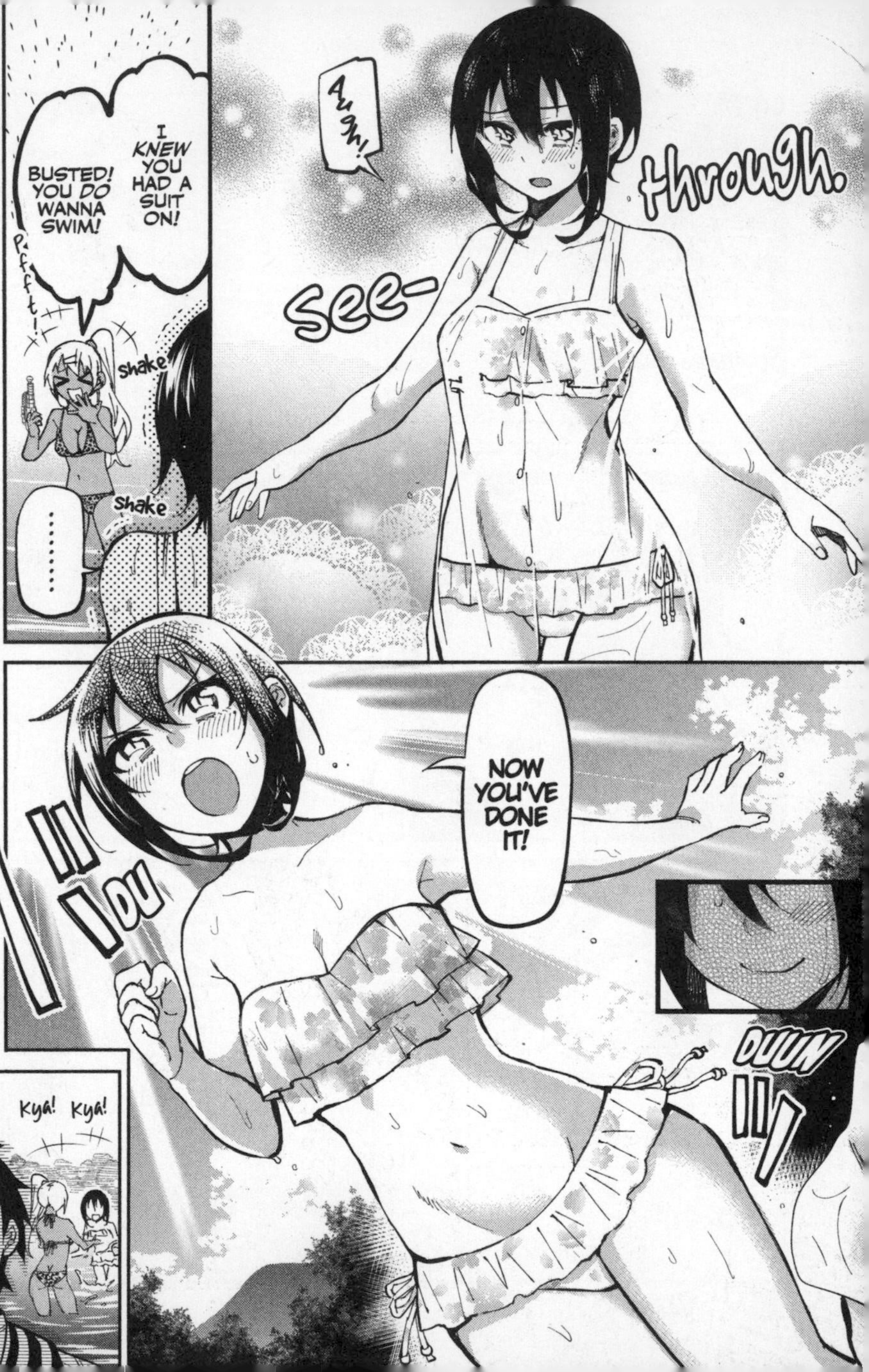
Augh!
see-
through.
I KNEW YOU HAD A SUIT ON!
BUSTED! YOU DO WANNA SWIM!
Pffft!
shake
shake
......
NOW YOU'VE DONE IT!
DUUN
Kya! Kya!

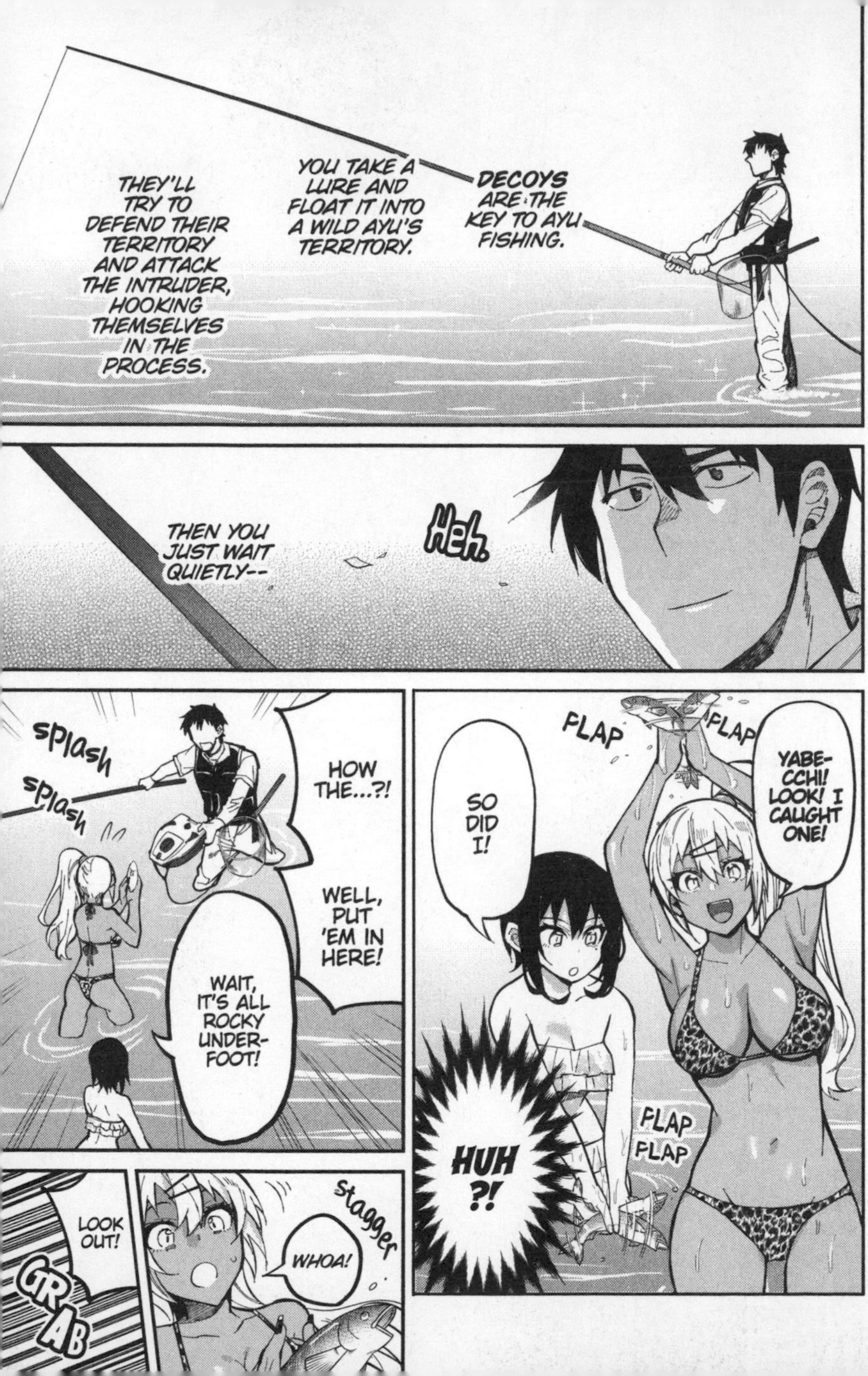
DECOYS ARE THE KEY TO AYU FISHING.
YOU TAKE A LURE AND FLOAT IT INTO A WILD AYU'S TERRITORY.
THEY'LL TRY TO DEFEND THEIR TERRITORY AND ATTACK THE INTRUDER, HOOKING THEMSELVES IN THE PROCESS.
Heh.
THEN YOU JUST WAIT QUIETLY--
FLAP FLAP
YABE-CCHI! LOOK! I CAUGHT ONE!
SO DID I!
FLAP FLAP
HUH?!
splash splash
HOW THE...?!
WELL, PUT 'EM IN HERE!
WAIT, IT'S ALL ROCKY UNDERFOOT!
stagger
WHOA!
LOOK OUT!
GRAB

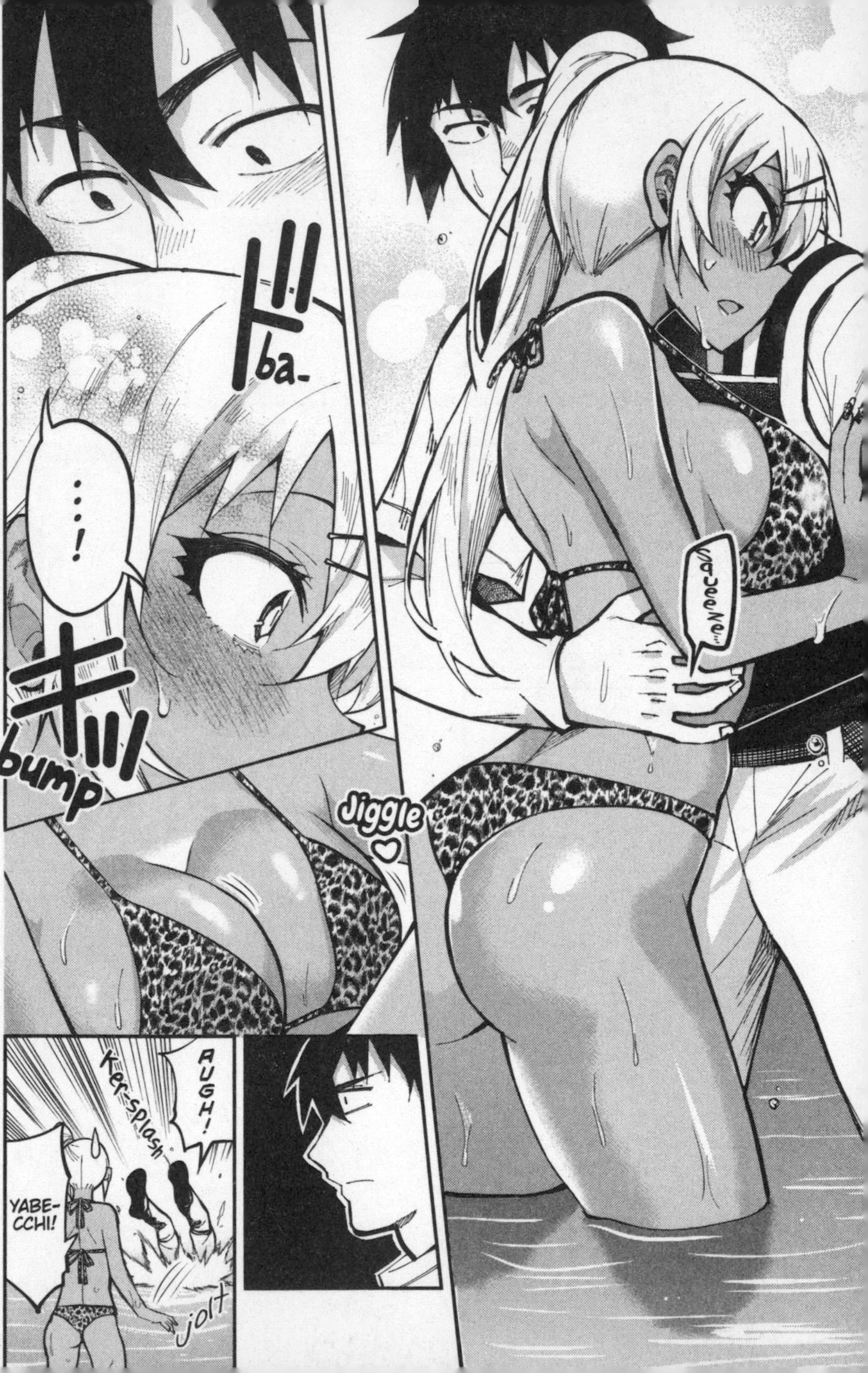
Squeeeze...
ba-
...!
bump
Jiggle ♥
AUGH!
Ker-splash
YABECCHI!
jolt

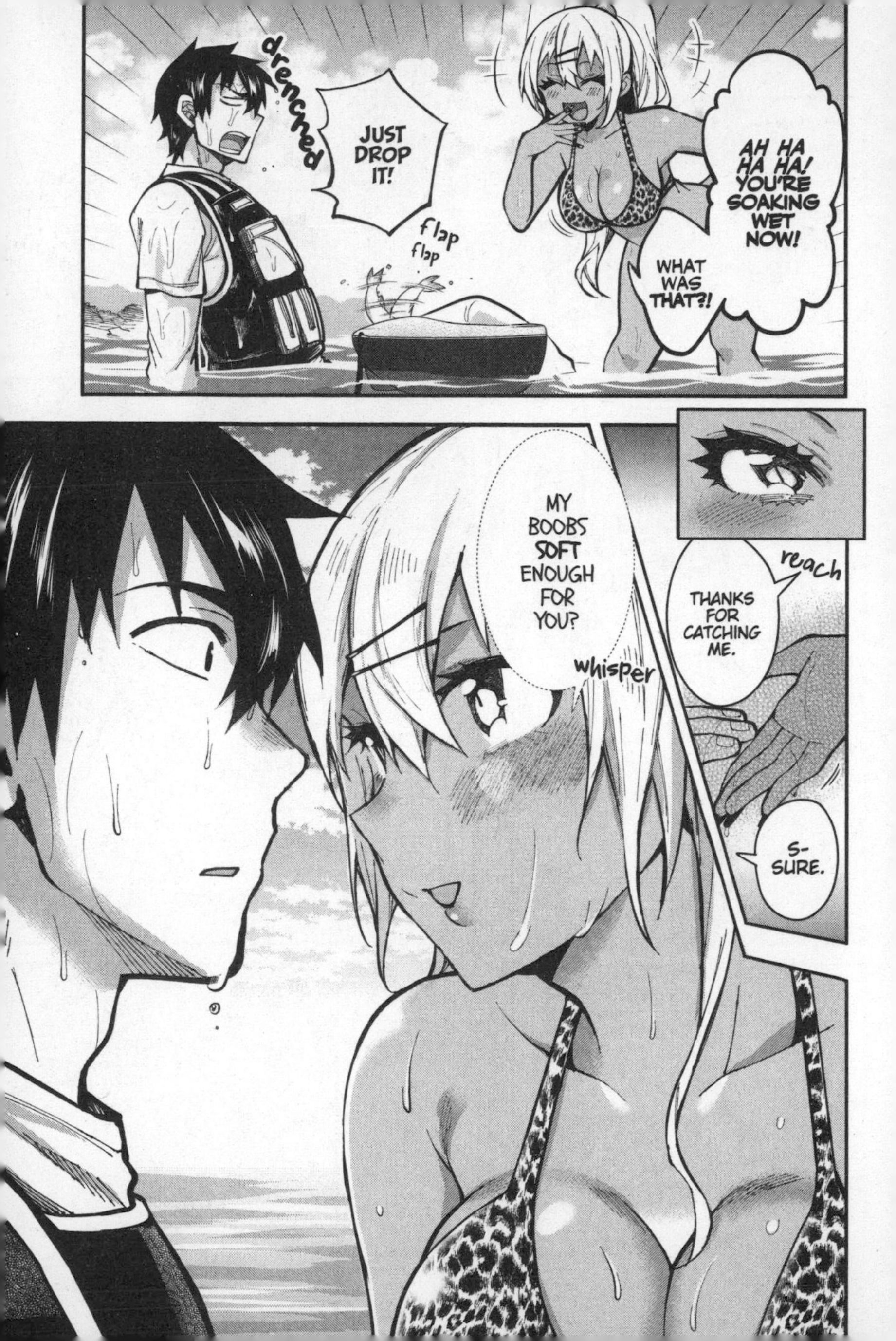
AH HA HA HA! YOU'RE SOAKING WET NOW!
WHAT WAS THAT?!
drenched
JUST DROP IT!
flap flap
reach
THANKS FOR CATCHING ME.
S-SURE.
MY BOOBS SOFT ENOUGH FOR YOU?
whisper

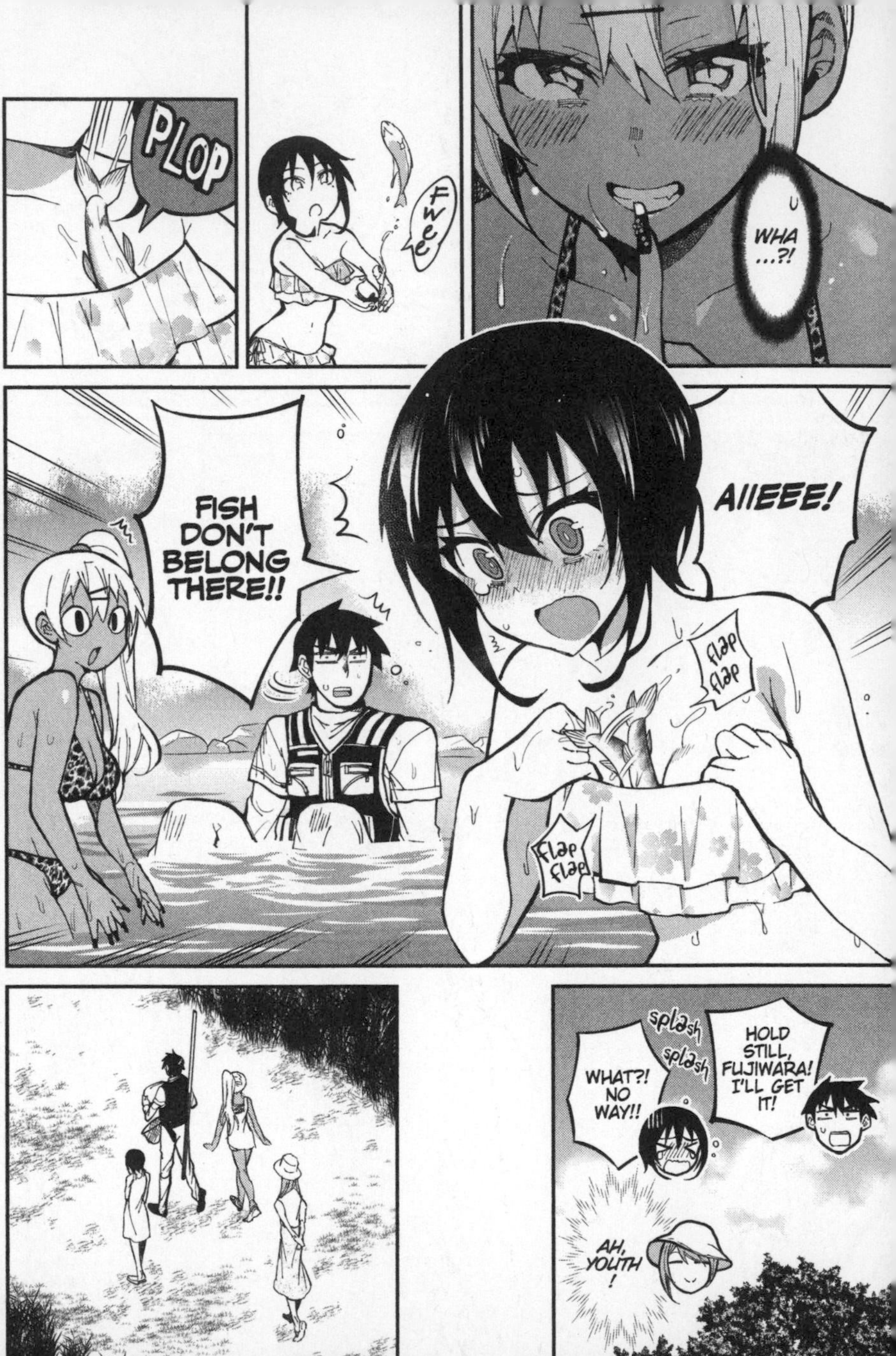
WHA ...?!
Fwee
PLOP
AIIEEE!
flap flap
FISH DON'T BELONG THERE!!
flap flap
HOLD STILL, FUJIWARA! I'LL GET IT!
splash splash
WHAT?! NO WAY!!
AH, YOUTH!

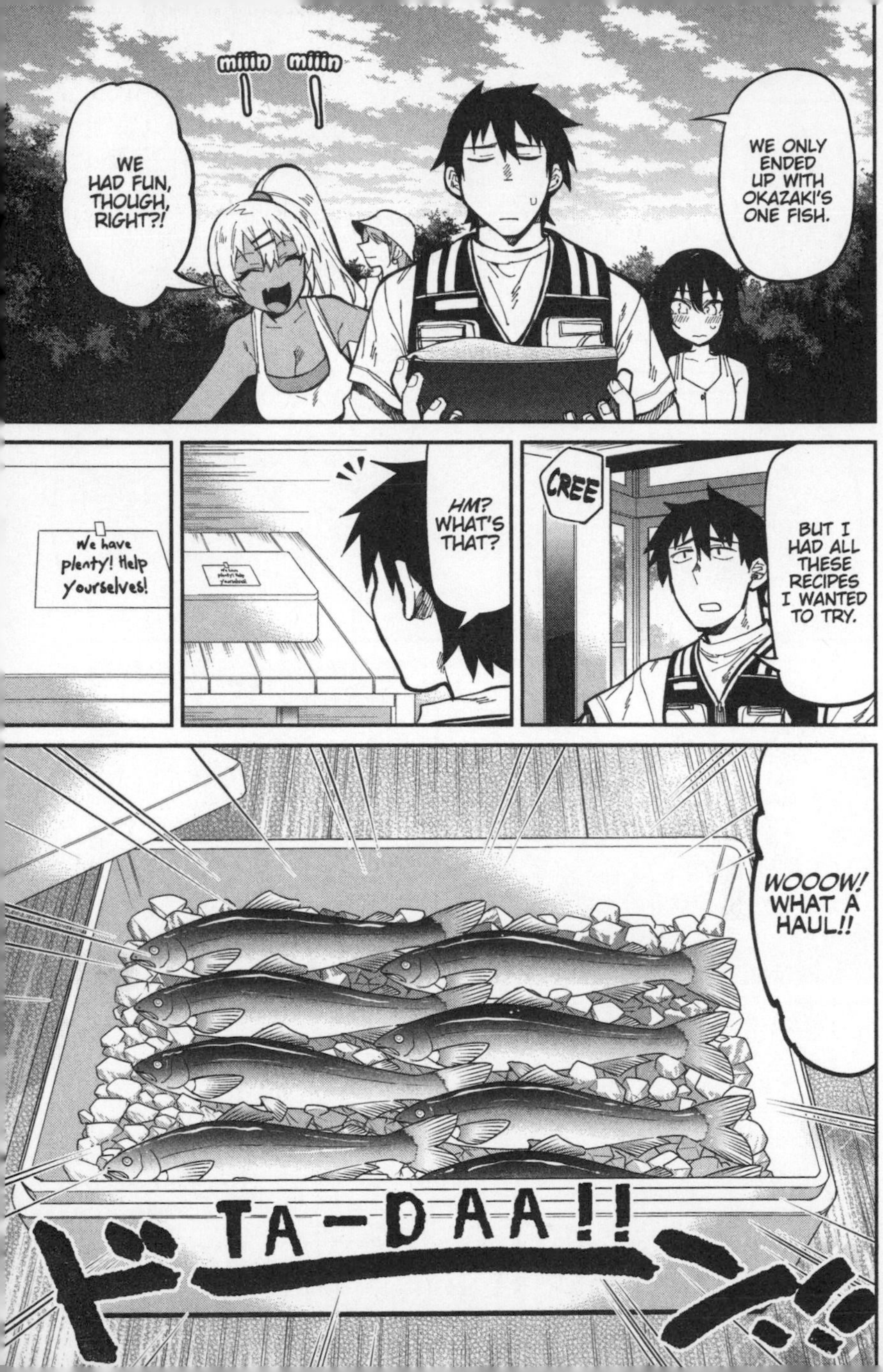
WE ONLY ENDED UP WITH OKAZAKI'S ONE FISH.
miiin miiin
WE HAD FUN, THOUGH, RIGHT?!
BUT I HAD ALL THESE RECIPES I WANTED TO TRY.
CREE
HM? WHAT'S THAT?
We have plenty! Help yourselves!
WOOOW! WHAT A HAUL!!
TA-DAA!!

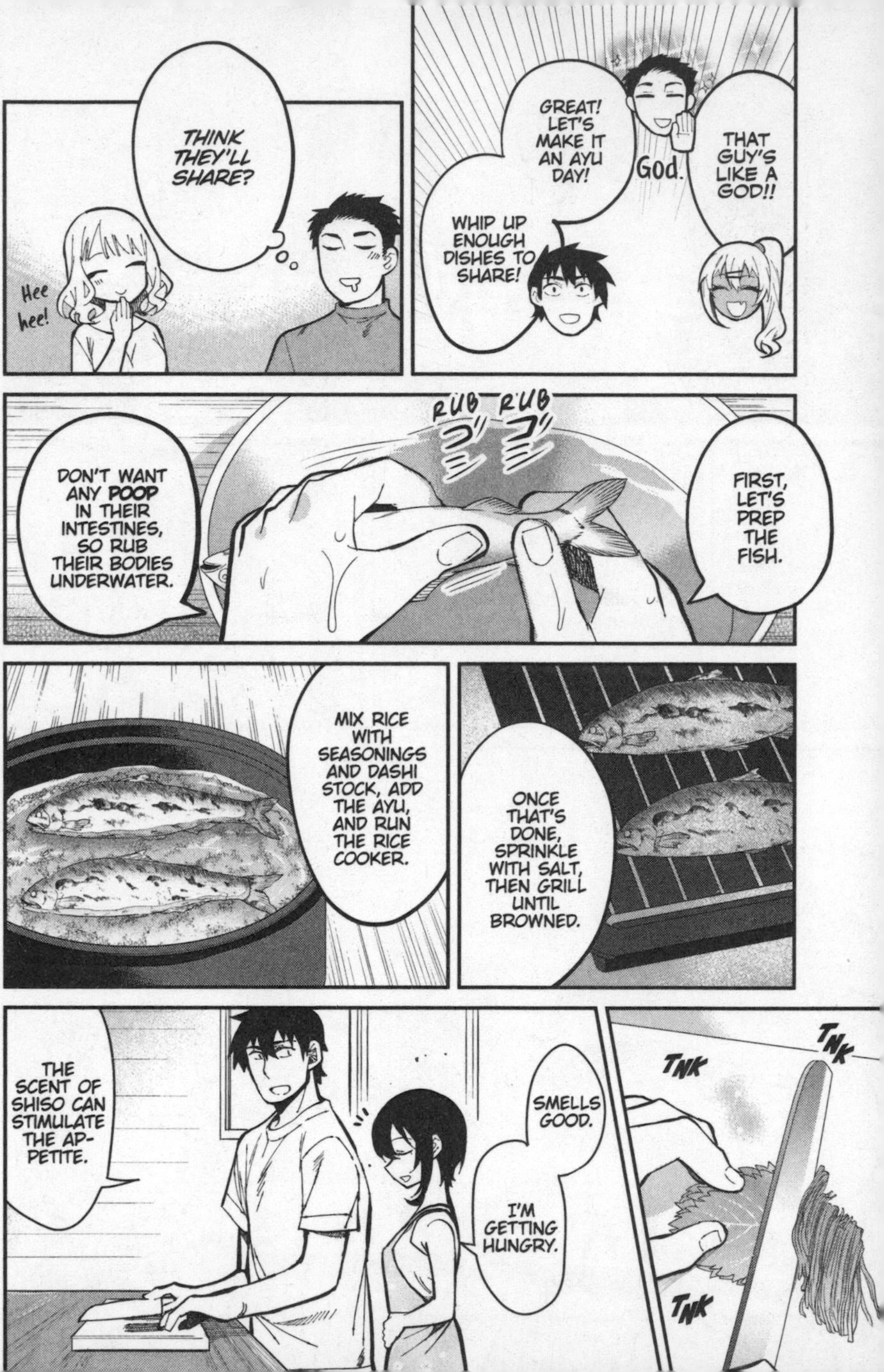
GREAT! LET'S MAKE IT AN AYU DAY!
WHIP UP ENOUGH DISHES TO SHARE!
God.
THAT GUY'S LIKE A GOD!!
THINK THEY'LL SHARE?
Hee hee!
FIRST, LET'S PREP THE FISH.
RUB RUB
DON'T WANT ANY POOP IN THEIR INTESTINES, SO RUB THEIR BODIES UNDERWATER.
ONCE THAT'S DONE, SPRINKLE WITH SALT, THEN GRILL UNTIL BROWNED.
MIX RICE WITH SEASONINGS AND DASHI STOCK, ADD THE AYU, AND RUN THE RICE COOKER.
TNK
TNK
TNK
SMELLS GOOD.
I'M GETTING HUNGRY.
THE SCENT OF SHISO CAN STIMULATE THE AP-PETITE.

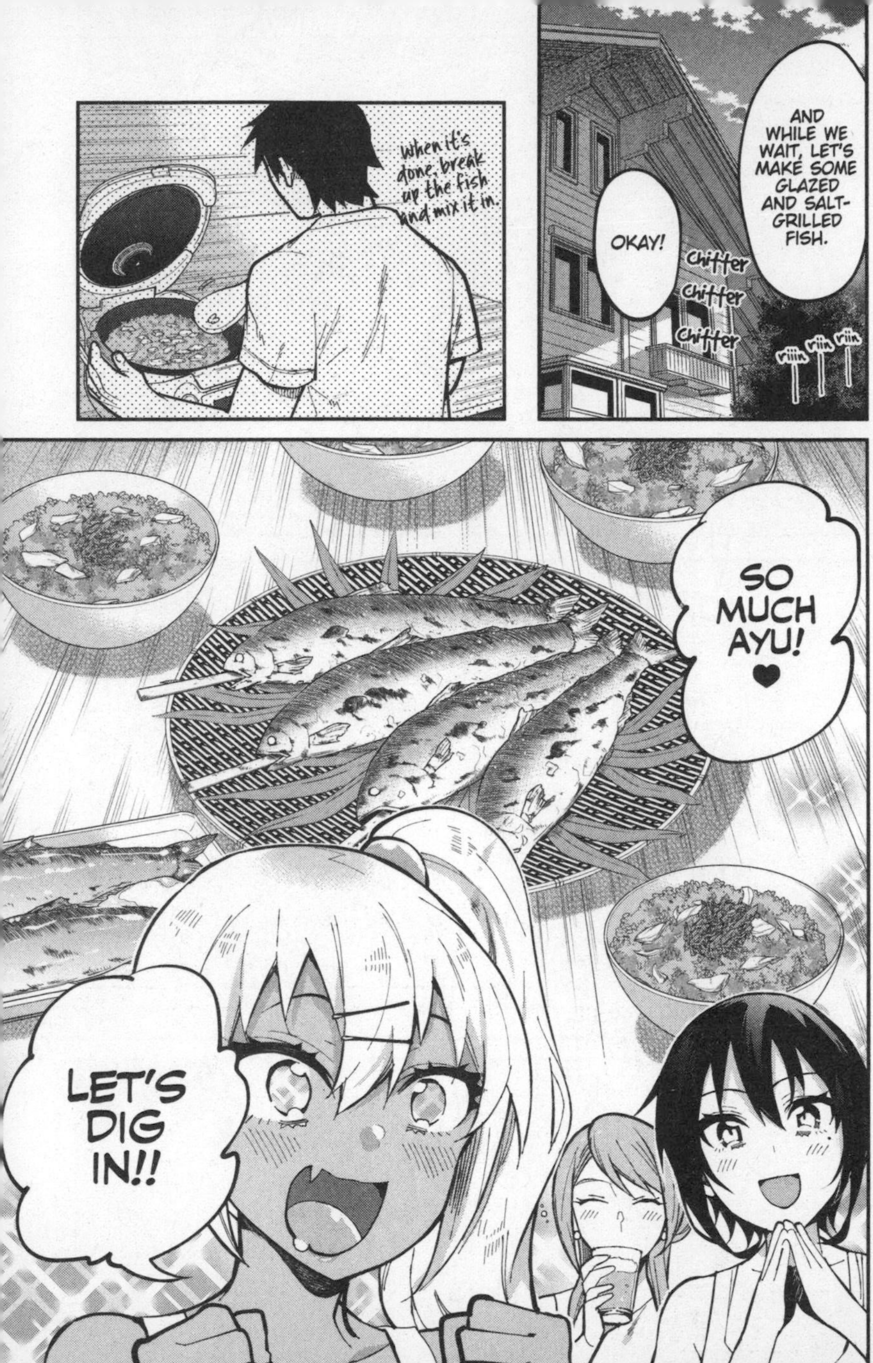
AND WHILE WE WAIT, LET'S MAKE SOME GLAZED AND SALT-GRILLED FISH.
OKAY!
chitter chitter chitter
riiin riiin riiin
when it's done, break up the fish and mix it in.
SO MUCH AYU! ♥
LET'S DIG IN!!

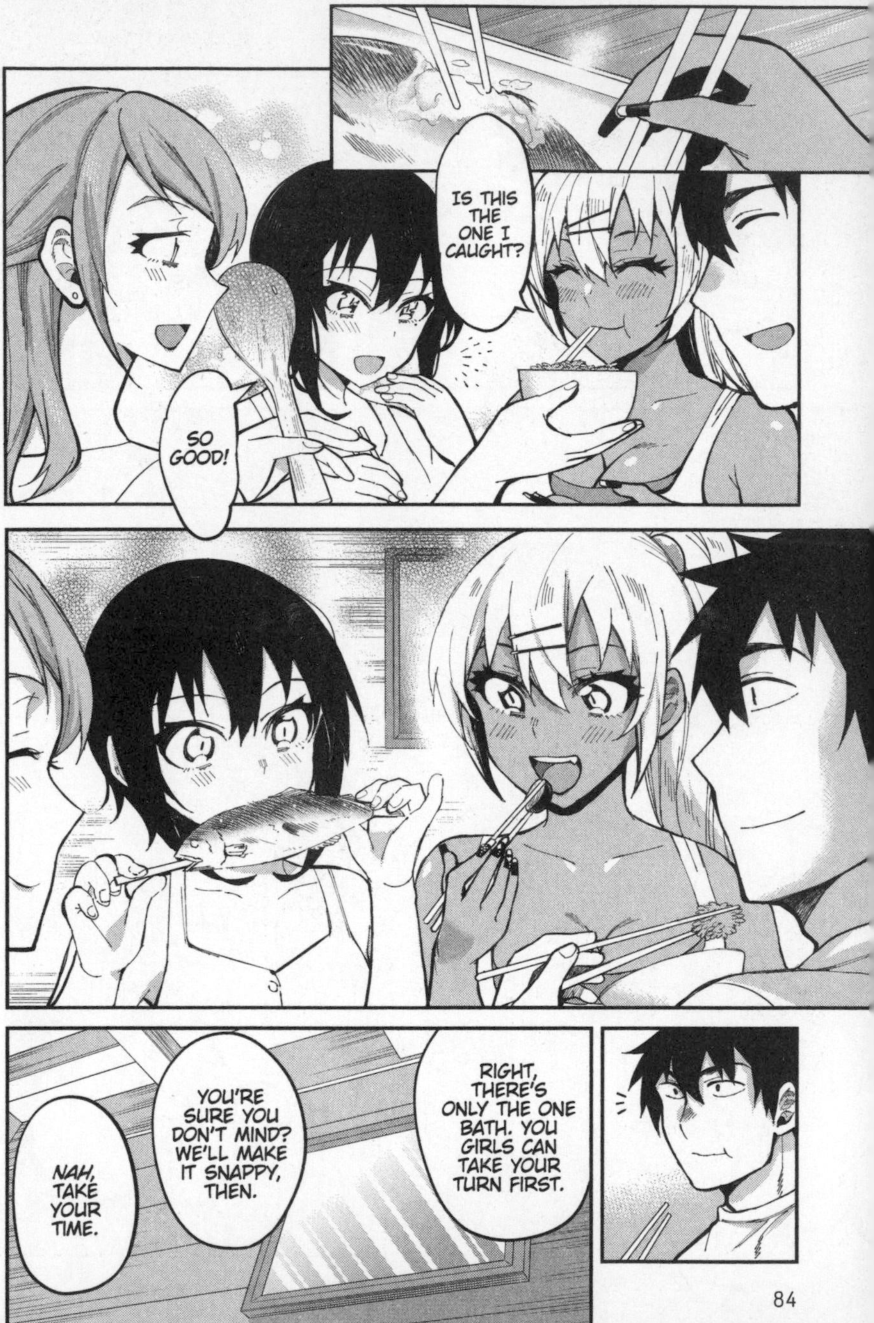
IS THIS THE ONE I CAUGHT?
SO GOOD!
RIGHT, THERE'S ONLY THE ONE BATH. YOU GIRLS CAN TAKE YOUR TURN FIRST.
YOU'RE SURE YOU DON'T MIND? WE'LL MAKE IT SNAPPY, THEN.
NAH, TAKE YOUR TIME.

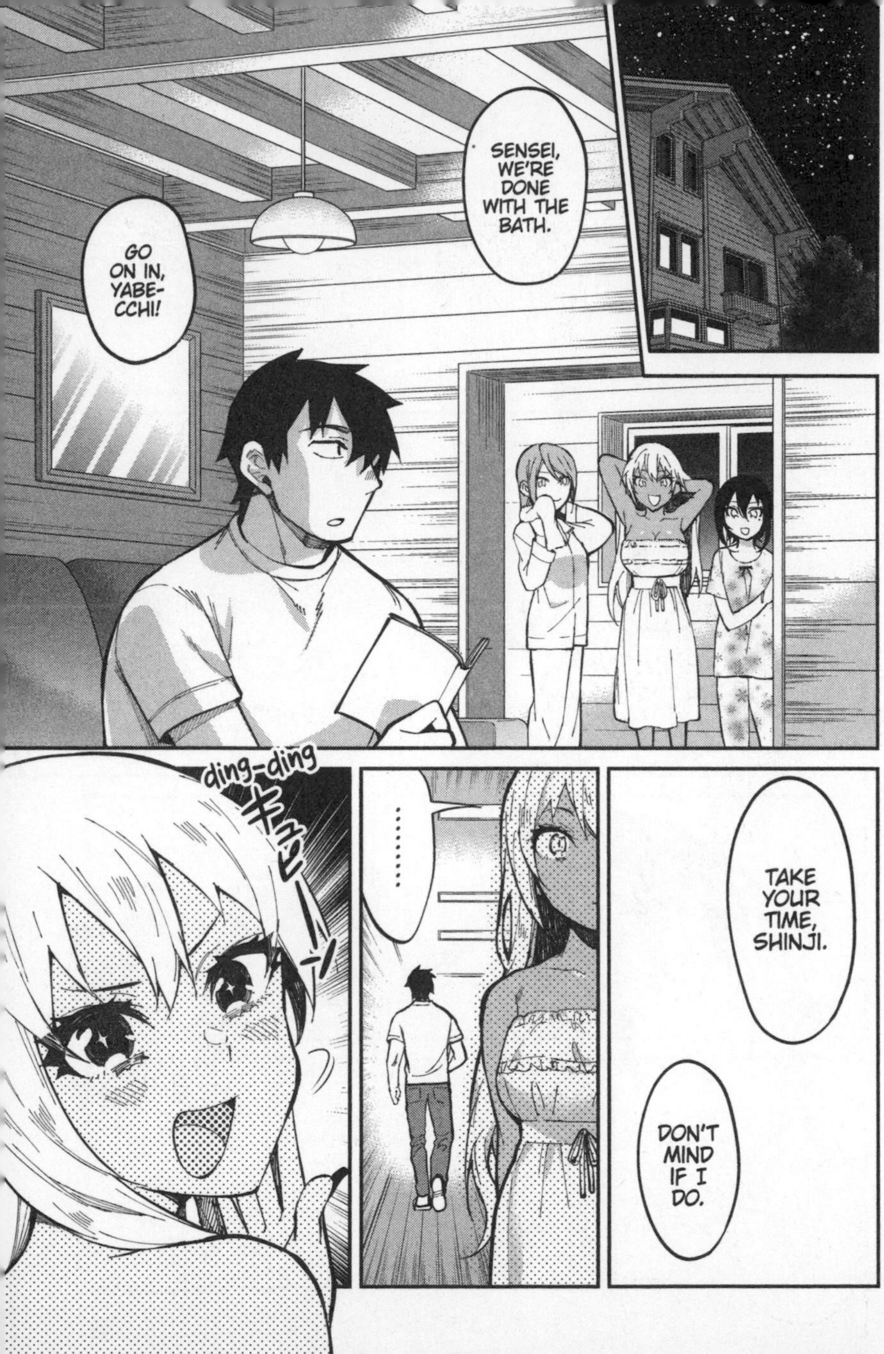
SENSEI, WE'RE DONE WITH THE BATH.
GO ON IN, YABECCHI!
TAKE YOUR TIME, SHINJI.
DON'T MIND IF I DO.
......
ding-ding

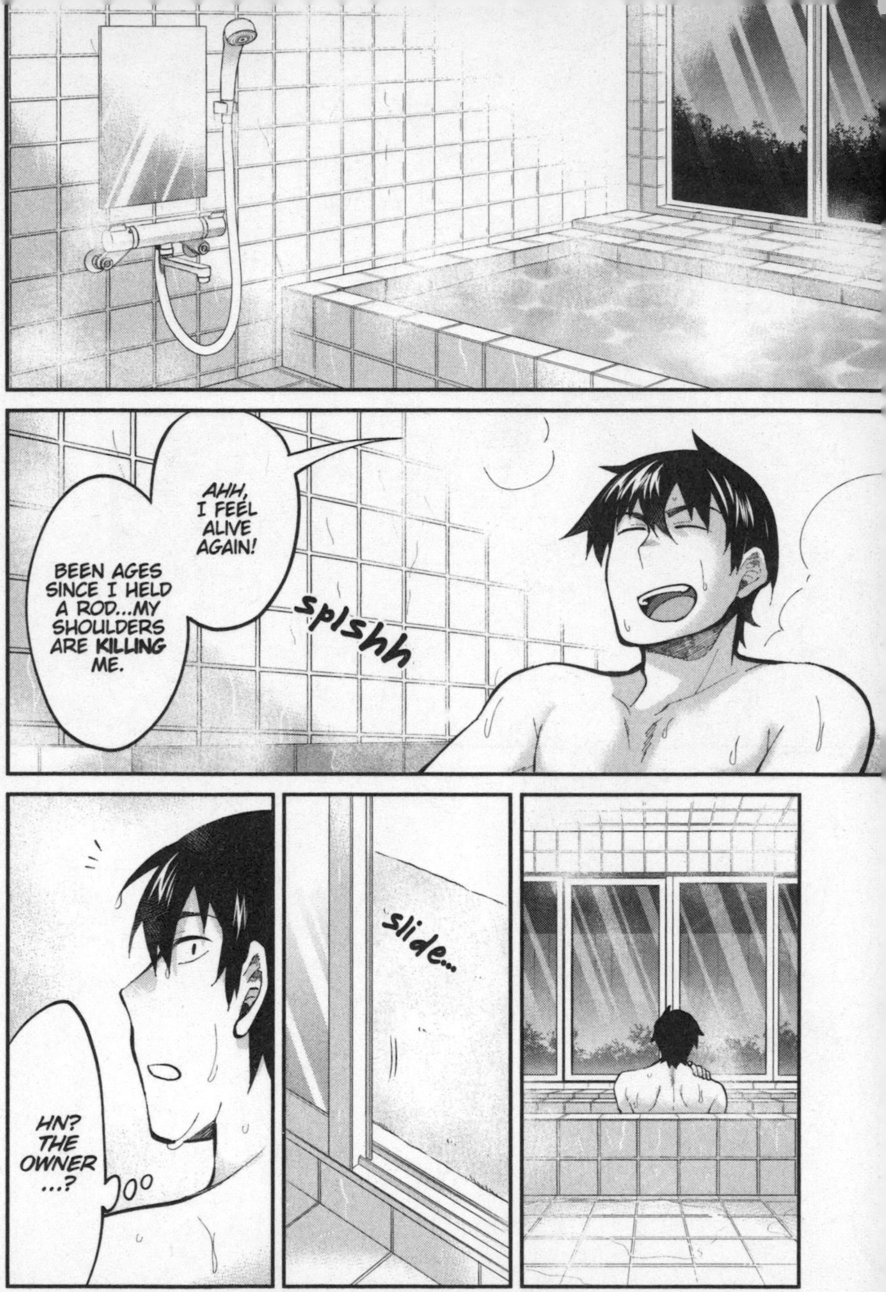
AHH, I FEEL ALIVE AGAIN!
BEEN AGES SINCE I HELD A ROD...MY SHOULDERS ARE KILLING ME.
splshh
slide...
HN? THE OWNER ...?

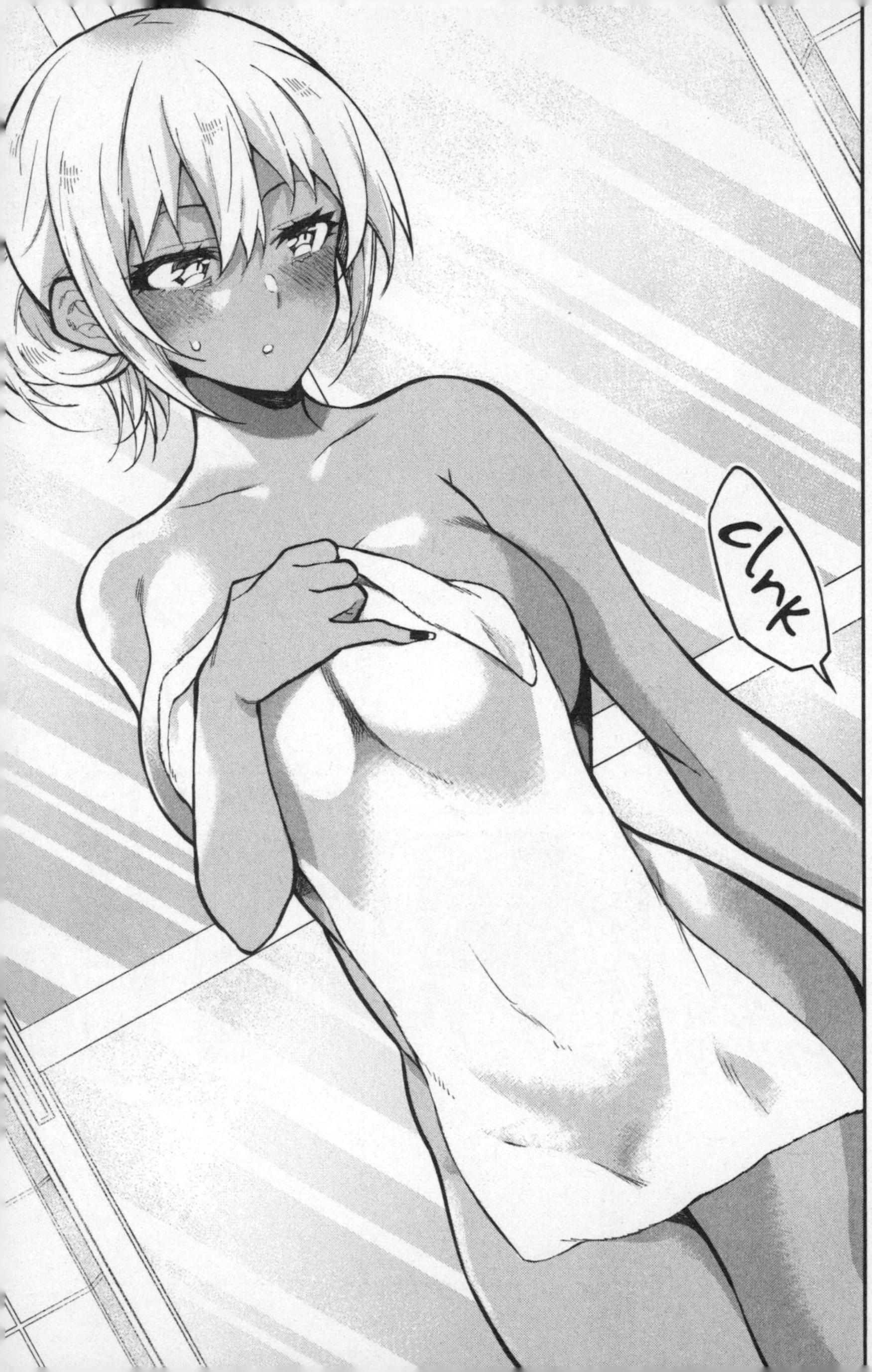
clnk

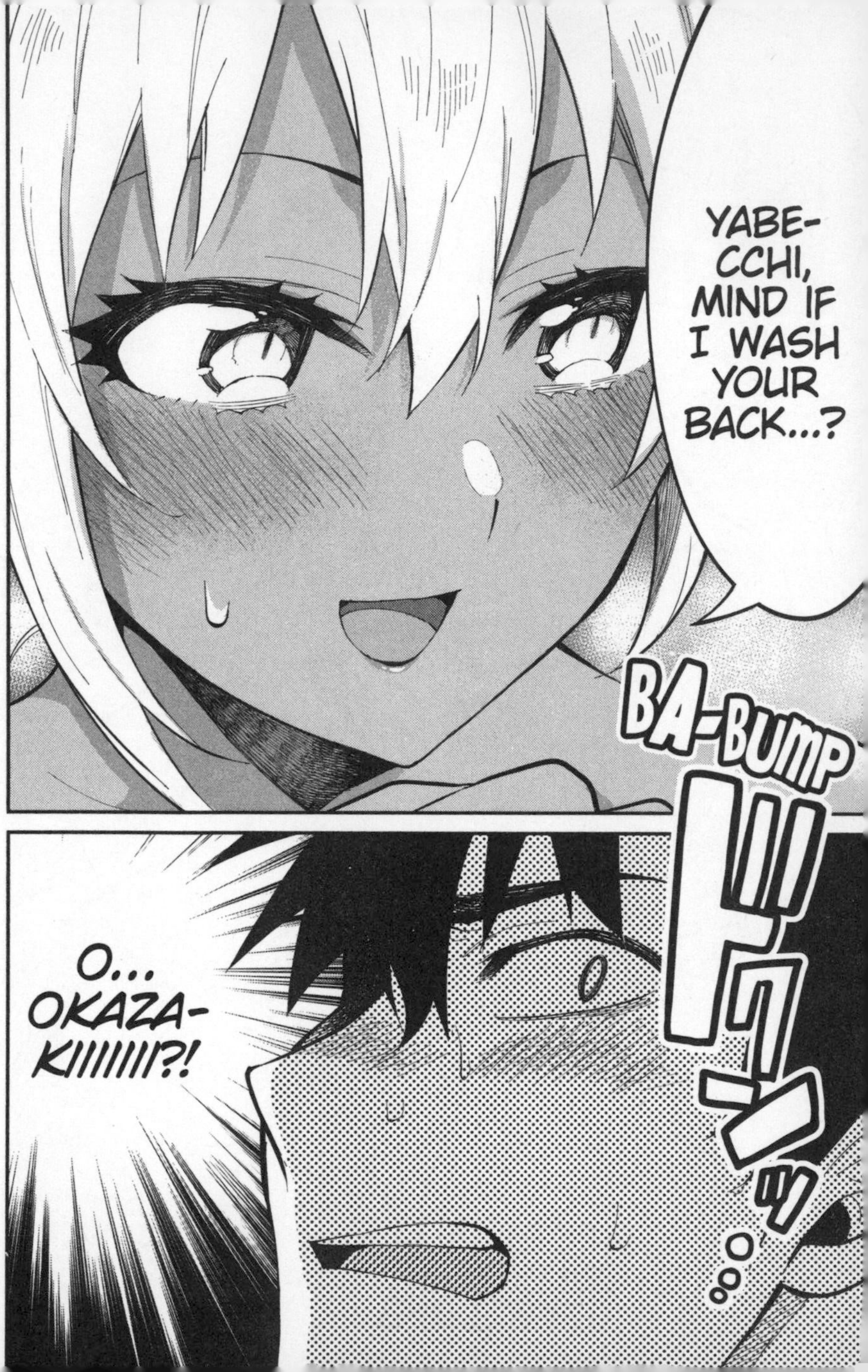
YABE-CCHI, MIND IF I WASH YOUR BACK...?
BA-BUMP
O... OKAZA-KIIIIIII?!

Gal Gohan

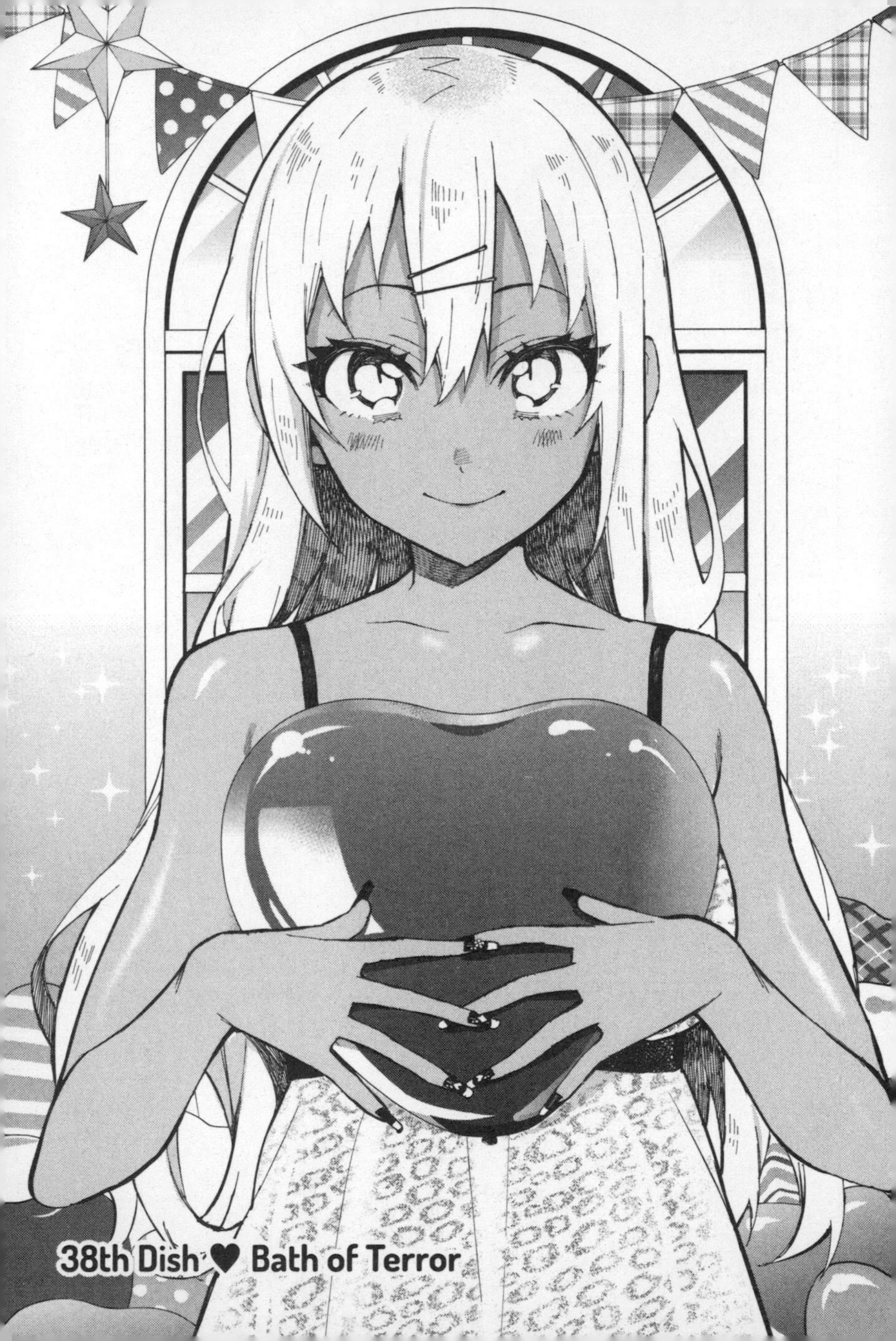
38th Dish ♥ Bath of Terror

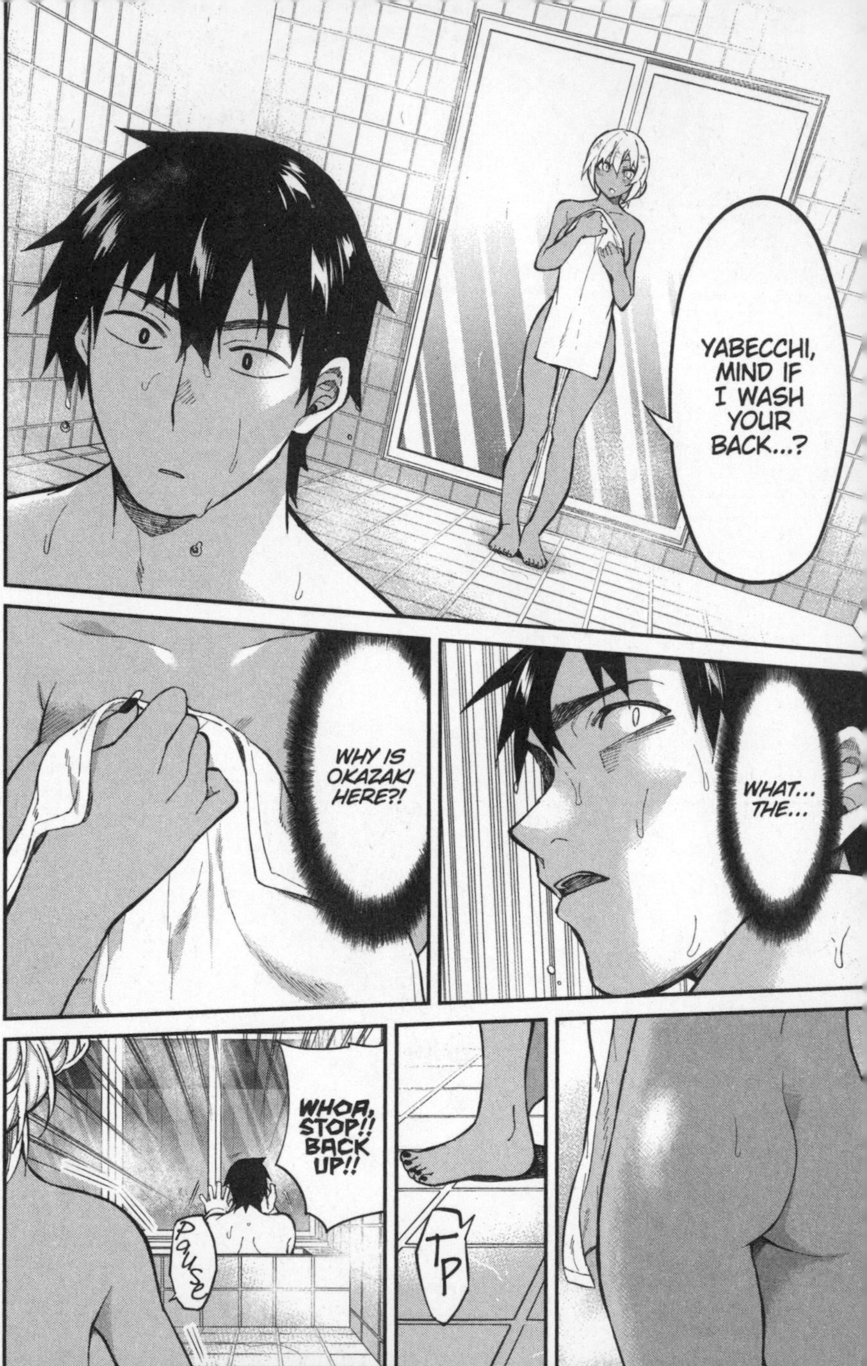
YABECCHI, MIND IF I WASH YOUR BACK...?
WHAT... THE...
WHY IS OKAZAKI HERE?!
TP
WHOA, STOP!! BACK UP!!
Pause

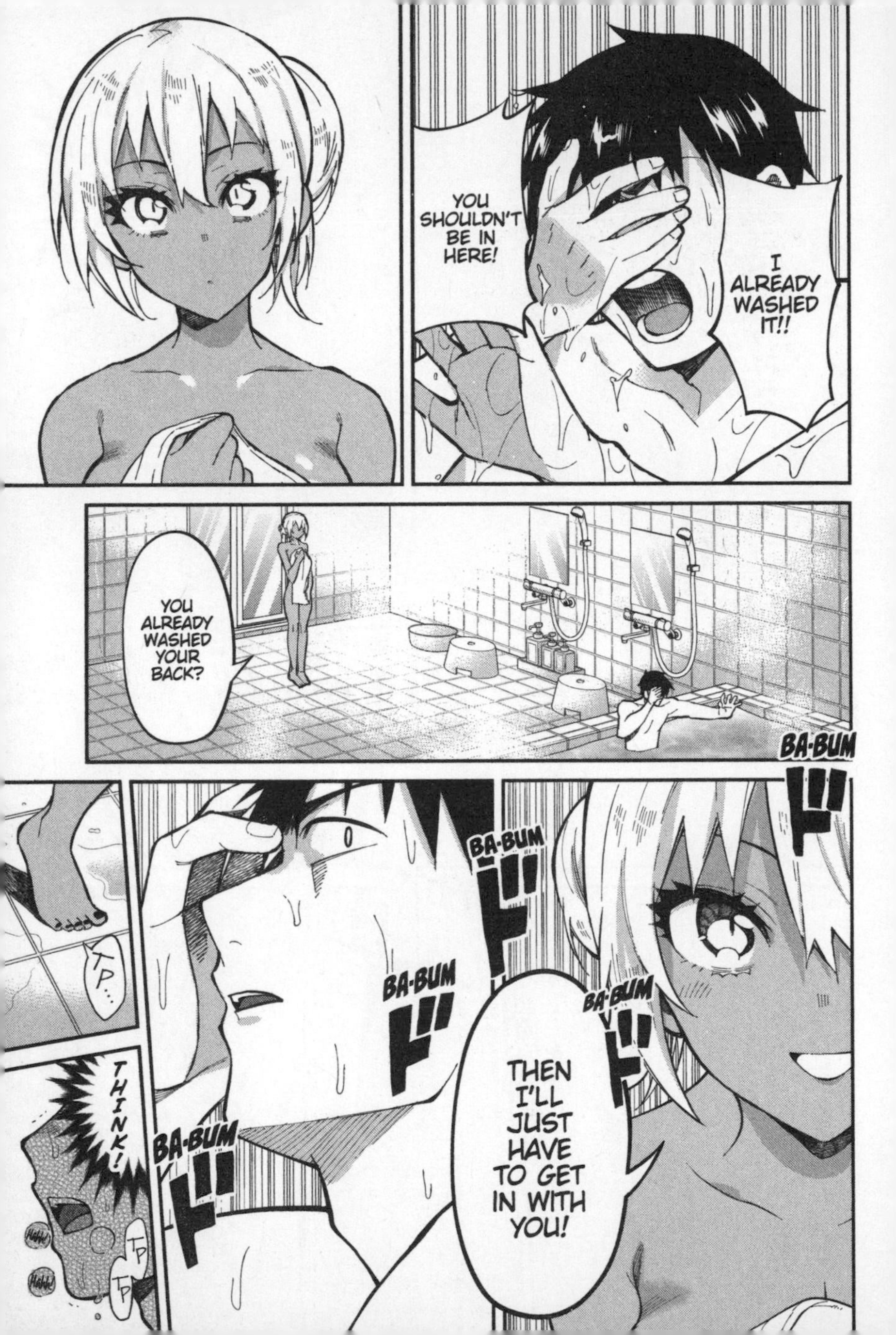
YOU SHOULDN'T BE IN HERE!
I ALREADY WASHED IT!!
YOU ALREADY WASHED YOUR BACK?
BA-BUM
BA-BUM
BA-BUM
THEN I'LL JUST HAVE TO GET IN WITH YOU!
BA-BUM
BA-BUM
TP...
THINK!
HAH!
HAH!
TP
TP

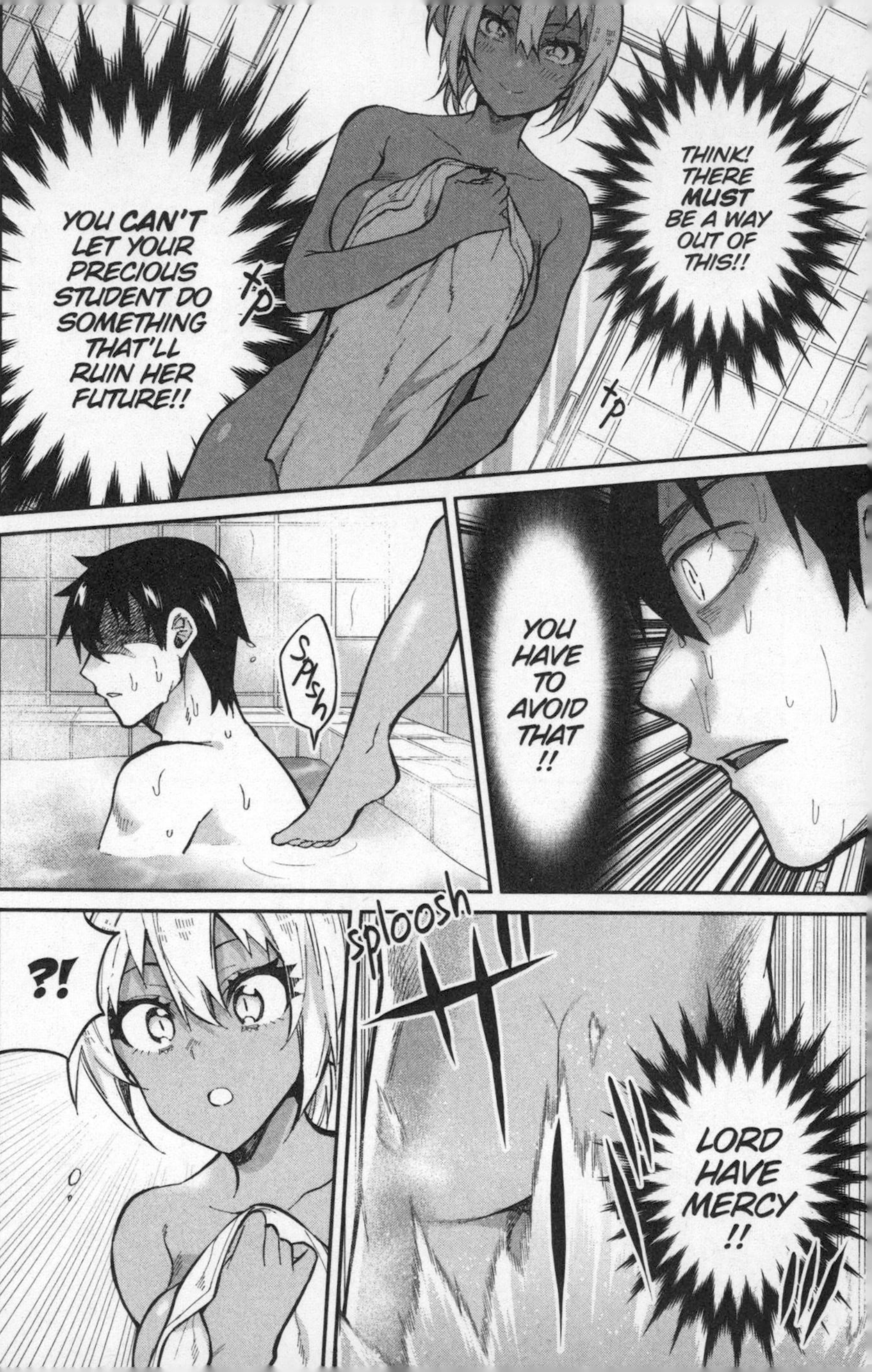
THINK! THERE MUST BE A WAY OUT OF THIS!!
tp
YOU CAN'T LET YOUR PRECIOUS STUDENT DO SOMETHING THAT'LL RUIN HER FUTURE!!
tp
YOU HAVE TO AVOID THAT!!
Splsh
sploosh
?!
LORD HAVE MERCY!!

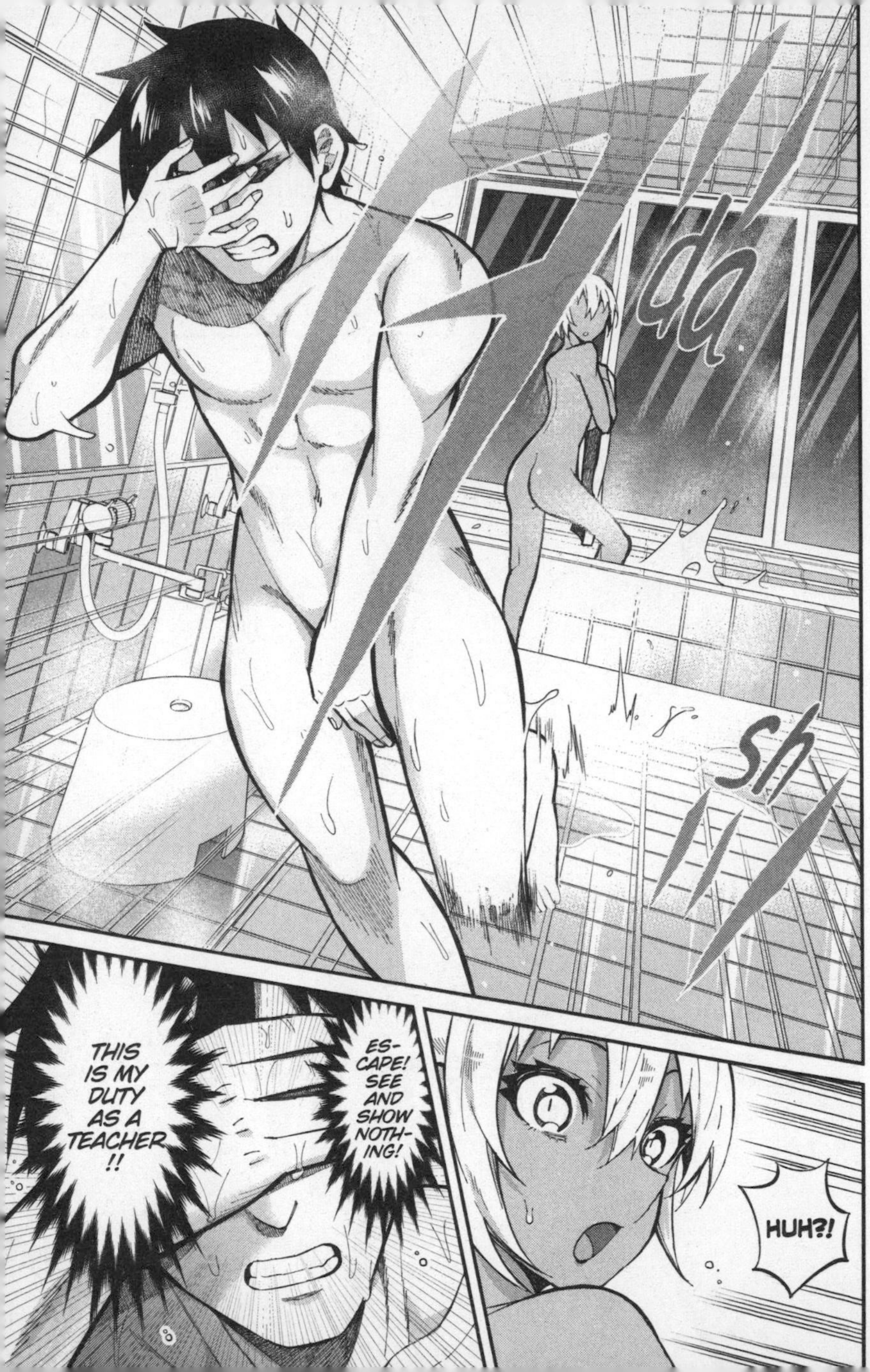
HUH?!
ES-CAPE! SEE AND SHOW NOTHING!
THIS IS MY DUTY AS A TEACHER!!

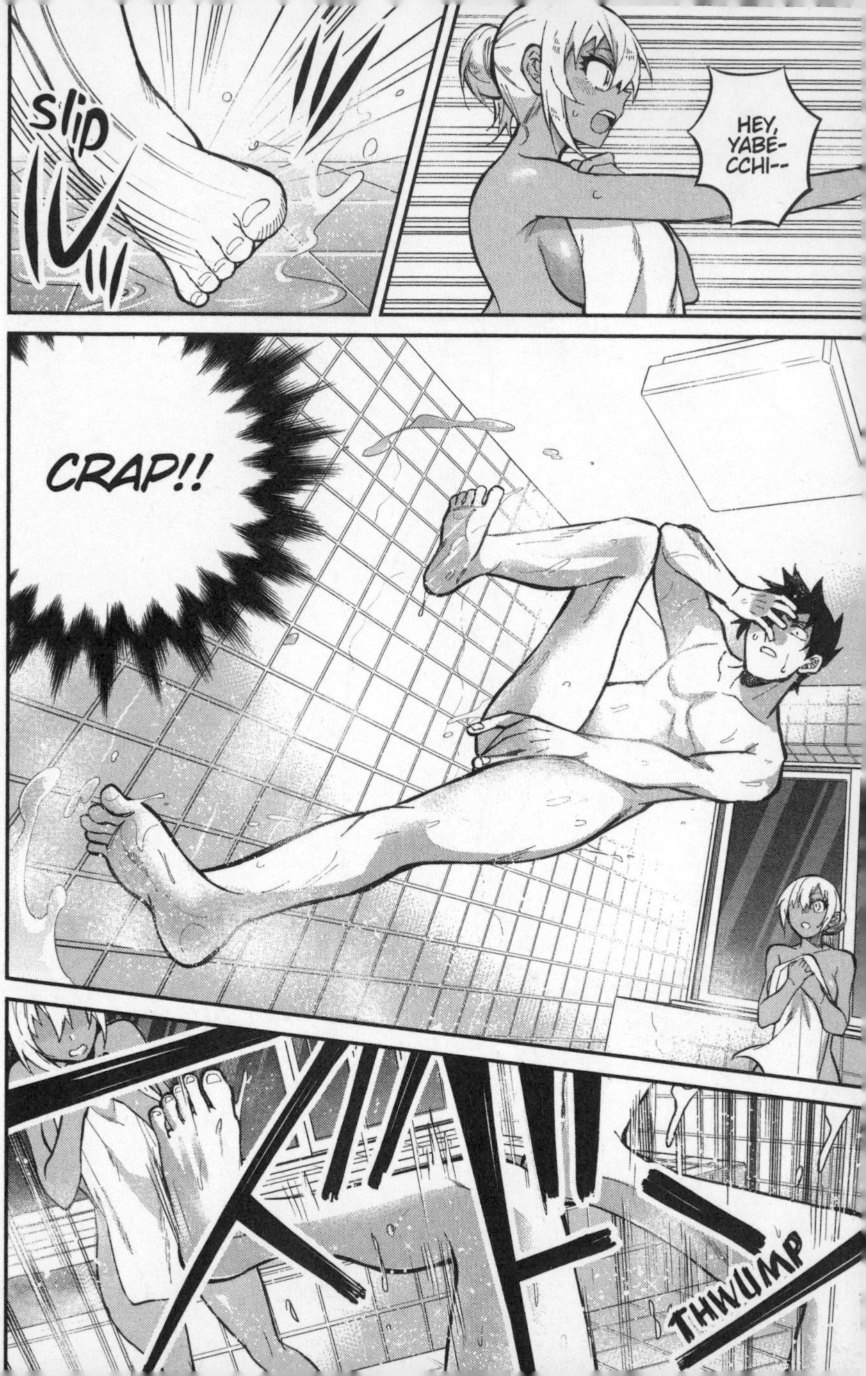
HEY, YABE-CCHI--
slip
CRAP!!
THWUMP

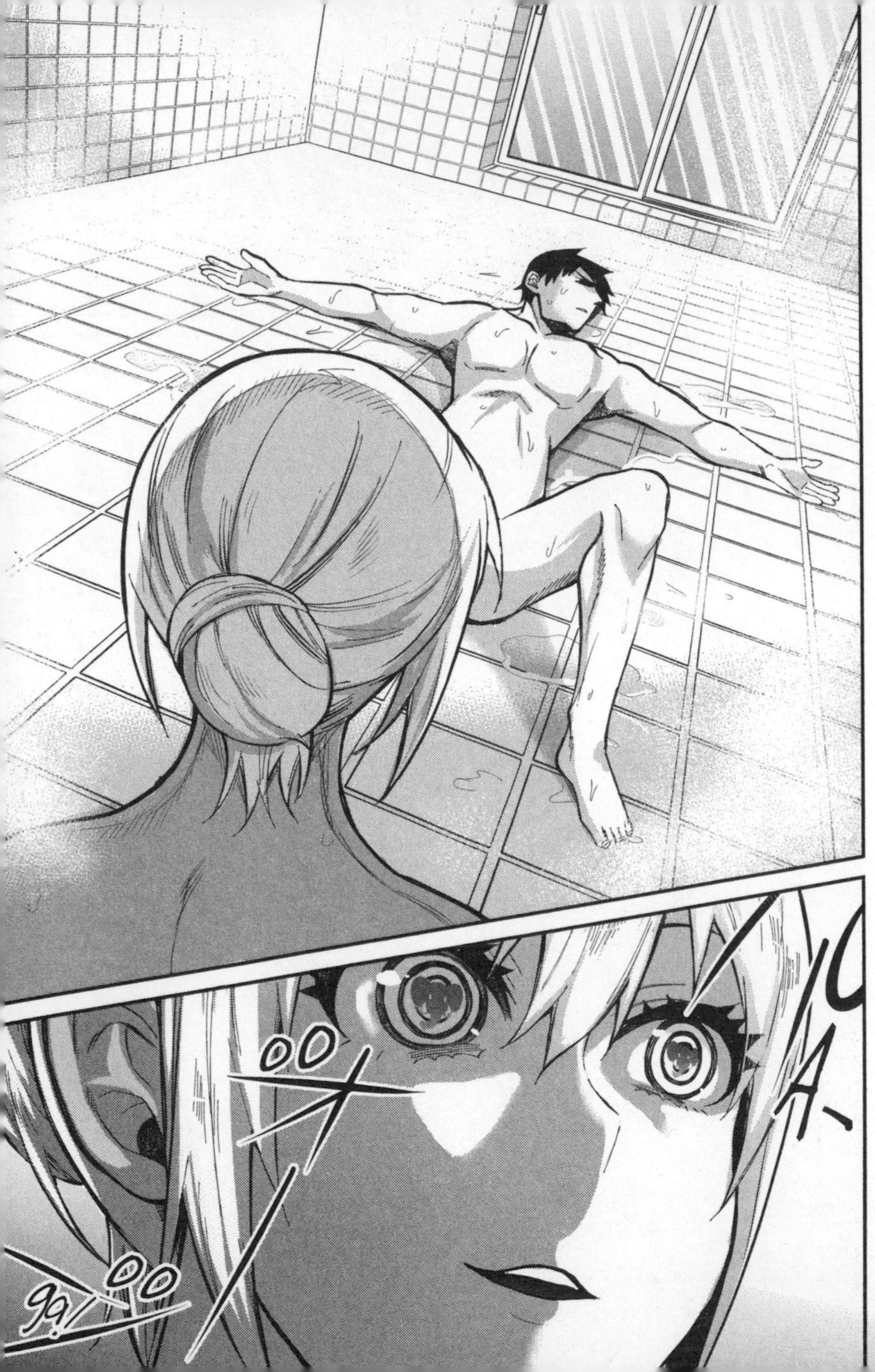
ga!

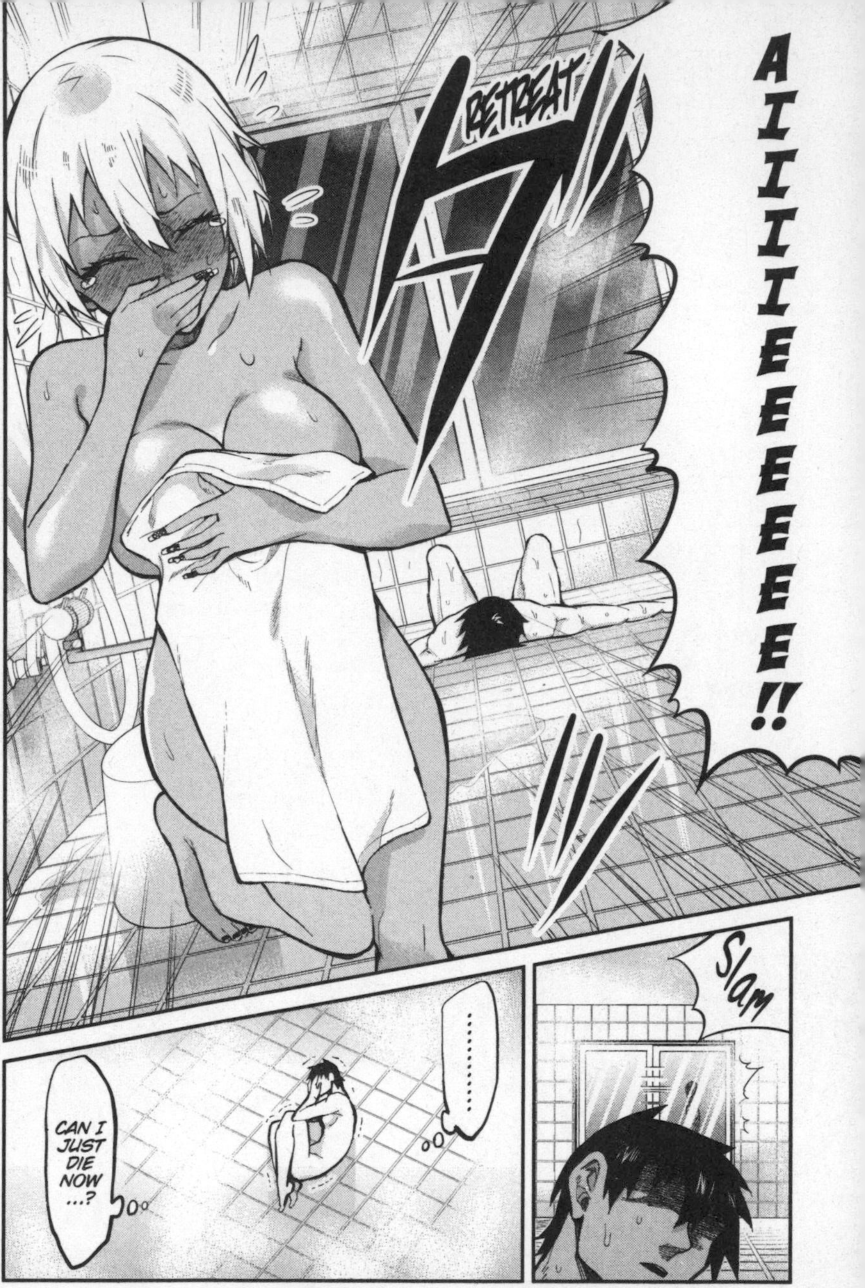
AIIIIEEEEEE!!
RETREAT
Slam
......
CAN I JUST DIE NOW ...?

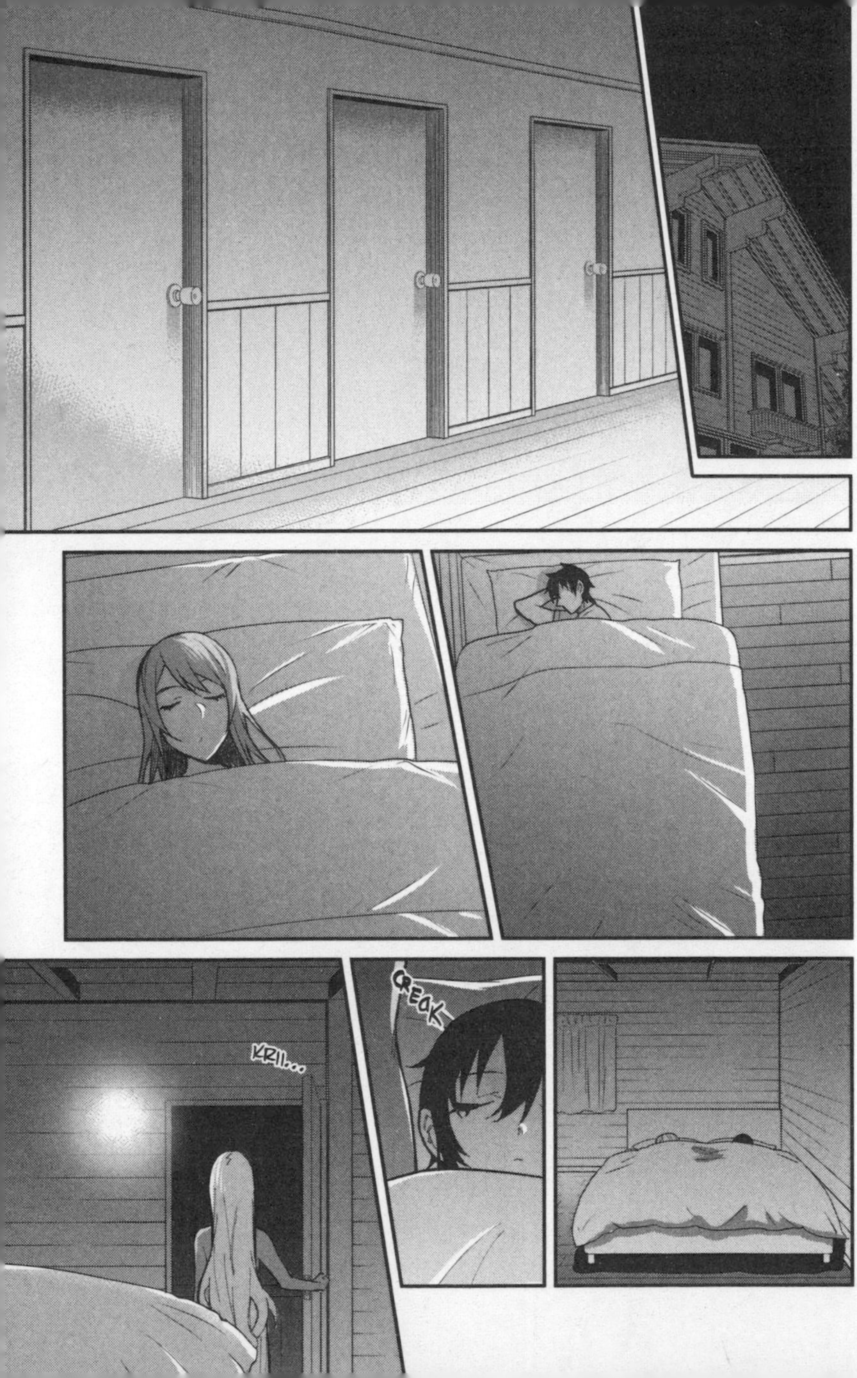
CREAK
KRII...

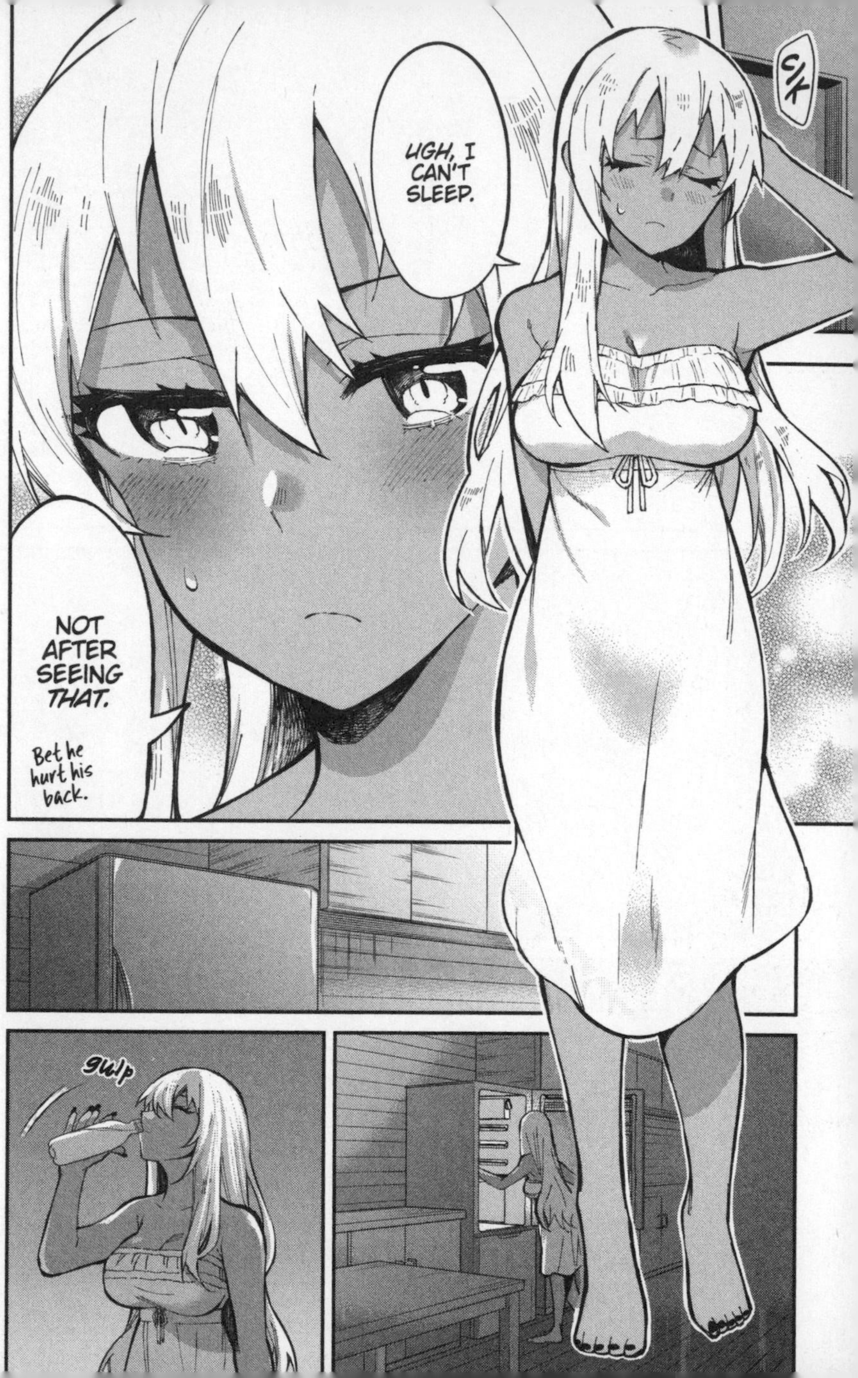
C/K
UGH, I CAN'T SLEEP.
NOT AFTER SEEING THAT.
Bet he hurt his back.
gulp

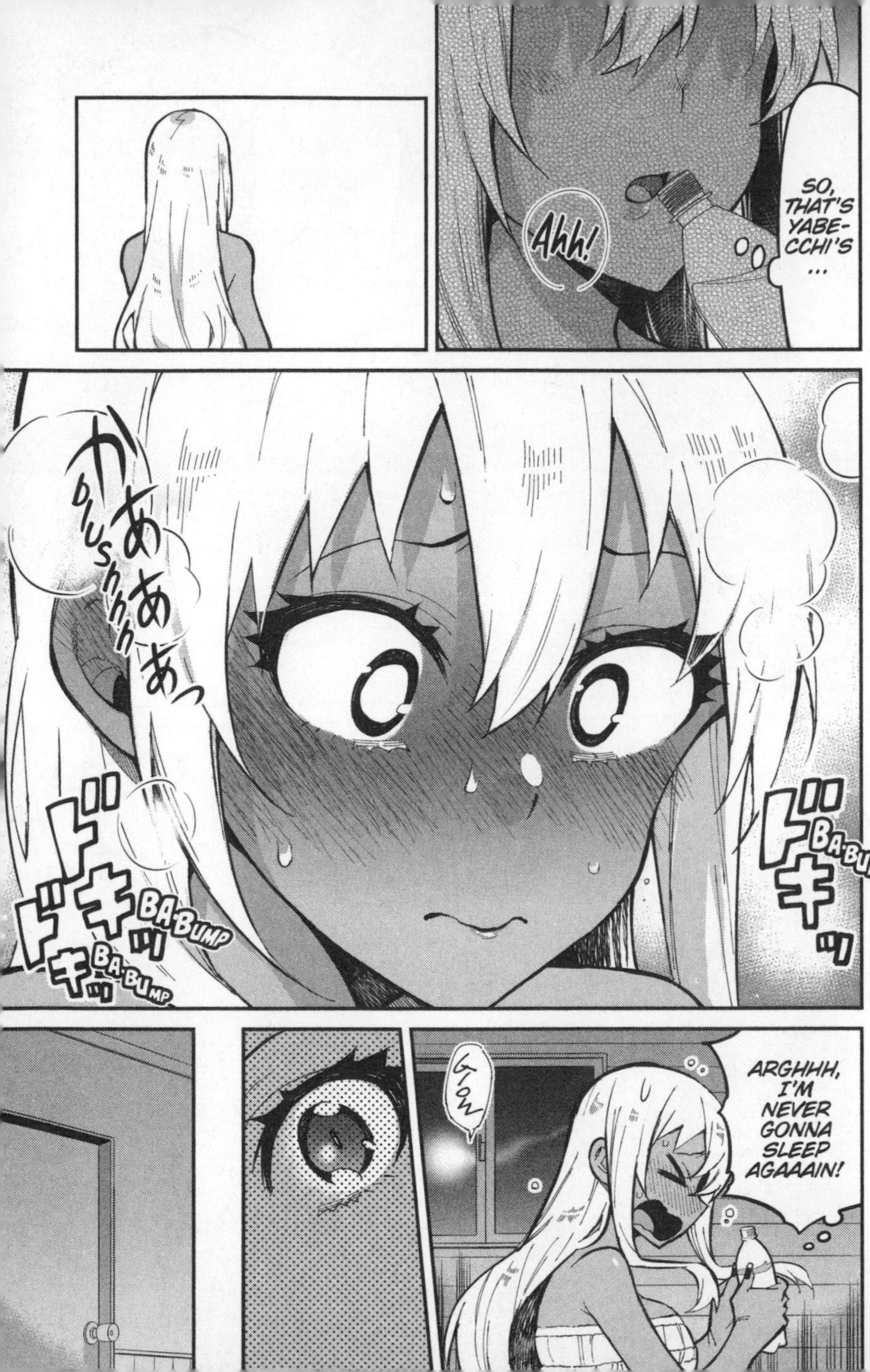

SO, THAT'S YABE-CCHI'S...
Ahh!
かあああっ
BLUSHHHH
ドキッ
BA-BUMP
ドキッ
BA-BUMP
ドキッ
BA-BUMP
ARGHHH, I'M NEVER GONNA SLEEP AGAAAIN!
GLOW

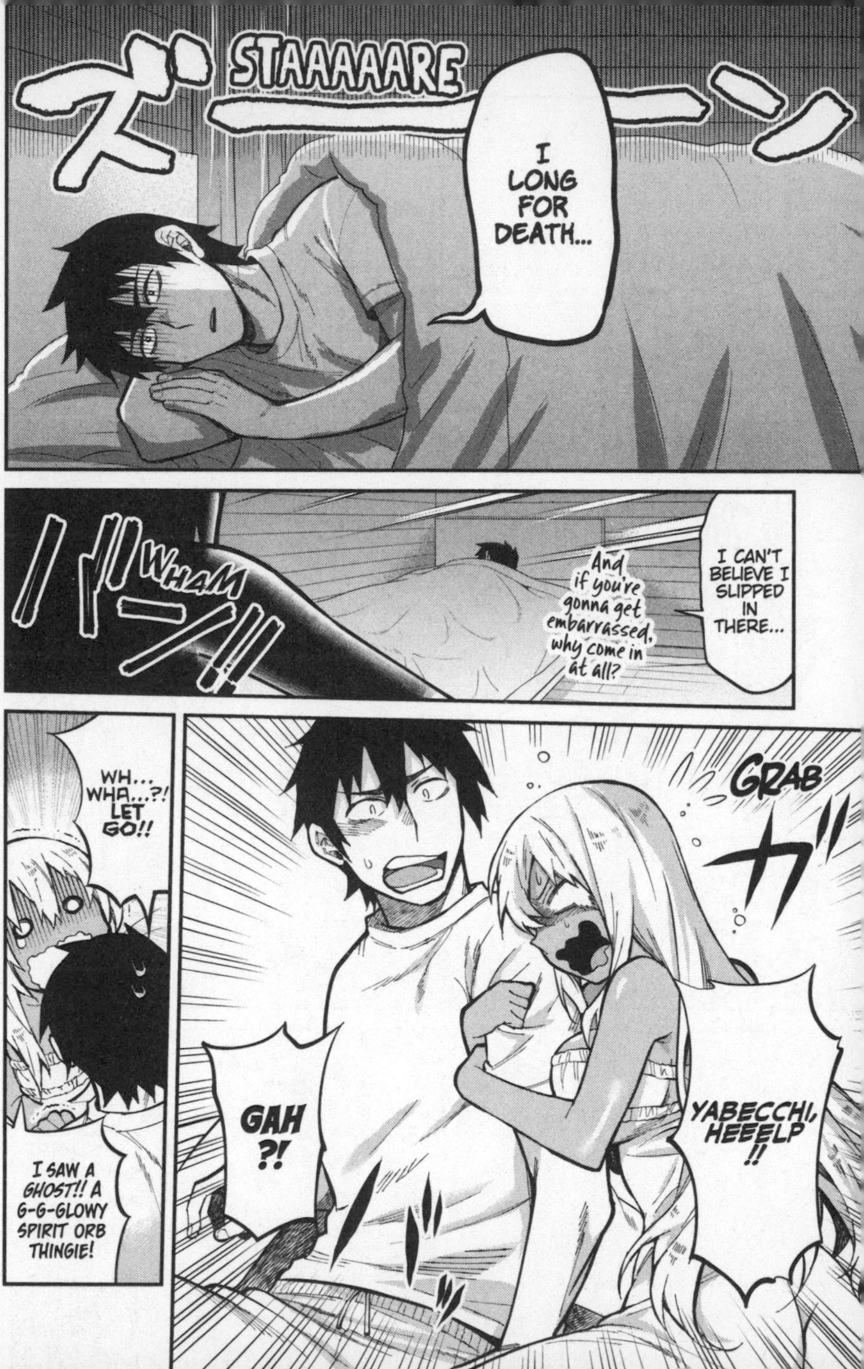
STAAAAARE
I LONG FOR DEATH...
I CAN'T BELIEVE I SLIPPED IN THERE...
And if you're gonna get embarrassed, why come in at all?
WHAM
GRAB
YABECCHI, HEEELP!!
GAH?!
WH... WHA...?! LET GO!!
I SAW A GHOST!! A G-G-GLOWY SPIRIT ORB THINGIE!

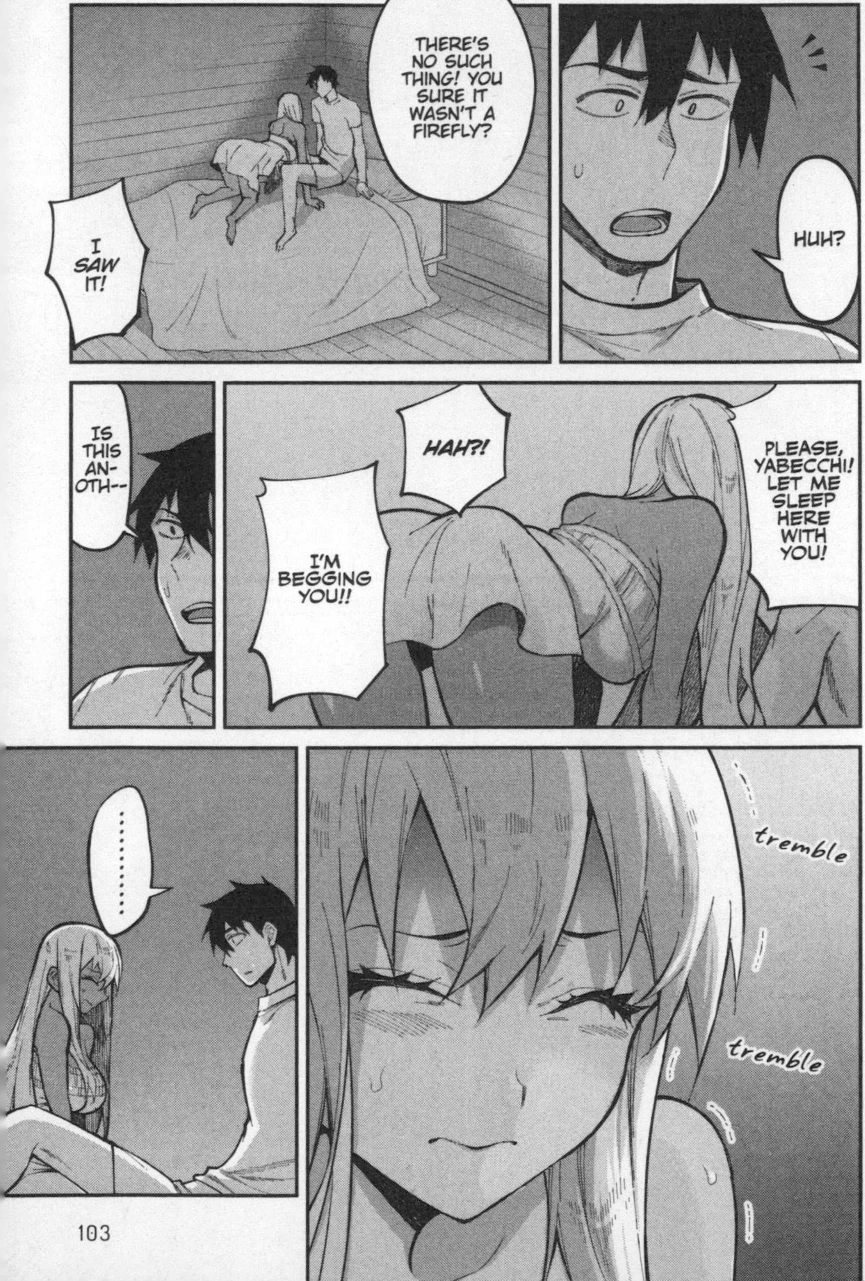
HUH?
THERE'S NO SUCH THING! YOU SURE IT WASN'T A FIREFLY?
I SAW IT!
PLEASE, YABECCHI! LET ME SLEEP HERE WITH YOU!
HAH?!
I'M BEGGING YOU!!
IS THIS AN-OTH--
tremble
tremble
....

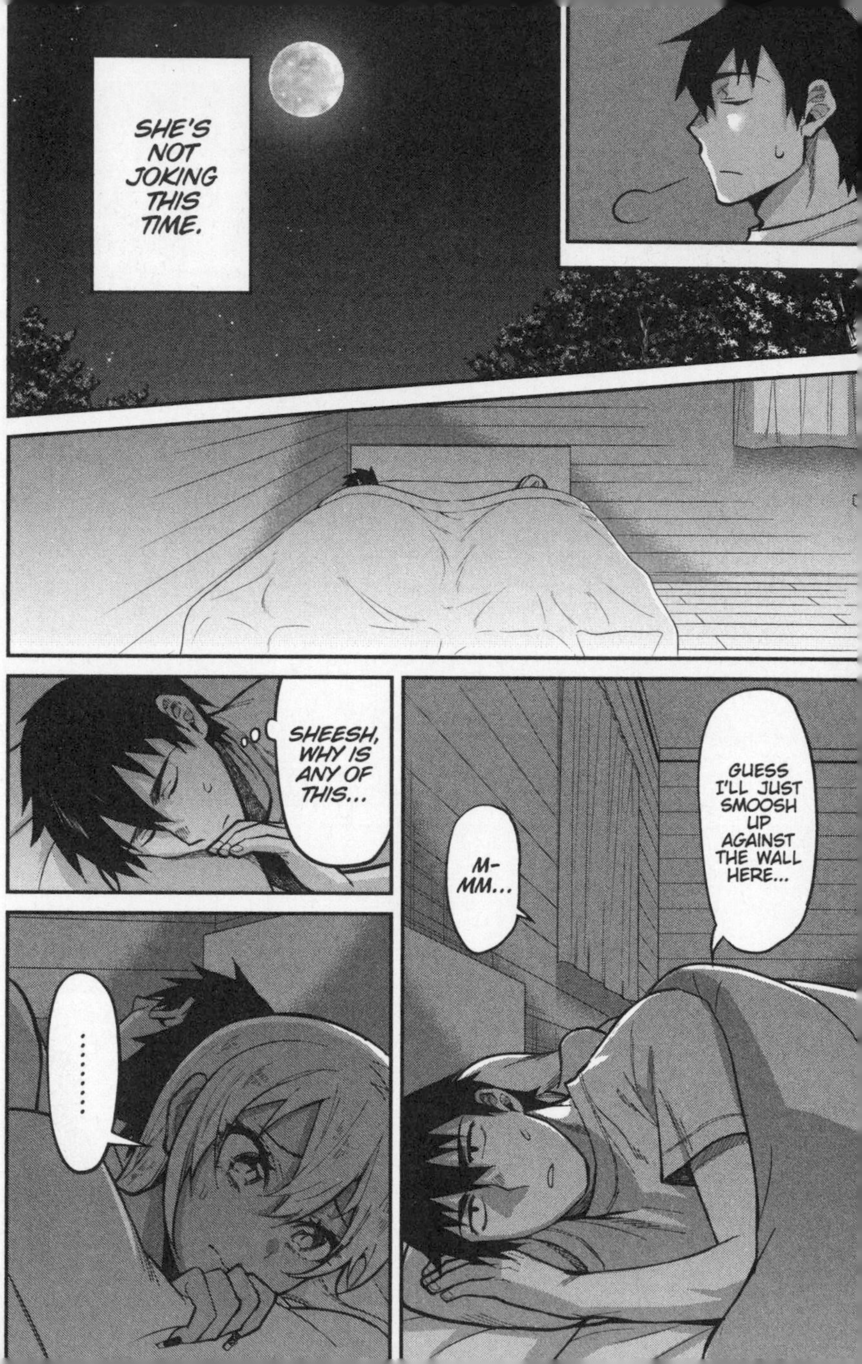
SHE'S NOT JOKING THIS TIME.
GUESS I'LL JUST SMOOSH UP AGAINST THE WALL HERE...
M-MM...
SHEESH, WHY IS ANY OF THIS...
....

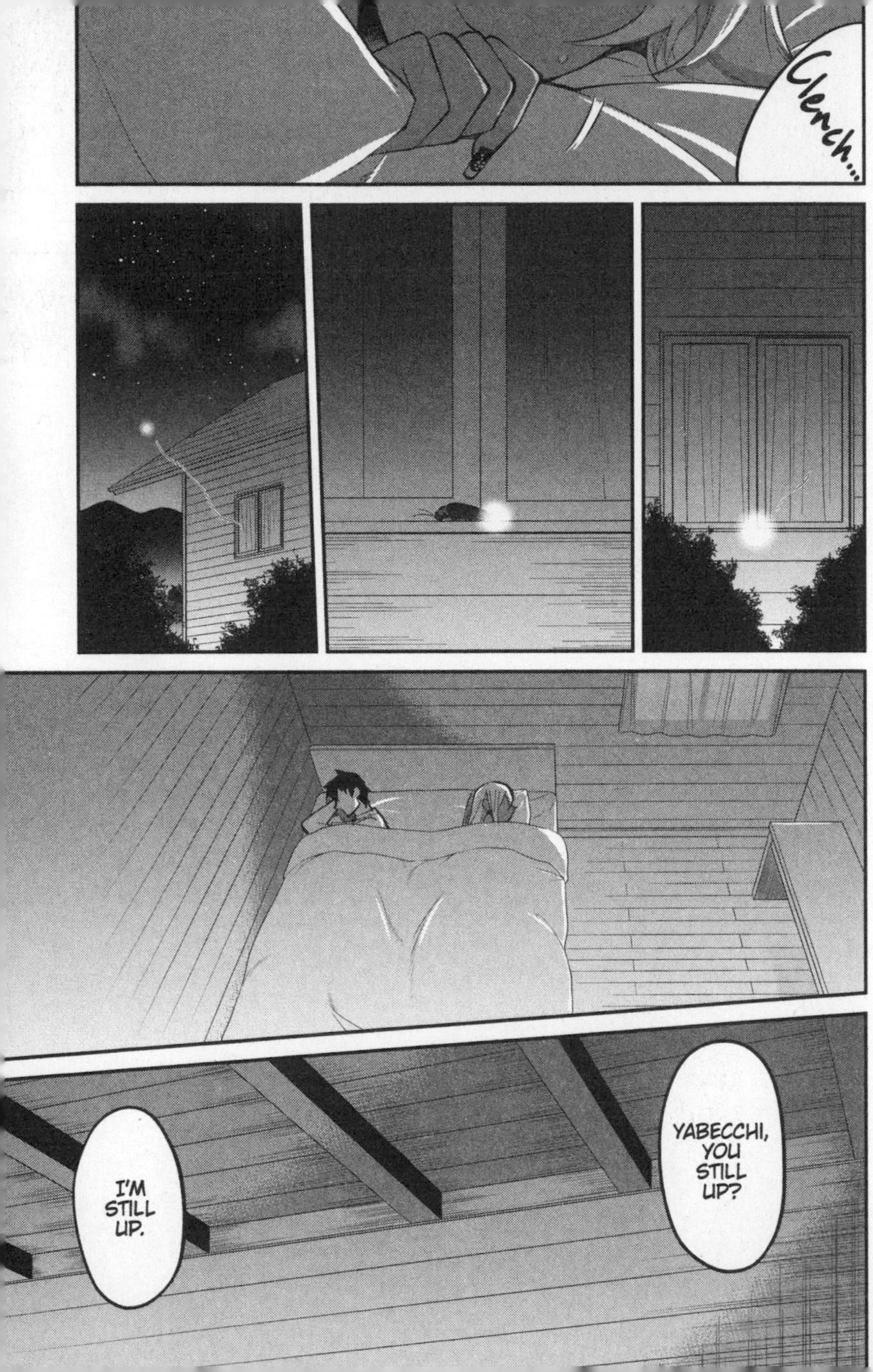
Clench...
YABECCHI, YOU STILL UP?
I'M STILL UP.

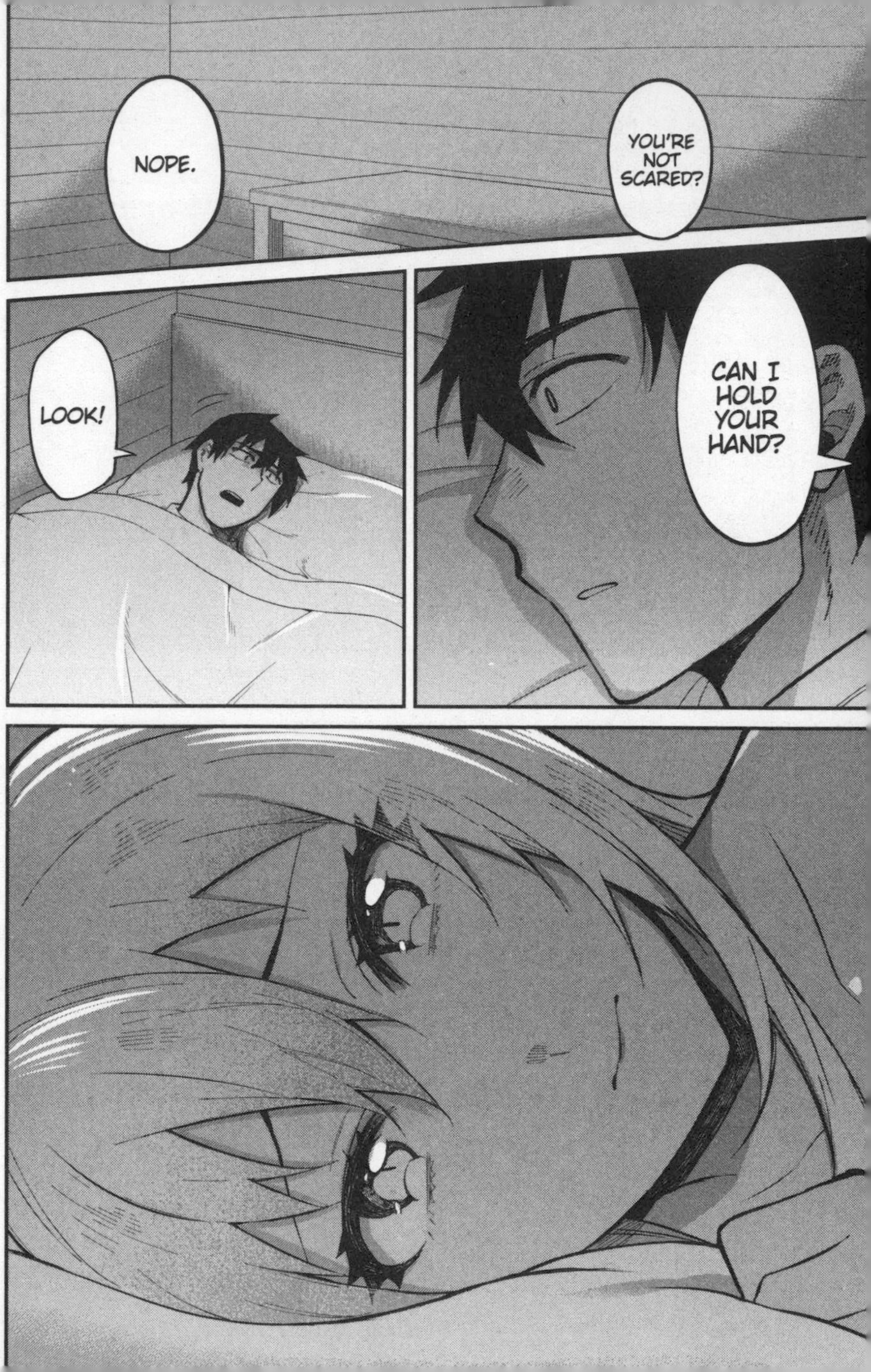
YOU'RE NOT SCARED?
NOPE.
CAN I HOLD YOUR HAND?
LOOK!

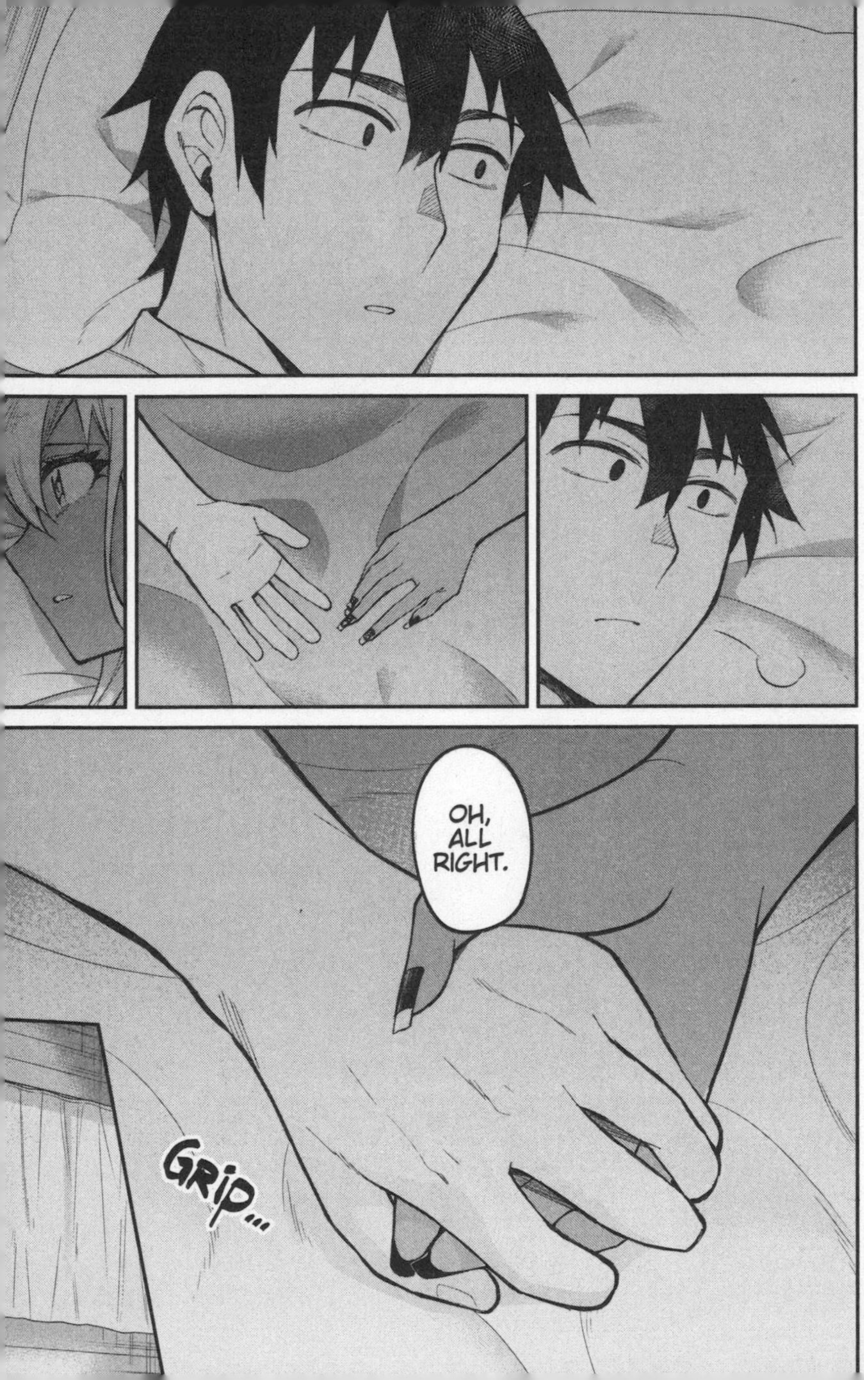
OH, ALL RIGHT.
Grip...

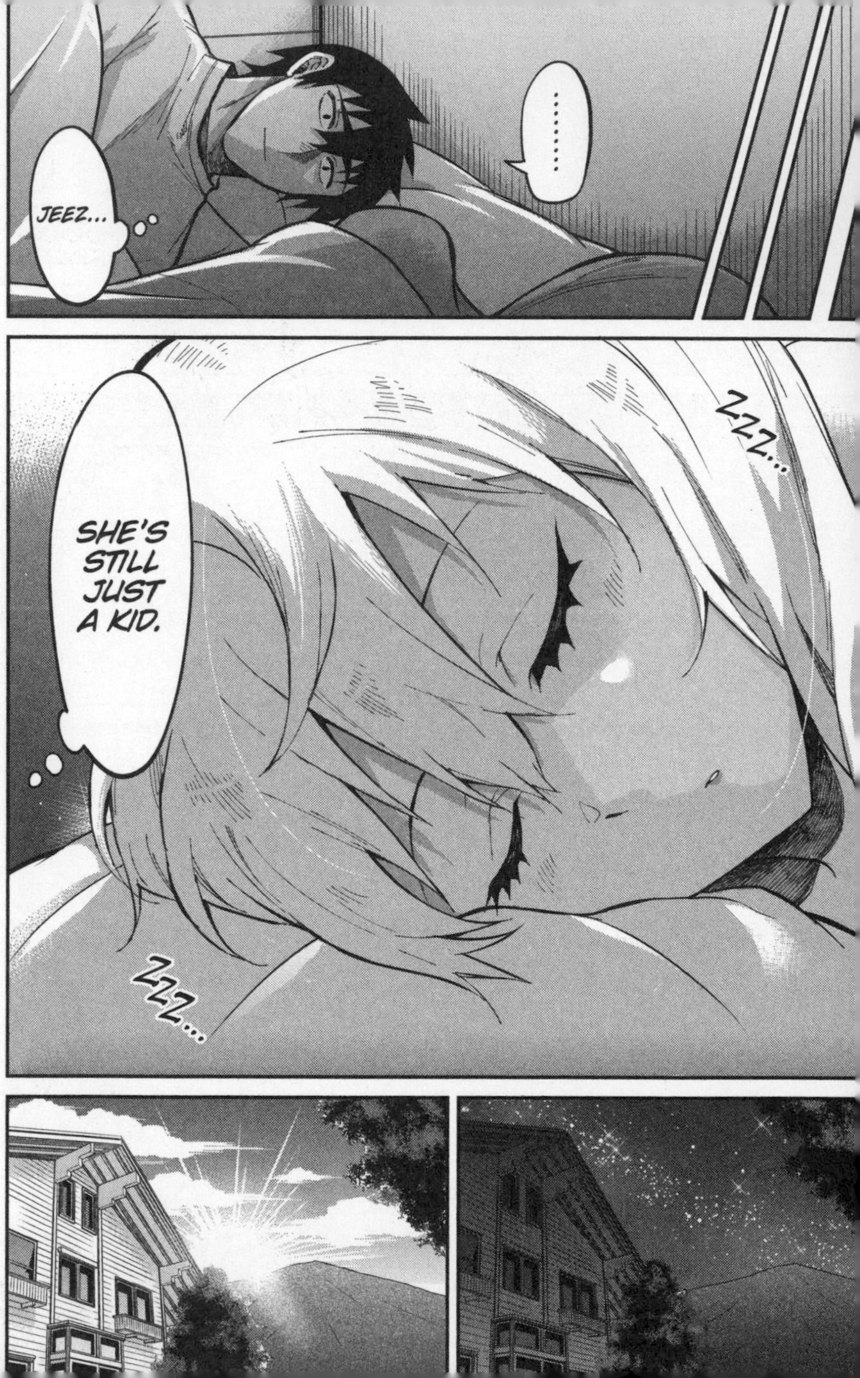
......
JEEZ...
ZZZ...
SHE'S STILL JUST A KID.
ZZZ...

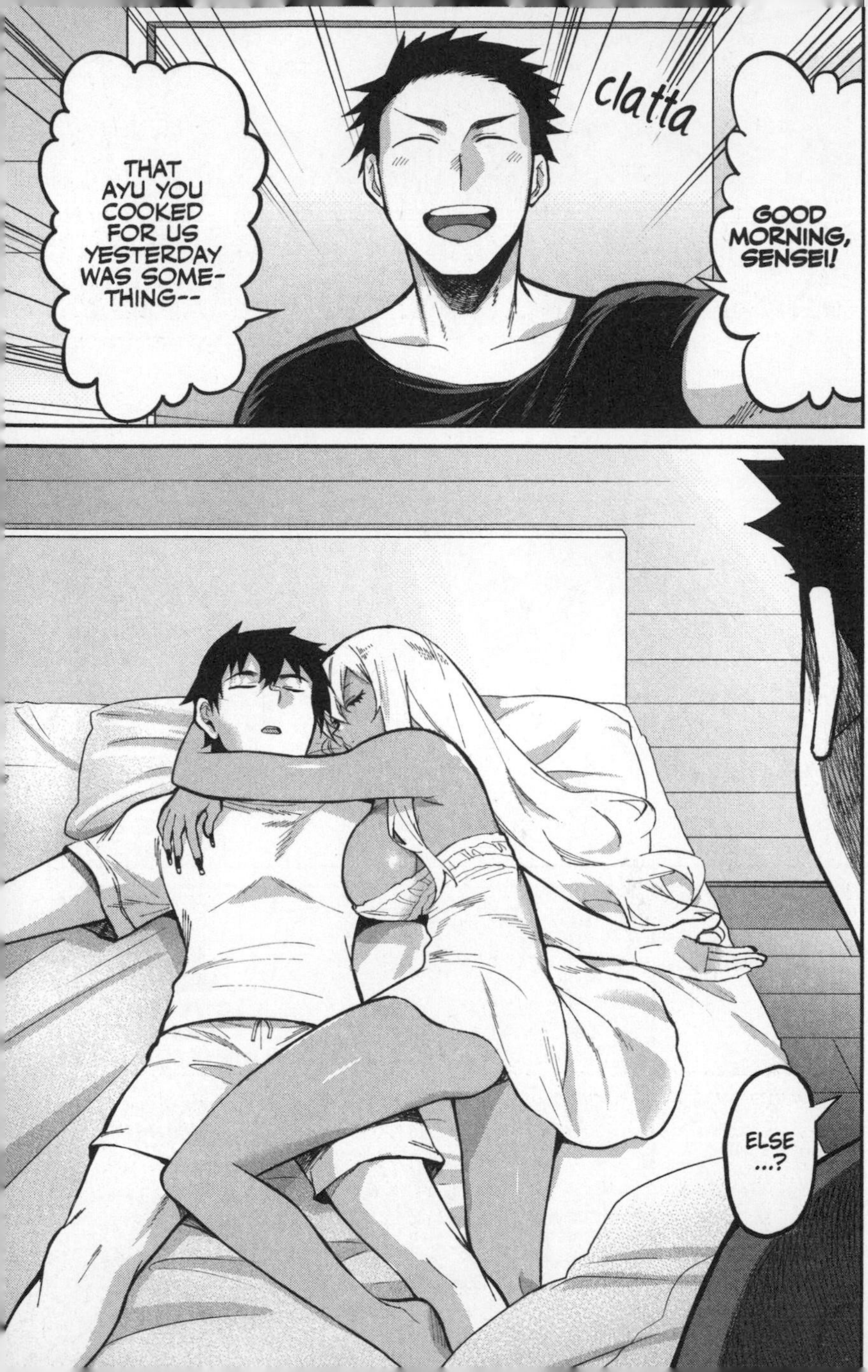
GOOD MORNING, SENSEI!
clatta
THAT AYU YOU COOKED FOR US YESTERDAY WAS SOME-THING--
ELSE ...?

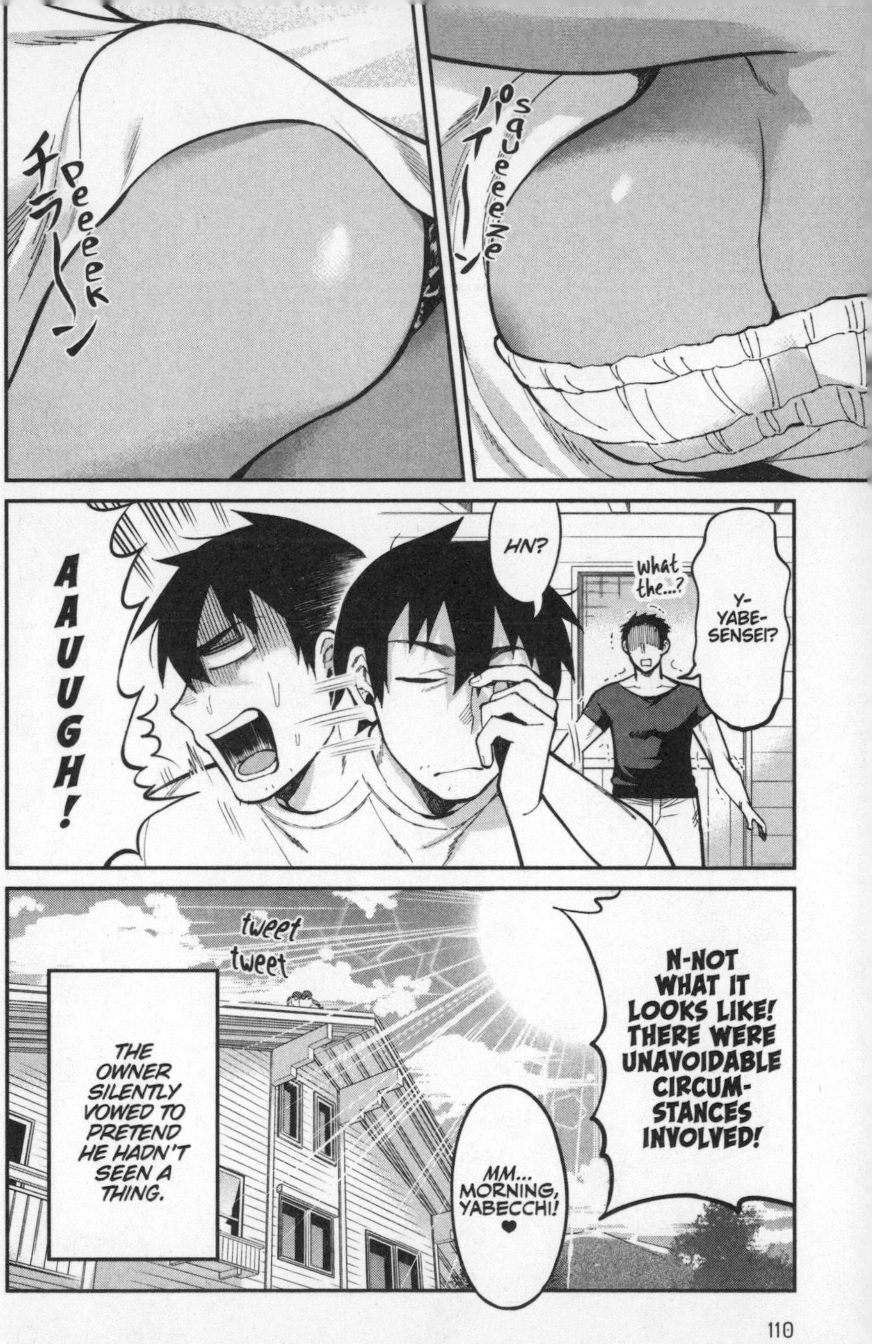
squeeeeze
パイーン
peeeek
チラーン
Y-YABE-SENSEI?
what the...?
HN?
AAUUGH!
N-NOT WHAT IT LOOKS LIKE! THERE WERE UNAVOIDABLE CIRCUM-STANCES INVOLVED!
MM... MORNING, YABECCHI! ♥
tweet tweet
THE OWNER SILENTLY VOWED TO PRETEND HE HADN'T SEEN A THING.

Gal
Gohan

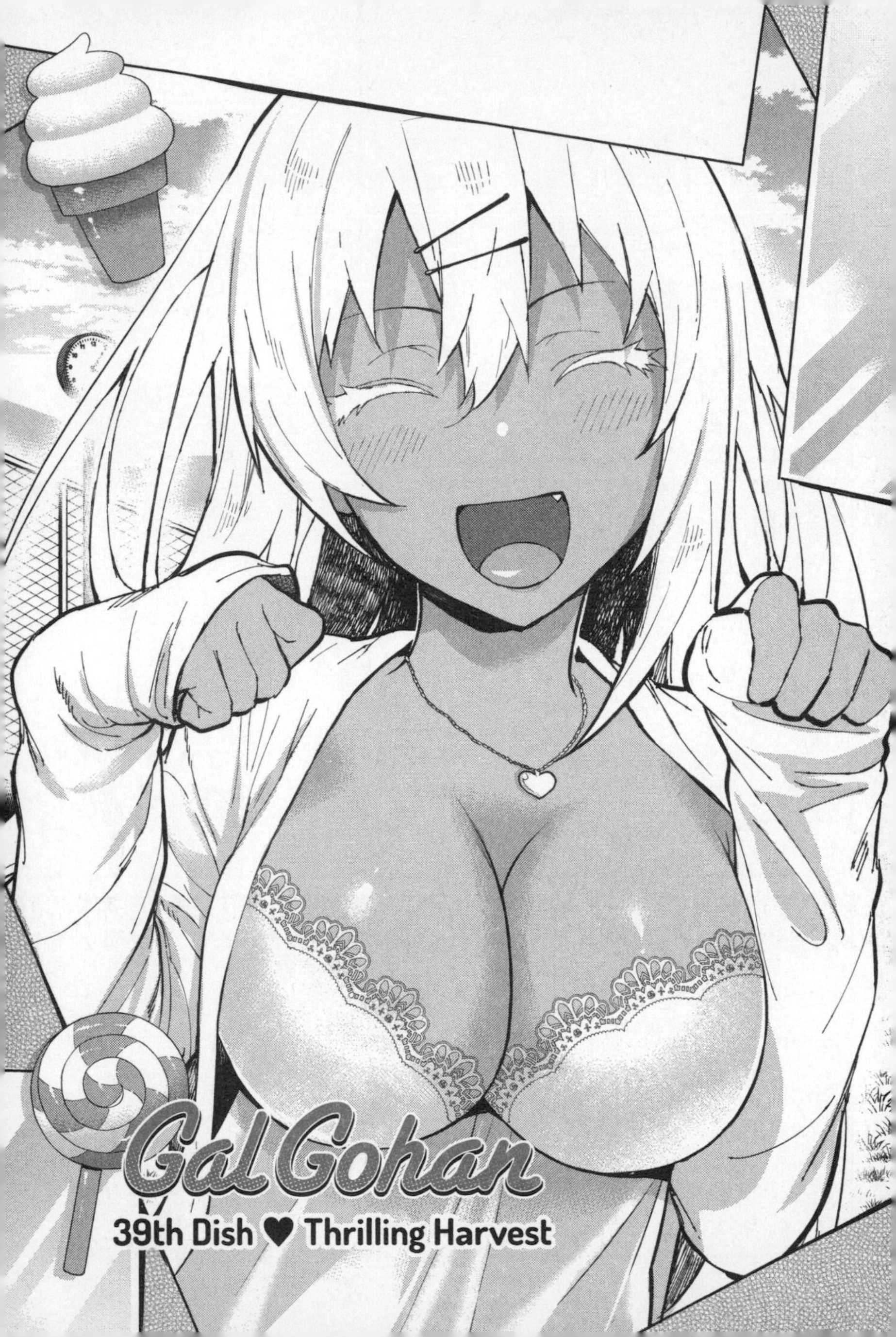
Gal Gohan
39th Dish ♥ Thrilling Harvest

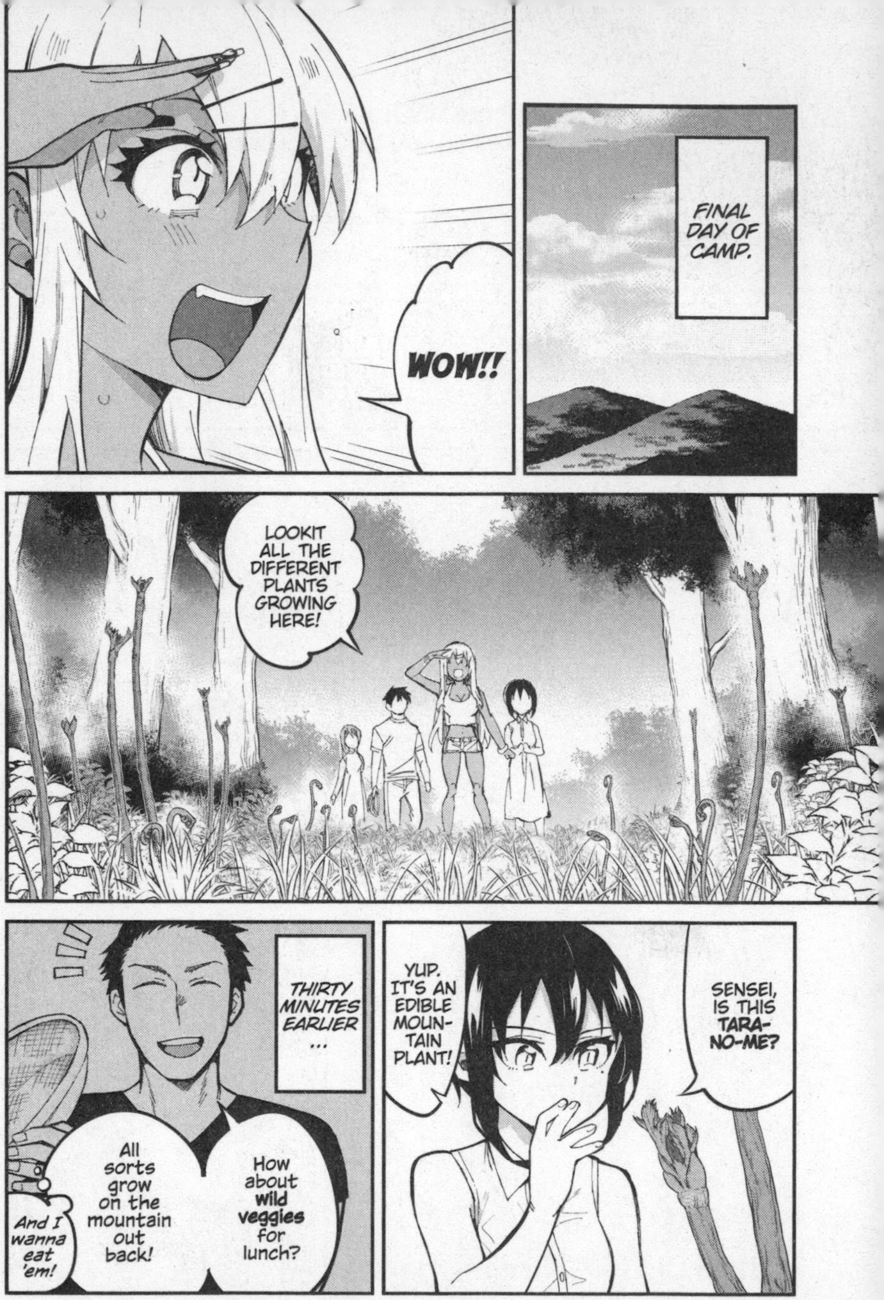
FINAL DAY OF CAMP.
WOW!!
LOOKIT ALL THE DIFFERENT PLANTS GROWING HERE!
SENSEI, IS THIS TARA-NO-ME?
YUP. IT'S AN EDIBLE MOUN-TAIN PLANT!
THIRTY MINUTES EARLIER ...
How about **wild veggies** for lunch?
All sorts grow on the mountain out back!
And I wanna eat 'em!

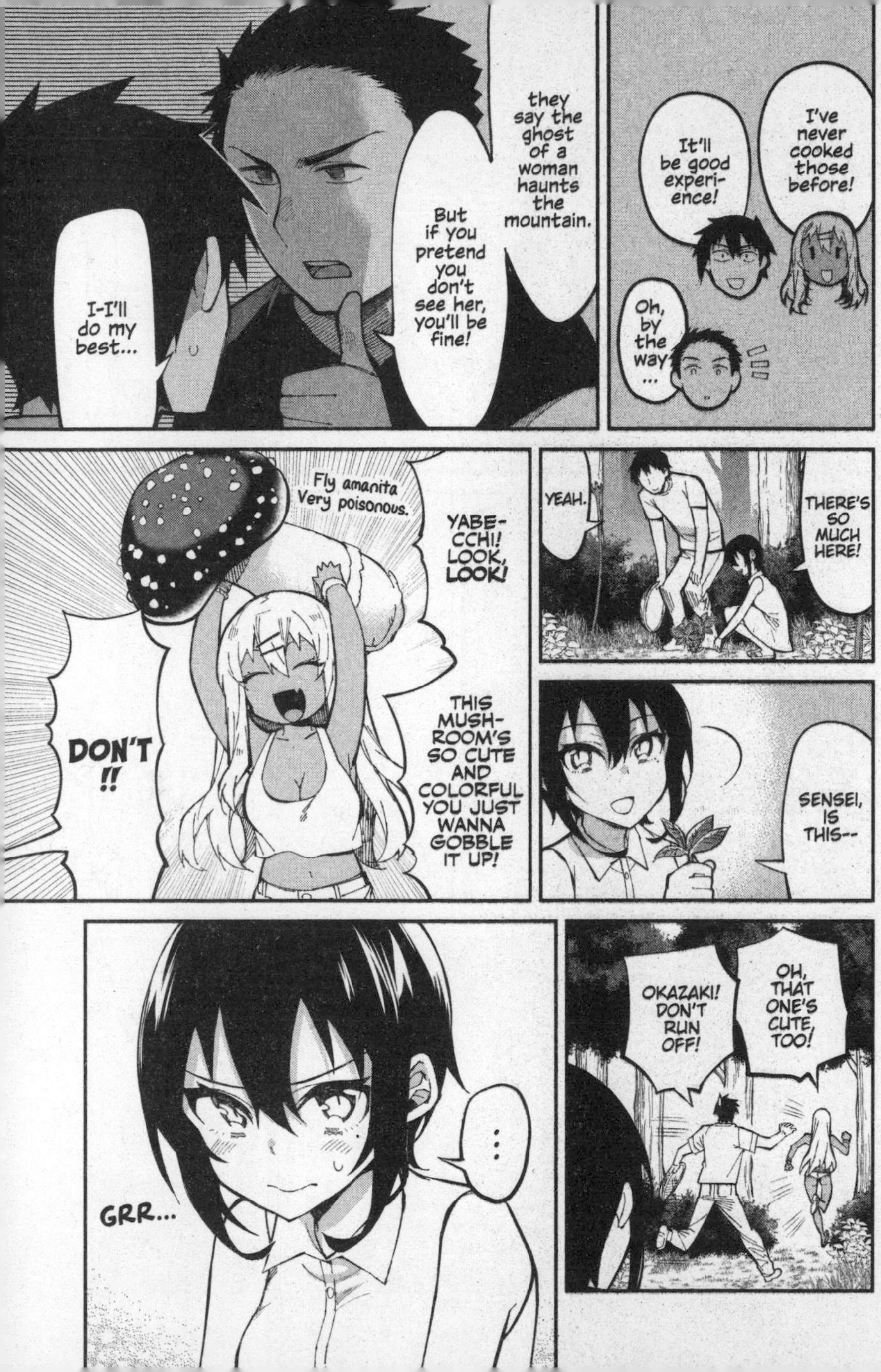
I've never cooked those before!
It'll be good experience!
Oh, by the way...
they say the ghost of a woman haunts the mountain.
But if you pretend you don't see her, you'll be fine!
I-I'll do my best...
THERE'S SO MUCH HERE!
YEAH.
SENSEI, IS THIS--
YABE-CCHI! LOOK, LOOK!
THIS MUSHROOM'S SO CUTE AND COLORFUL YOU JUST WANNA GOBBLE IT UP!
Fly amanita Very poisonous.
DON'T!!
OH, THAT ONE'S CUTE, TOO!
OKAZAKI! DON'T RUN OFF!
...
GRR...

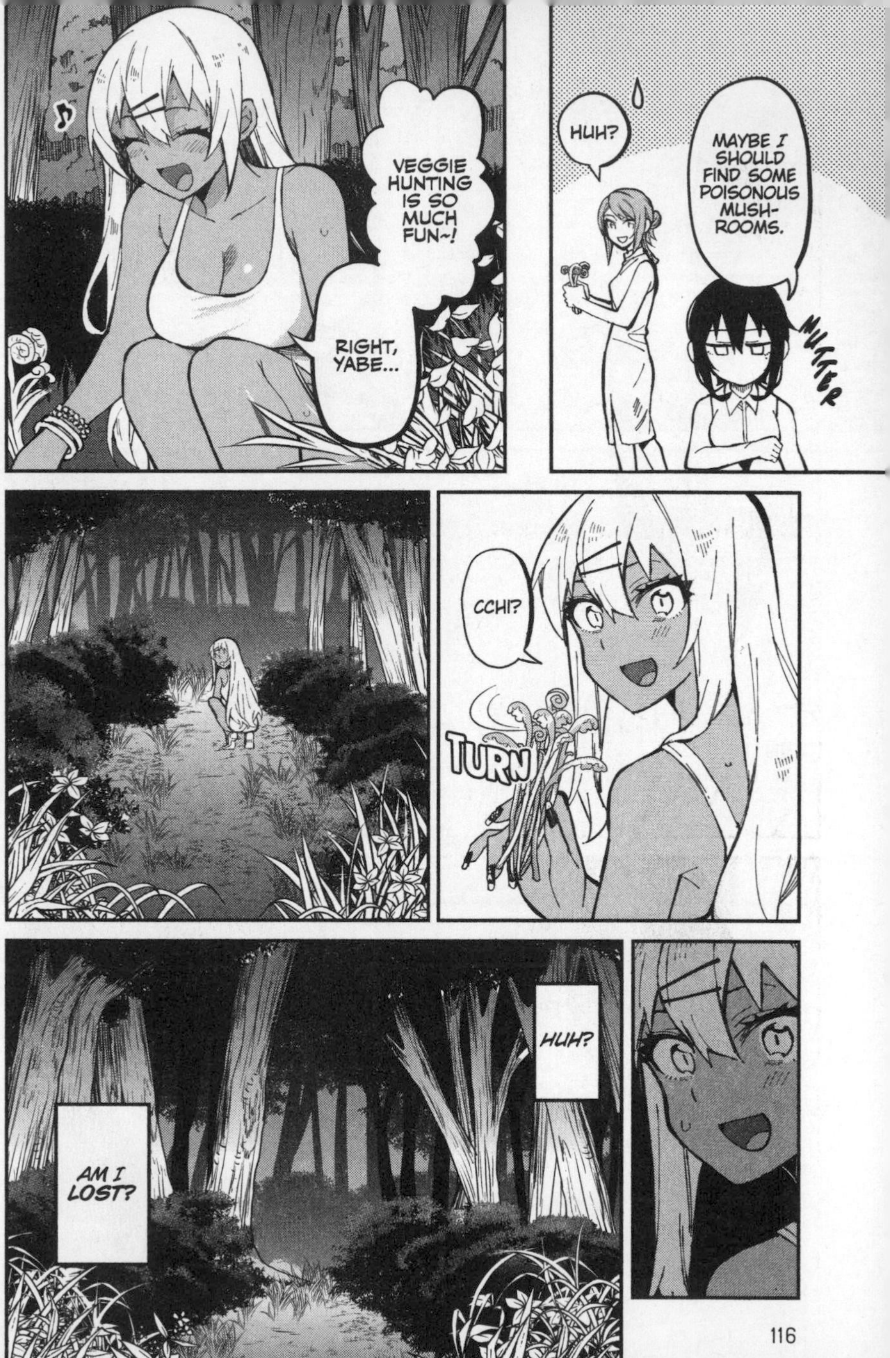
MAYBE I SHOULD FIND SOME POISONOUS MUSH-ROOMS.
HUH?
MUTTER
VEGGIE HUNTING IS SO MUCH FUN~!
RIGHT, YABE...
CCHI?
TURN
HUH?
AM I LOST?

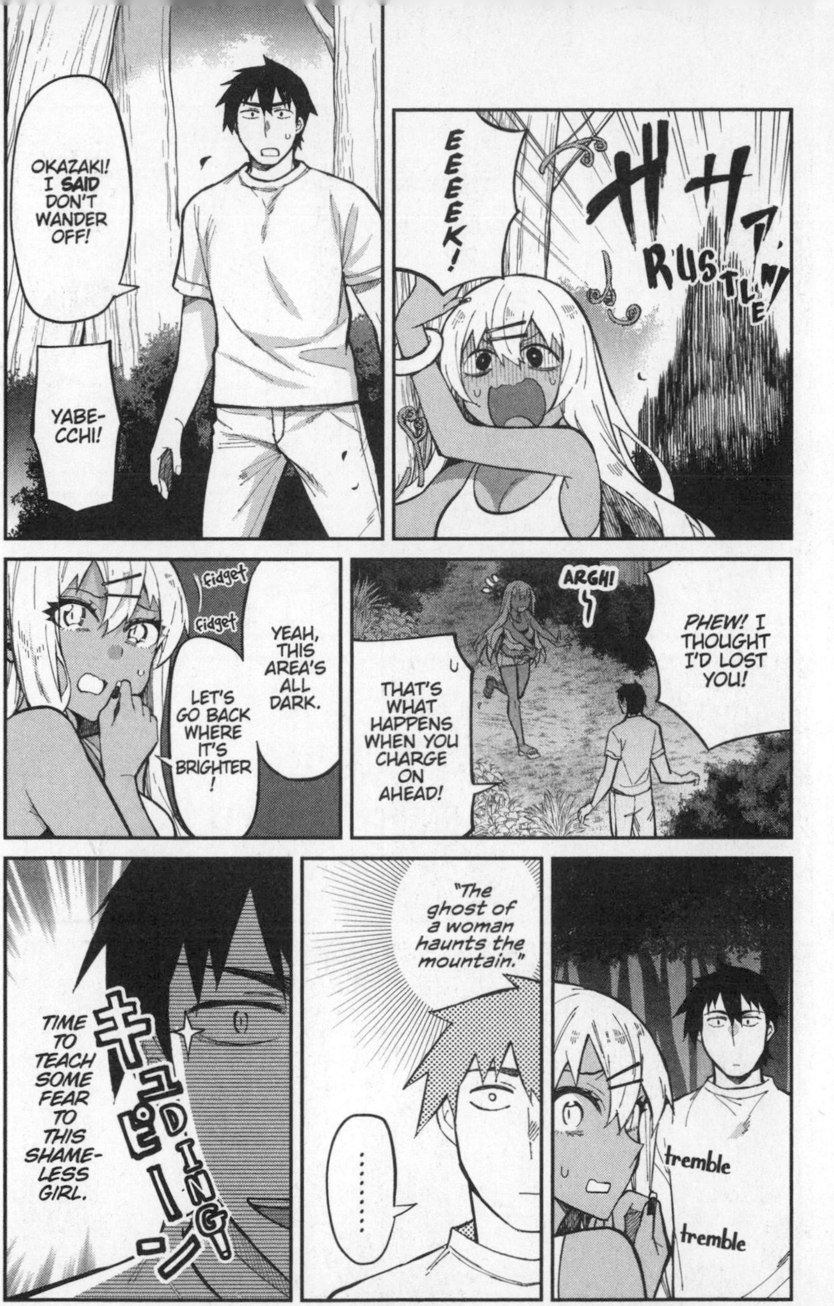
RUSTLE
EEEEK!
OKAZAKI! I SAID DON'T WANDER OFF!
YABE-CCHI!
PHEW! I THOUGHT I'D LOST YOU!
ARGH!
THAT'S WHAT HAPPENS WHEN YOU CHARGE ON AHEAD!
fidget
fidget
YEAH, THIS AREA'S ALL DARK.
LET'S GO BACK WHERE IT'S BRIGHTER!
tremble
tremble
"The ghost of a woman haunts the mountain."
......
DING!
TIME TO TEACH SOME FEAR TO THIS SHAMELESS GIRL.

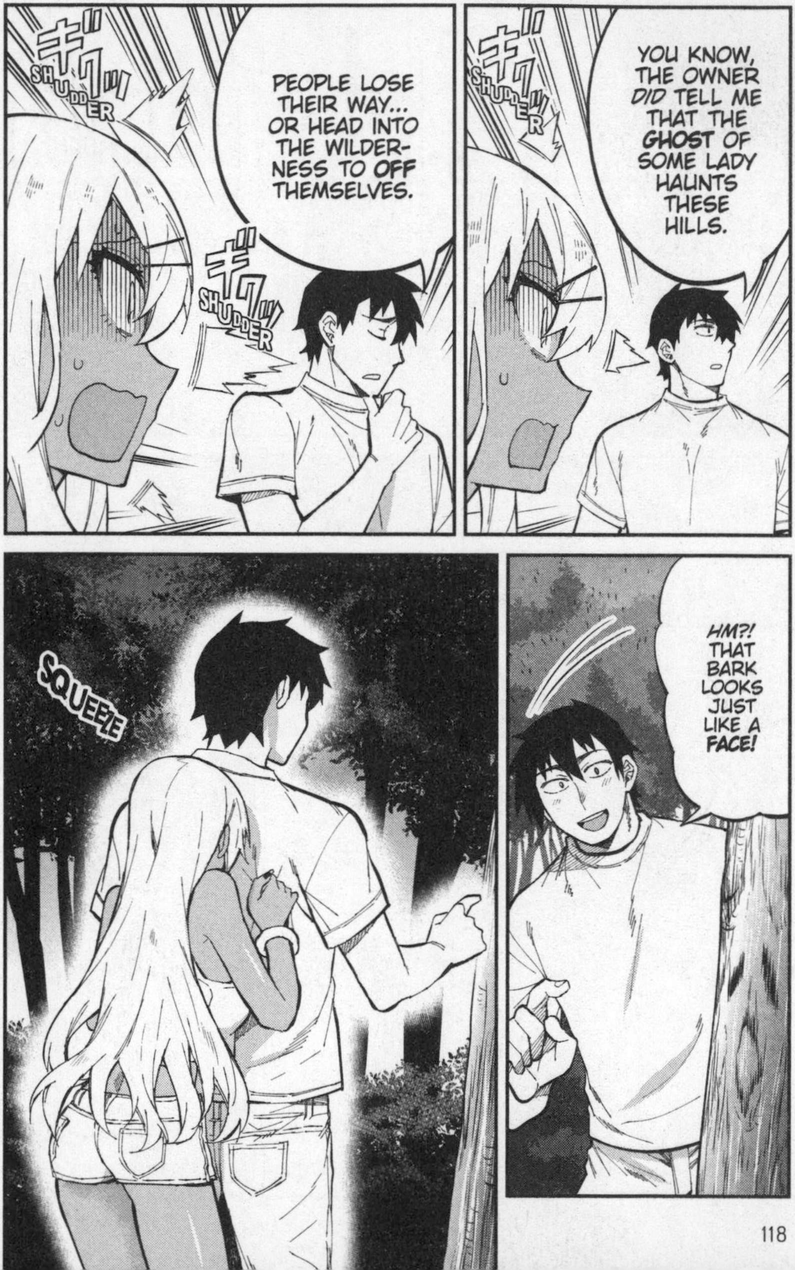
SHUDDER
YOU KNOW, THE OWNER *DID* TELL ME THAT THE **GHOST** OF SOME LADY HAUNTS THESE HILLS.
SHUDDER
PEOPLE LOSE THEIR WAY... OR HEAD INTO THE WILDER-NESS TO **OFF** THEMSELVES.
SHUDDER
HM?! THAT BARK LOOKS JUST LIKE A **FACE!**
SQUEEZE

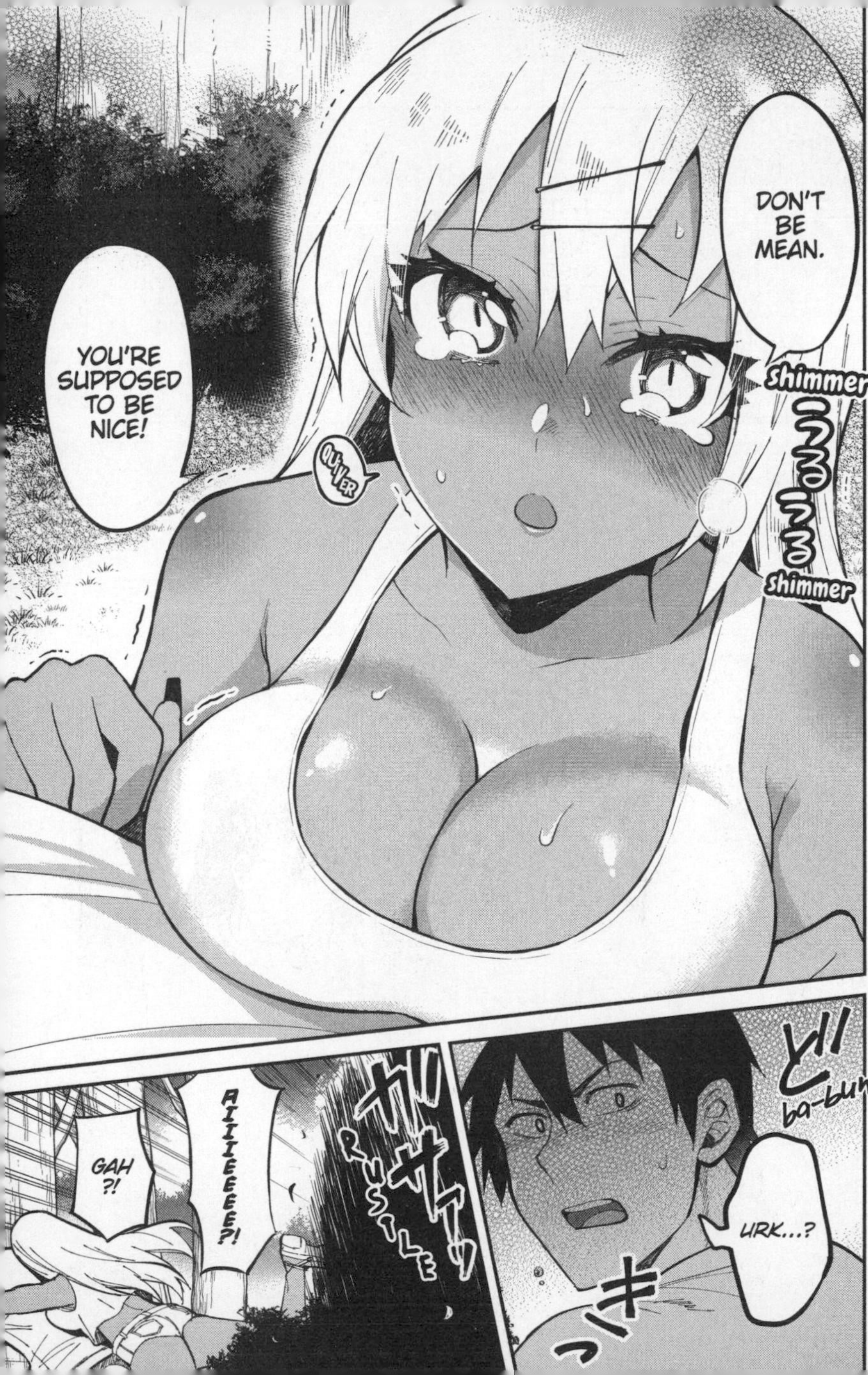
DON'T BE MEAN.
shimmer うるうる shimmer
YOU'RE SUPPOSED TO BE NICE!
QUIVER
ba-bump
URK...?
RUSTLE
AIIIEEEEE?!
GAH ?!

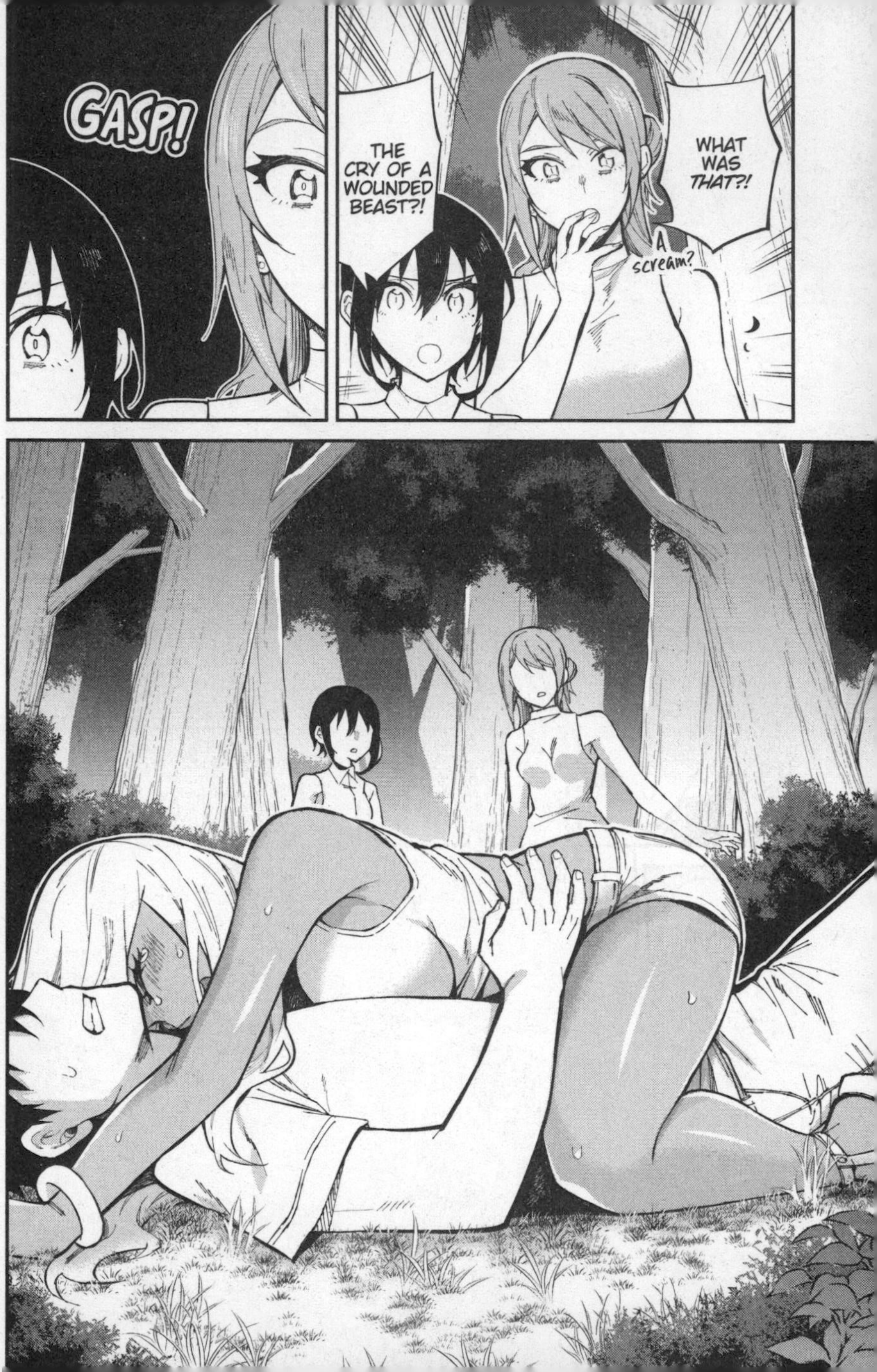
WHAT WAS THAT?!
THE CRY OF A WOUNDED BEAST?!
A scream?
GASP!

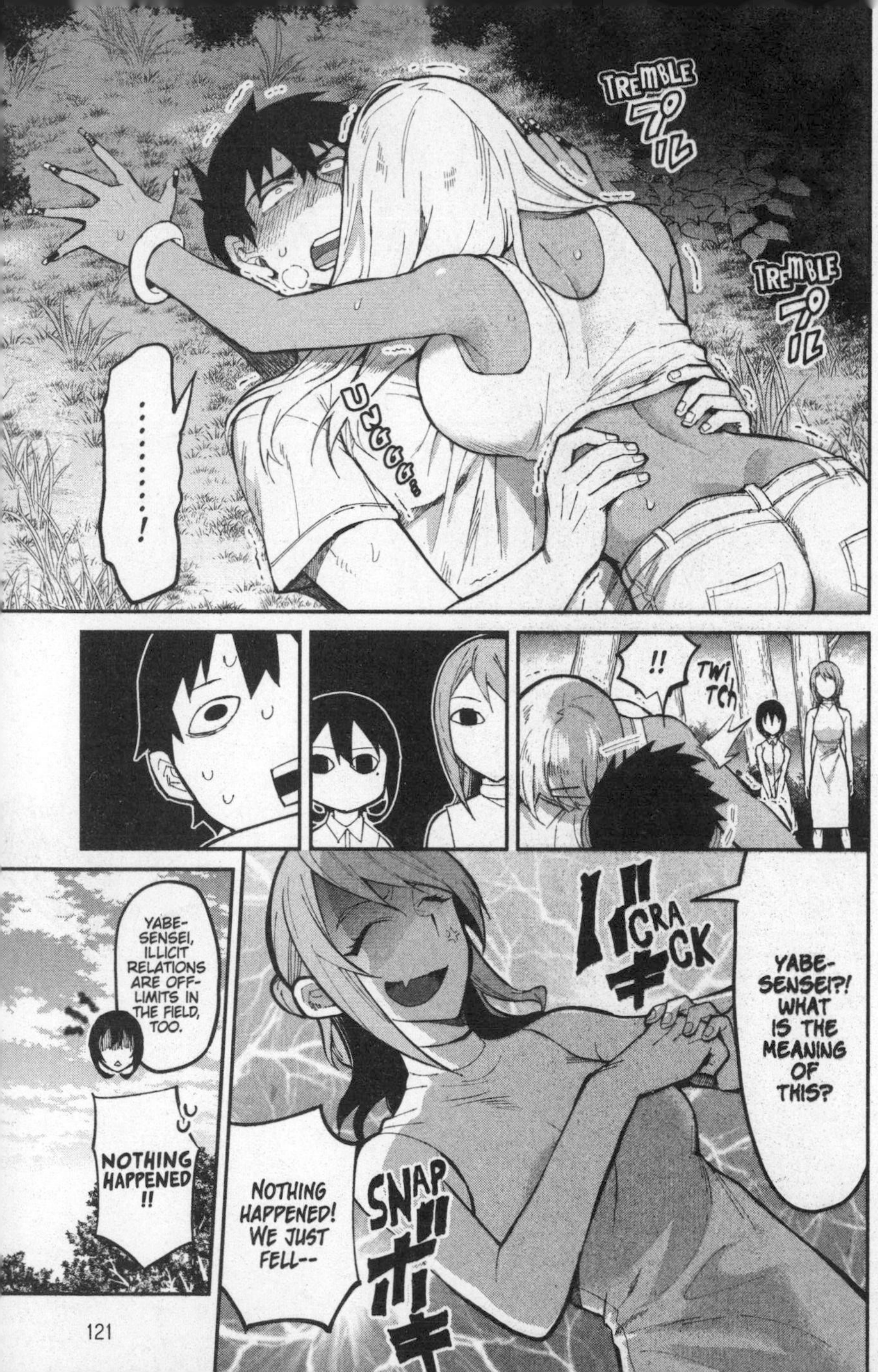
TREMBLE
プル
TREMBLE
プル
UNGGG
......!
!!
TWITCH
YABE-SENSEI!?! WHAT IS THE MEANING OF THIS?
CRACK
NOTHING HAPPENED! WE JUST FELL--
SNAP
YABE-SENSEI, ILLICIT RELATIONS ARE OFF-LIMITS IN THE FIELD, TOO.
NOTHING HAPPENED!!

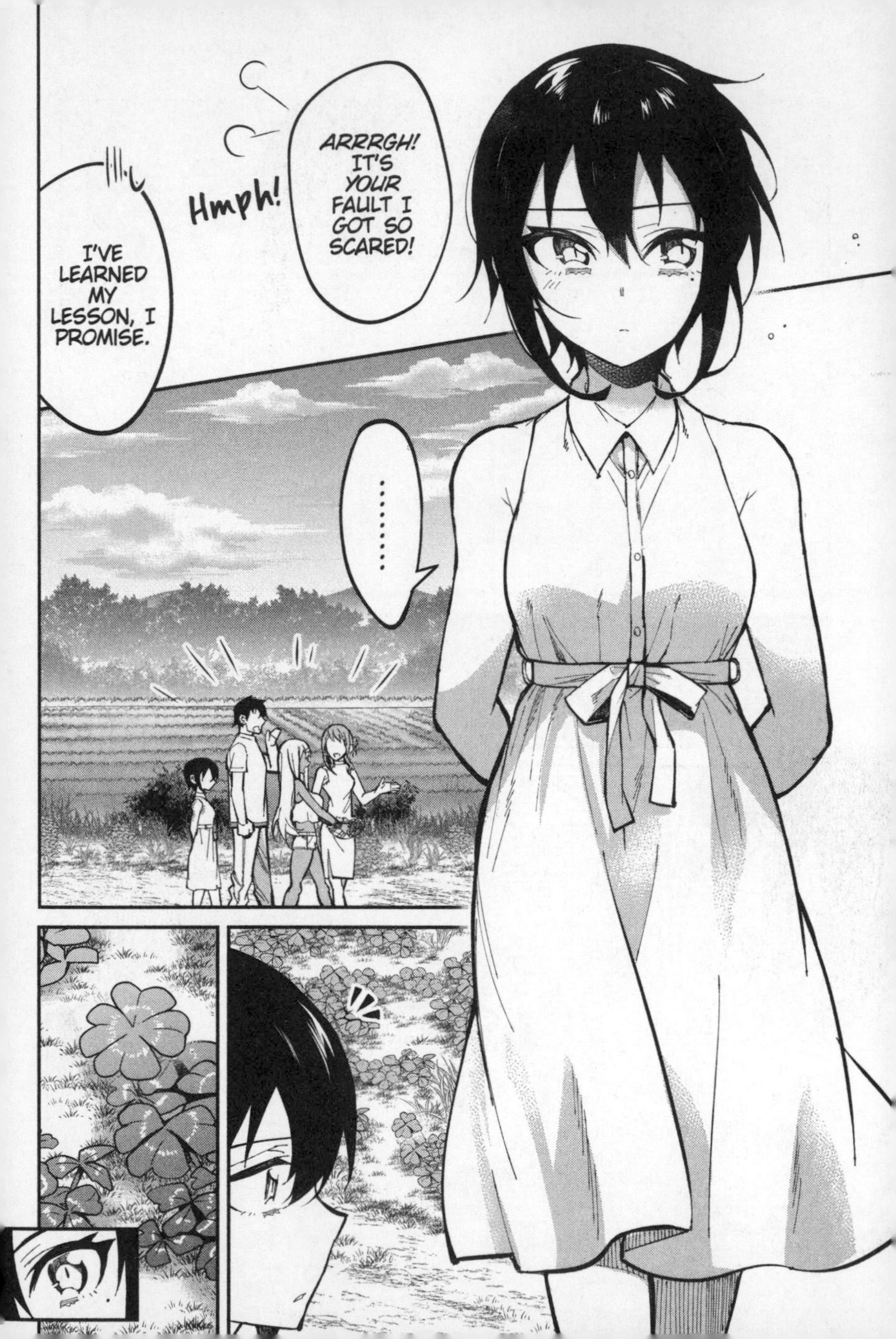
ARRRGH! IT'S YOUR FAULT I GOT SO SCARED!
Hmph!
I'VE LEARNED MY LESSON, I PROMISE.
......

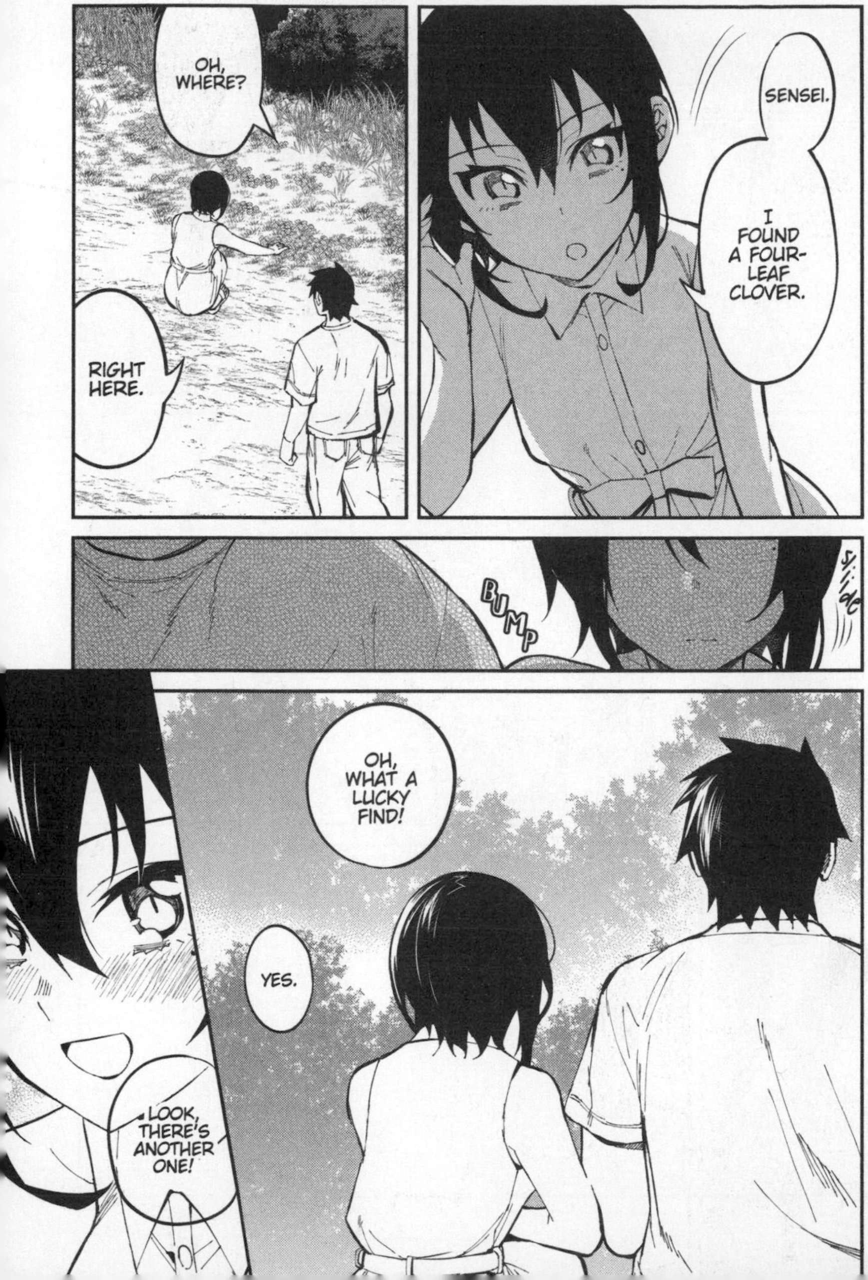
SENSEI.
I FOUND A FOUR-LEAF CLOVER.
OH, WHERE?
RIGHT HERE.
slide
BUMP
OH, WHAT A LUCKY FIND!
YES.
LOOK, THERE'S ANOTHER ONE!

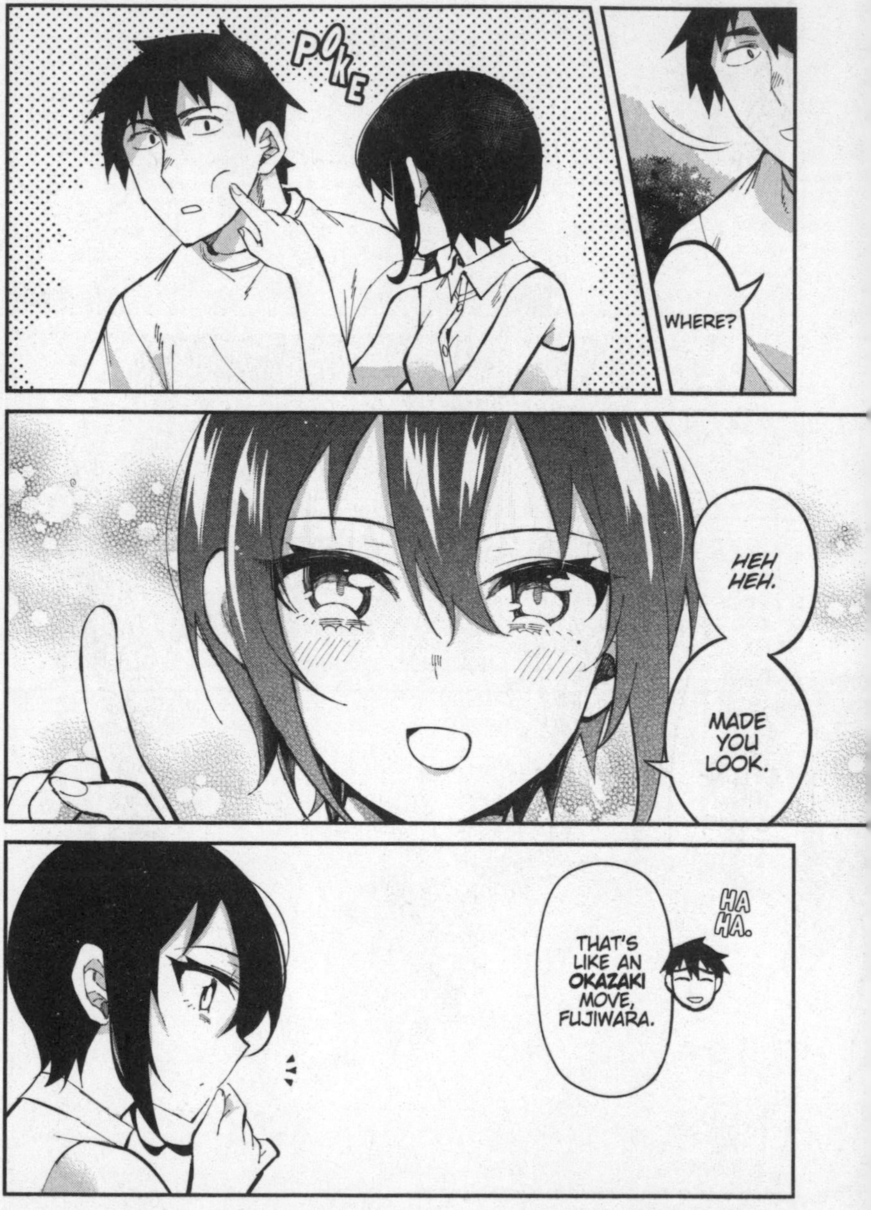
WHERE?
POKE
HEH HEH.
MADE YOU LOOK.
HA HA.
THAT'S LIKE AN OKAZAKI MOVE, FUJIWARA.

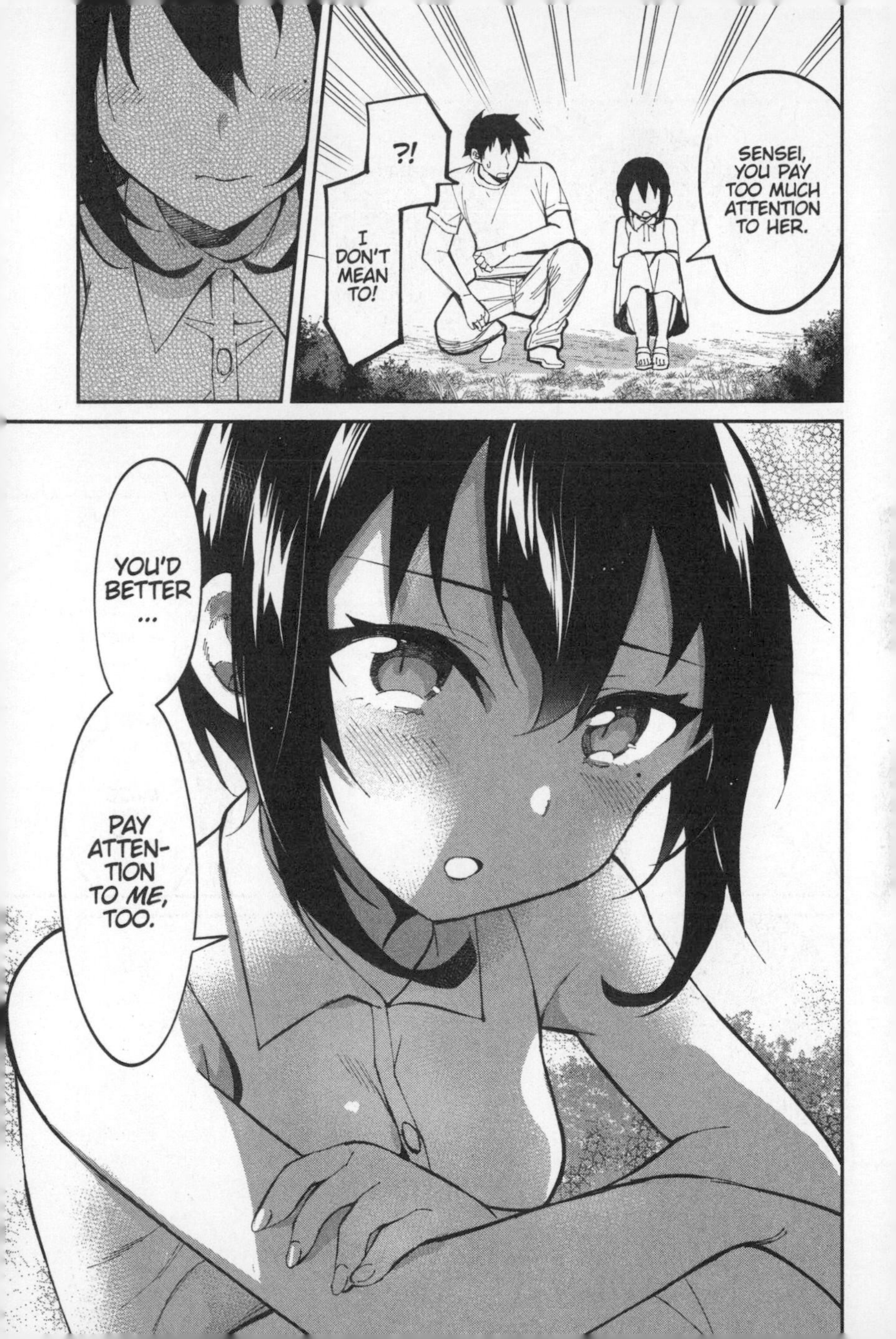
SENSEI, YOU PAY TOO MUCH ATTENTION TO HER.
?!
I DON'T MEAN TO!
YOU'D BETTER ...
PAY ATTEN- TION TO ME, TOO.

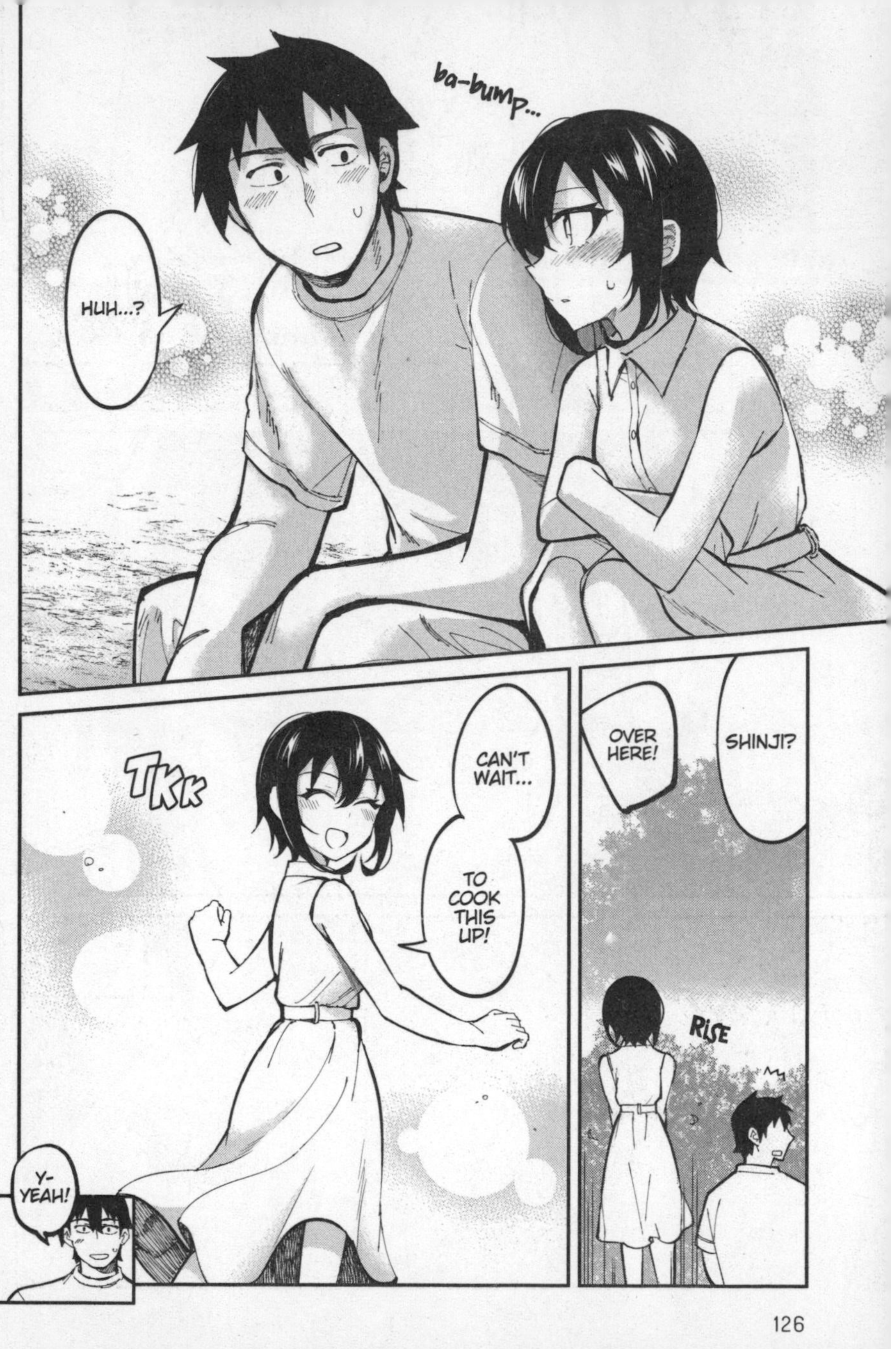
ba-bump...
HUH...?
SHINJI?
OVER HERE!
RISE
CAN'T WAIT...
TO COOK THIS UP!
TKK
Y-YEAH!

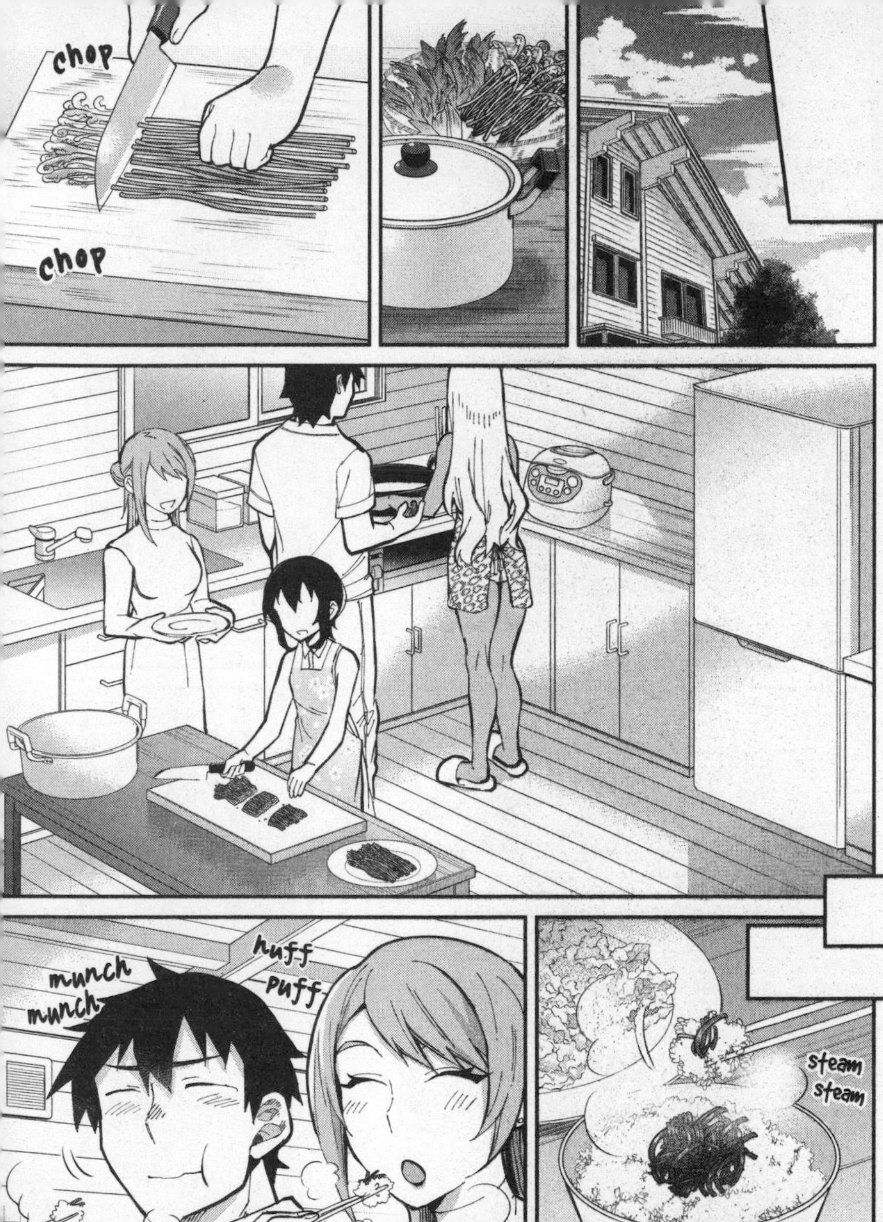
chop
chop
steam steam
huff puff
munch munch

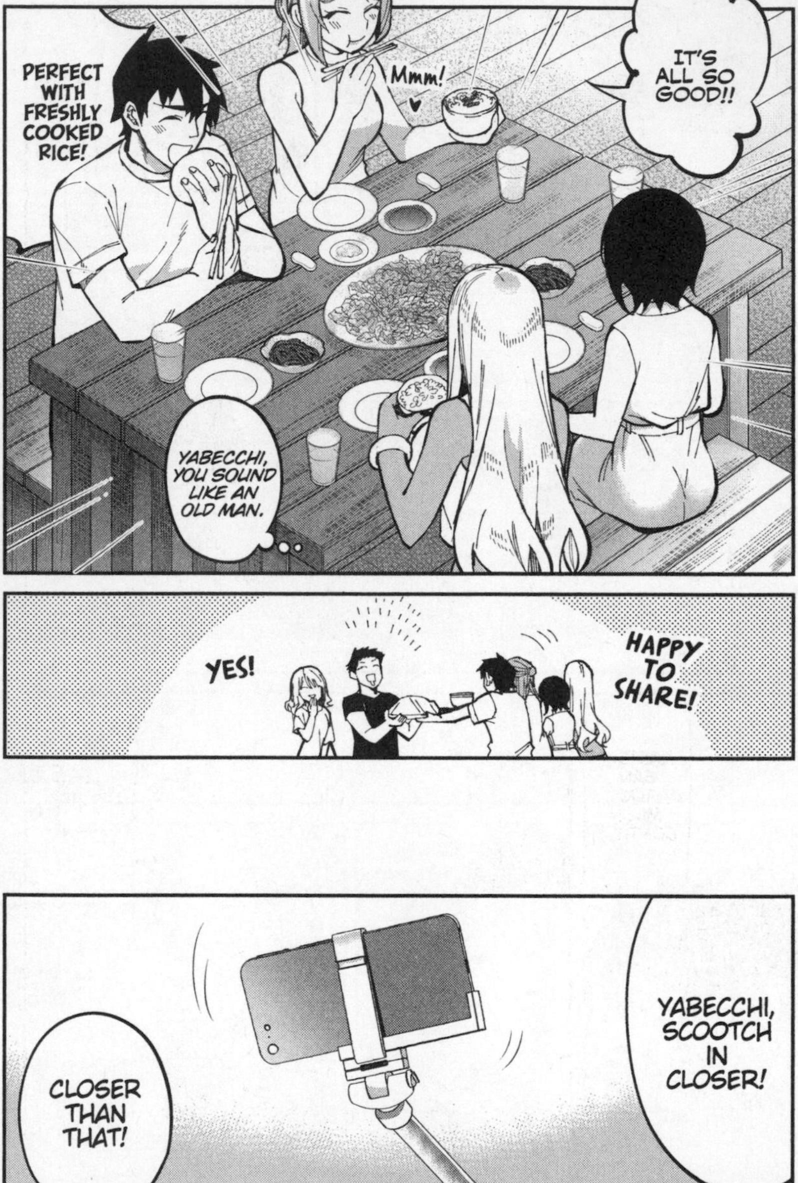
IT'S ALL SO GOOD!!
Mmm! ♥
PERFECT WITH FRESHLY COOKED RICE!
YABECCHI, YOU SOUND LIKE AN OLD MAN.
HAPPY TO SHARE!
YES!
YABECCHI, SCOOTCH IN CLOSER!
CLOSER THAN THAT!

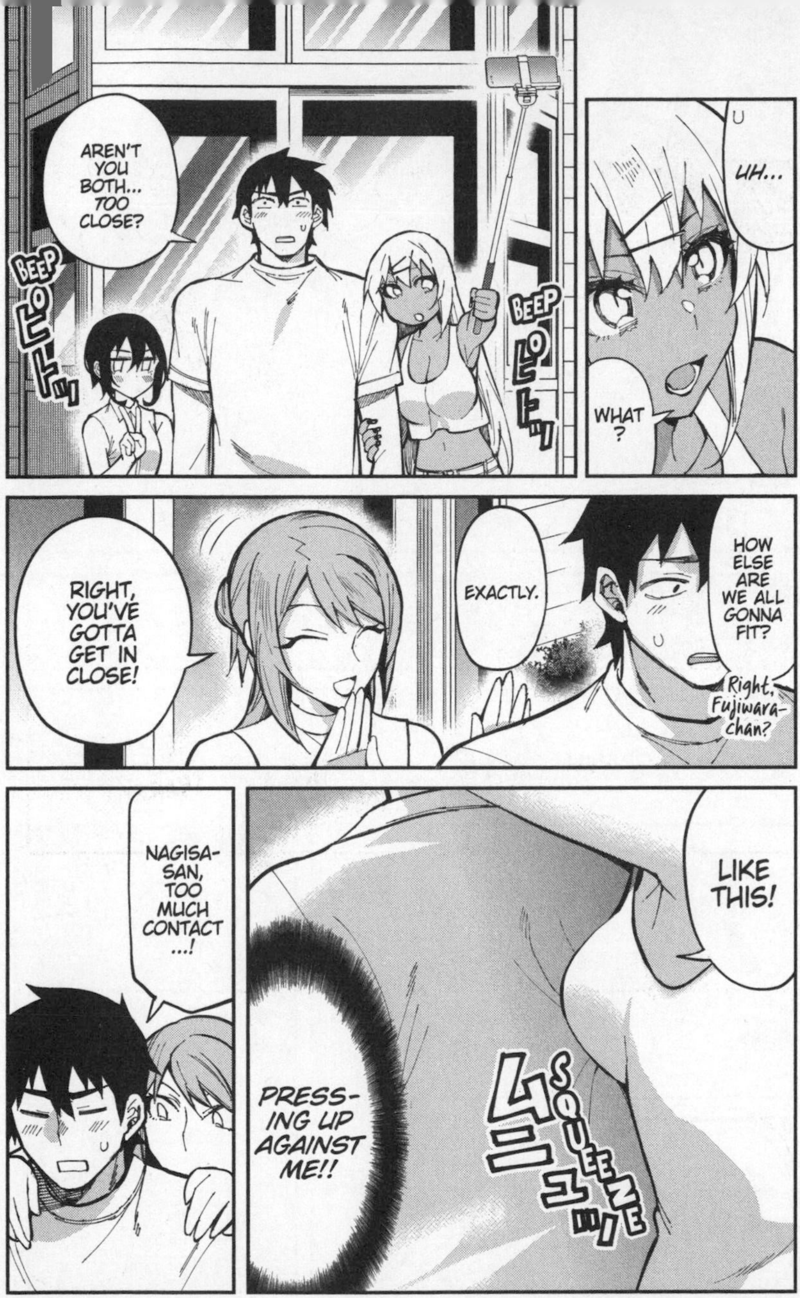
UH...
WHAT?
AREN'T YOU BOTH... TOO CLOSE?
BEEP
BEEP
HOW ELSE ARE WE ALL GONNA FIT?
Right, Fujiwara-chan?
EXACTLY.
RIGHT, YOU'VE GOTTA GET IN CLOSE!
LIKE THIS!
SQUEEZE
PRESSING-ING UP AGAINST ME!!
NAGISA-SAN, TOO MUCH CONTACT ...!

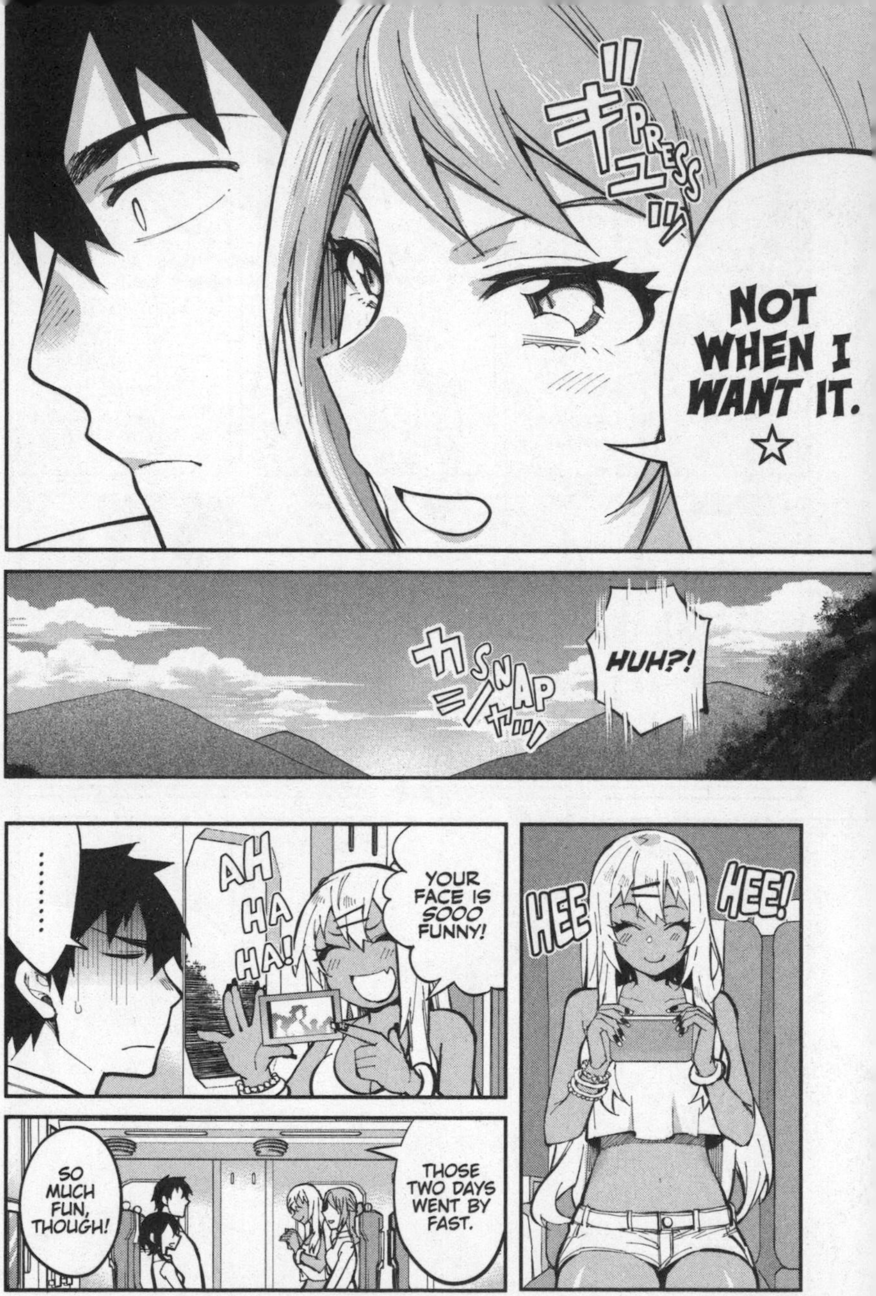
ギュッ
PRESS
NOT WHEN I WANT IT. ☆
カシャッ
SNAP
HUH?!
HEE HEE!
YOUR FACE IS SOOO FUNNY!
AH HA HA!
......
THOSE TWO DAYS WENT BY FAST.
SO MUCH FUN, THOUGH!

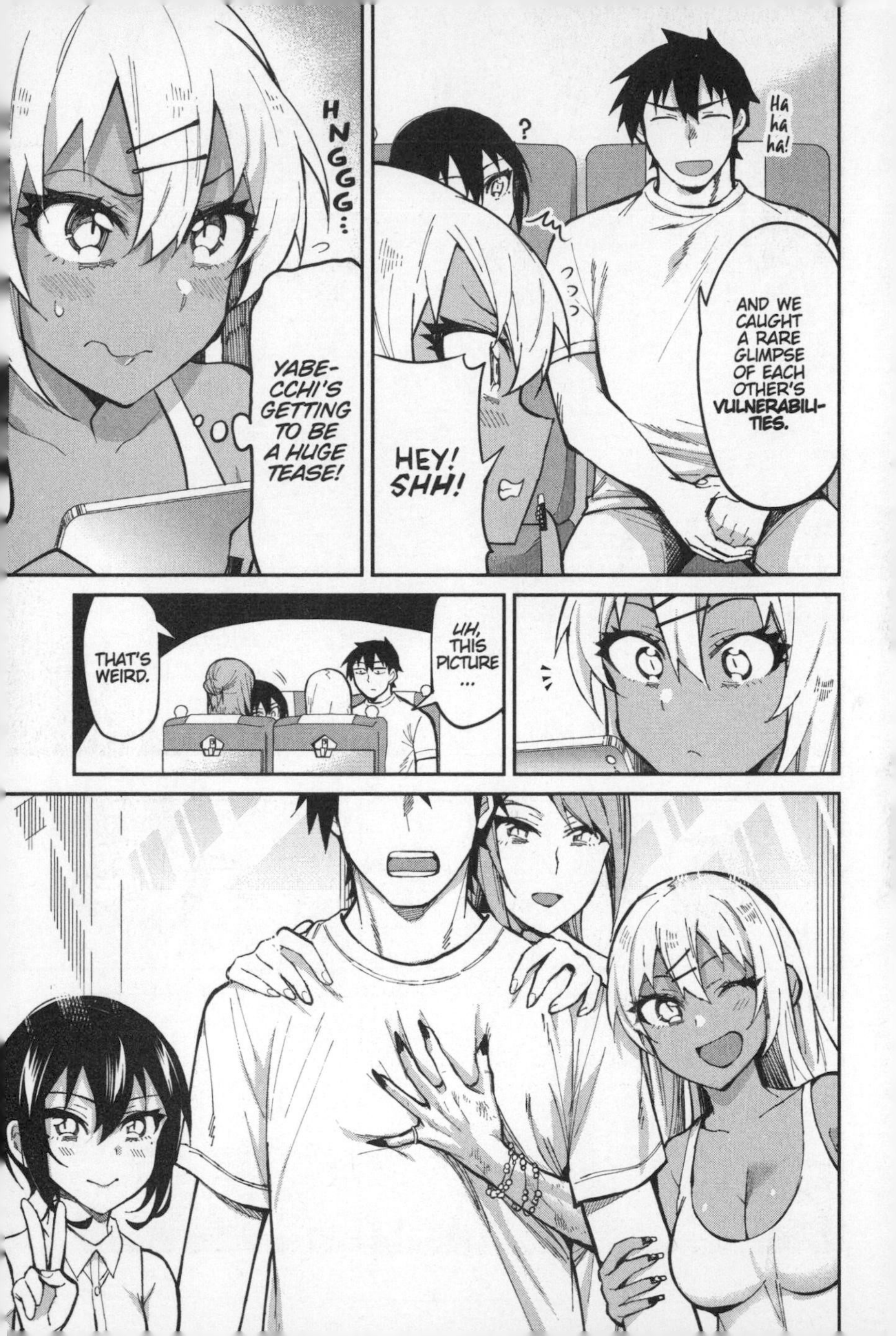
Ha ha ha!
?
AND WE CAUGHT A RARE GLIMPSE OF EACH OTHER'S VULNERABILI-TIES.
HEY! SHH!
HNGGG...
YABE-CCHI'S GETTING TO BE A HUGE TEASE!
UH, THIS PICTURE ...
THAT'S WEIRD.

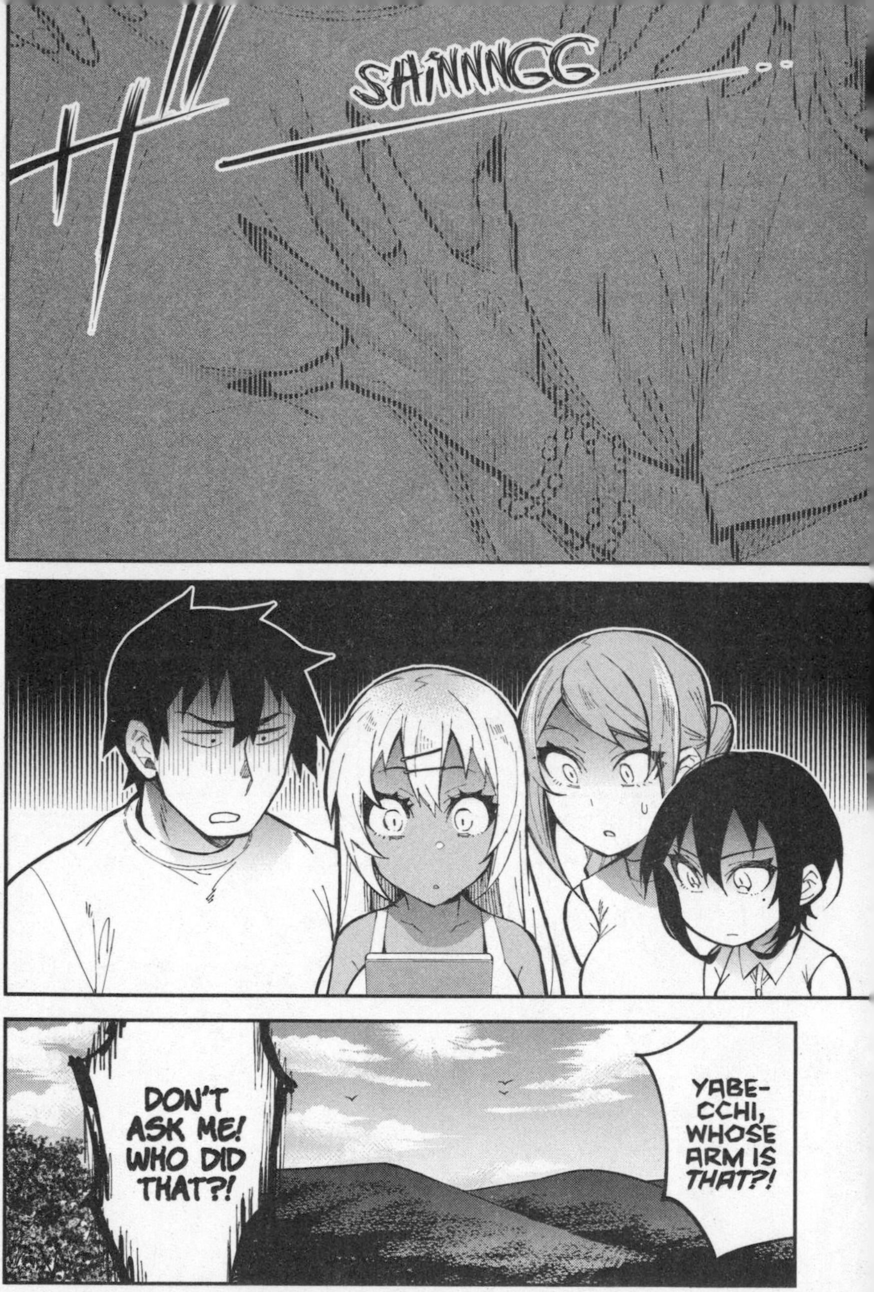
SHINNNGG
YABE-CCHI, WHOSE ARM IS THAT?!
DON'T ASK ME! WHO DID THAT?!

Gal
Gohan

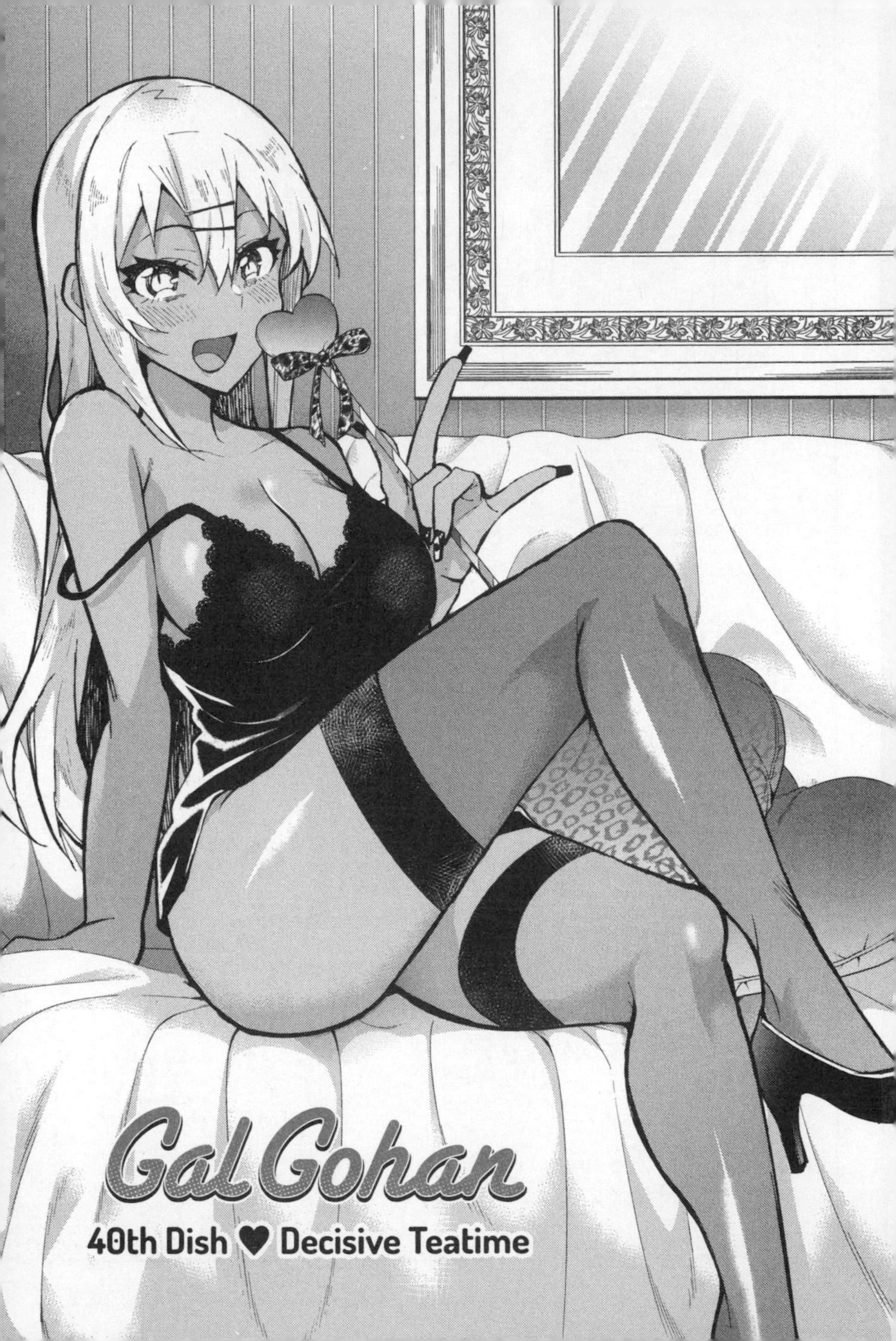
Gal Gohan
40th Dish ♥ Decisive Teatime

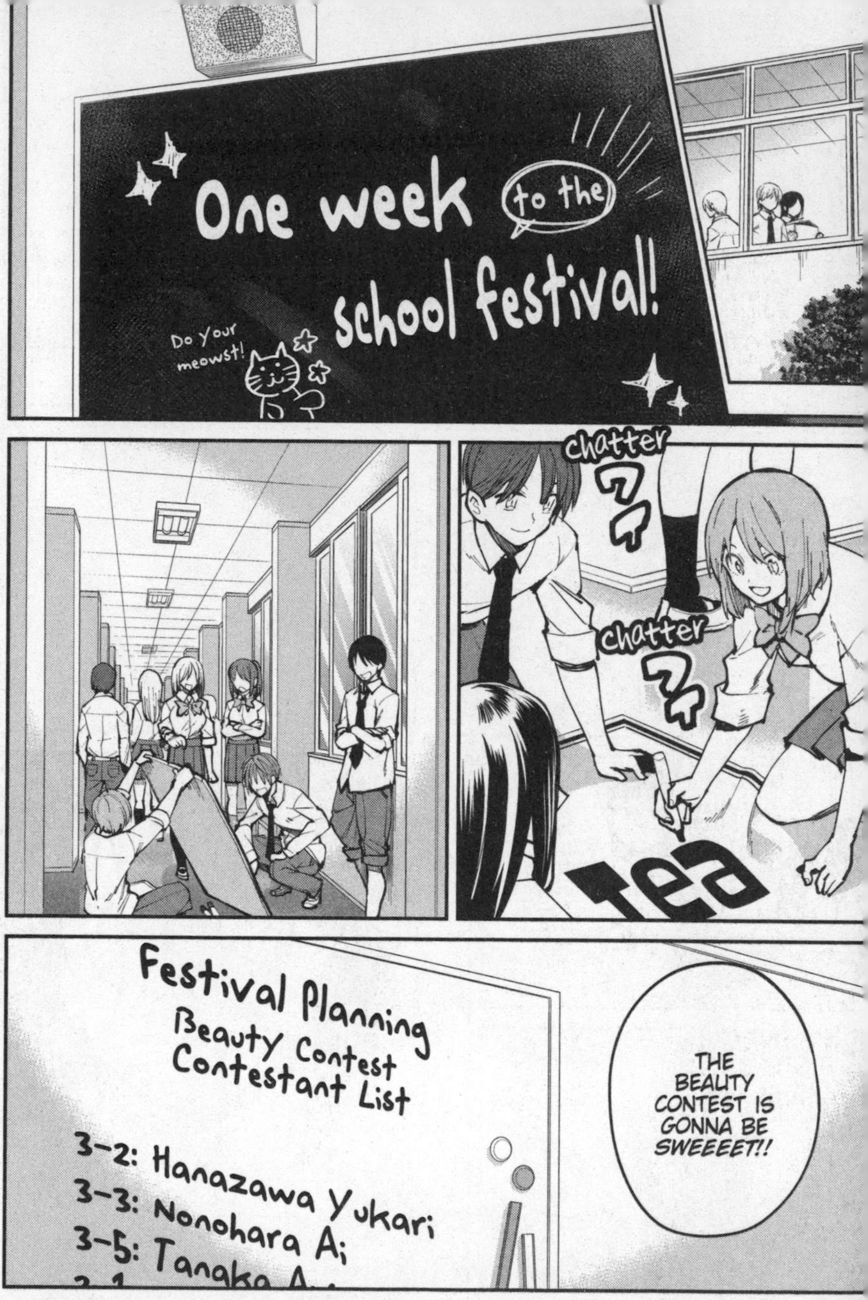

One week to the school festival!
Do your meowst!
chatter
chatter
tea
THE BEAUTY CONTEST IS GONNA BE SWEEEET!!
Festival Planning
Beauty Contest
Contestant List
3-2: Hanazawa Yukari
3-3: Nonohara Ai
3-5: Tanaka A

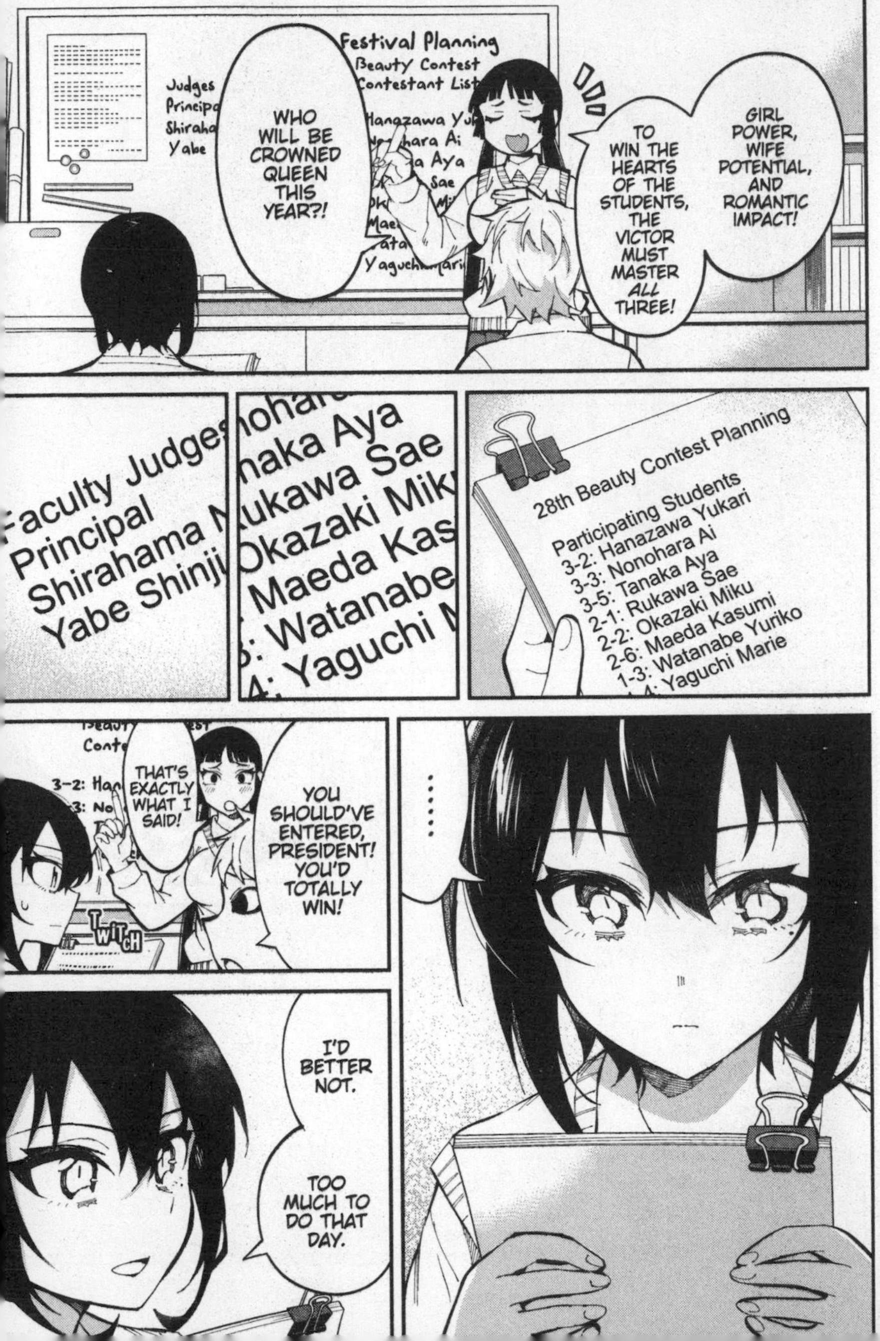
Festival Planning
Beauty Contest
Contestant List
Judges
GIRL POWER, WIFE POTENTIAL, AND ROMANTIC IMPACT!
TO WIN THE HEARTS OF THE STUDENTS, THE VICTOR MUST MASTER ALL THREE!
WHO WILL BE CROWNED QUEEN THIS YEAR?!
28th Beauty Contest Planning
Participating Students
3-2: Hanazawa Yukari
3-3: Nonohara Ai
3-5: Tanaka Aya
2-1: Rukawa Sae
2-2: Okazaki Miku
2-6: Maeda Kasumi
1-3: Watanabe Yuriko
Yaguchi Marie
Faculty Judges
Principal
......
YOU SHOULD'VE ENTERED, PRESIDENT! YOU'D TOTALLY WIN!
THAT'S EXACTLY WHAT I SAID!
TWITCH
I'D BETTER NOT.
TOO MUCH TO DO THAT DAY.

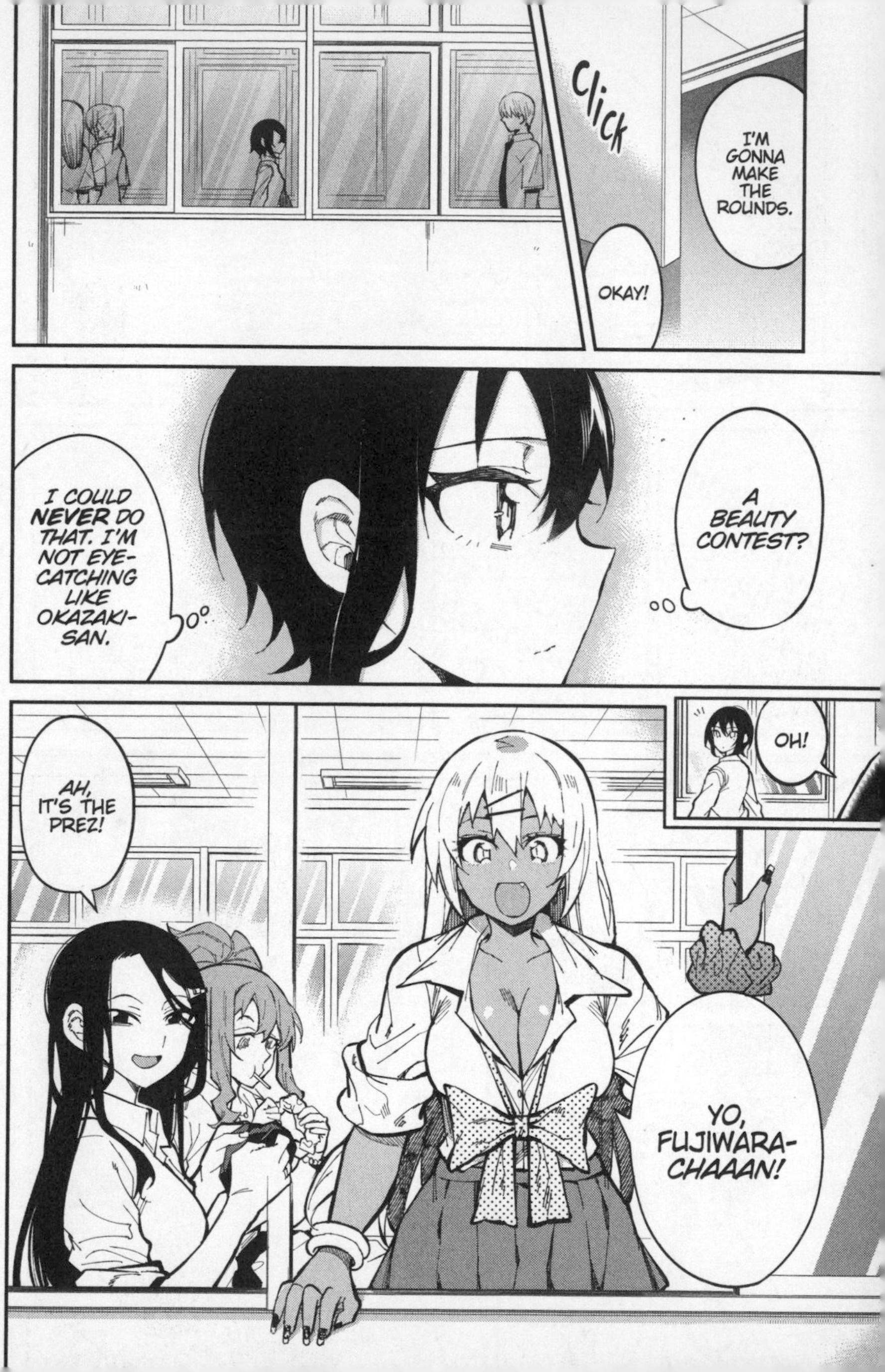
Click
I'M GONNA MAKE THE ROUNDS.
OKAY!
A BEAUTY CONTEST?
I COULD NEVER DO THAT. I'M NOT EYE-CATCHING LIKE OKAZAKI-SAN.
OH!
YO, FUJIWARA-CHAAAN!
AH, IT'S THE PREZ!

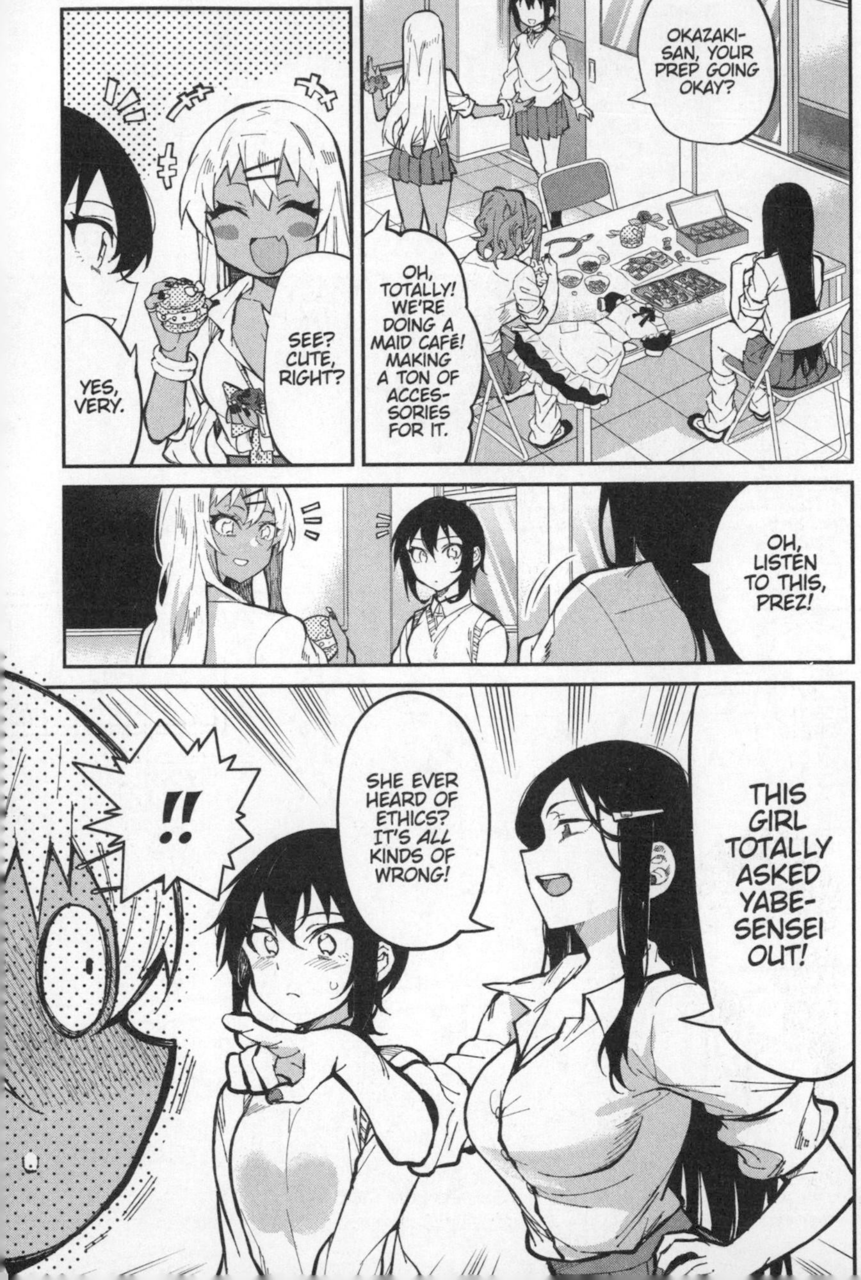
OKAZAKI-SAN, YOUR PREP GOING OKAY?
OH, TOTALLY! WE'RE DOING A MAID CAFÉ! MAKING A TON OF ACCESSORIES FOR IT.
SEE? CUTE, RIGHT?
YES, VERY.
OH, LISTEN TO THIS, PREZ!
THIS GIRL TOTALLY ASKED YABE-SENSEI OUT!
SHE EVER HEARD OF ETHICS? IT'S *ALL* KINDS OF WRONG!
!!

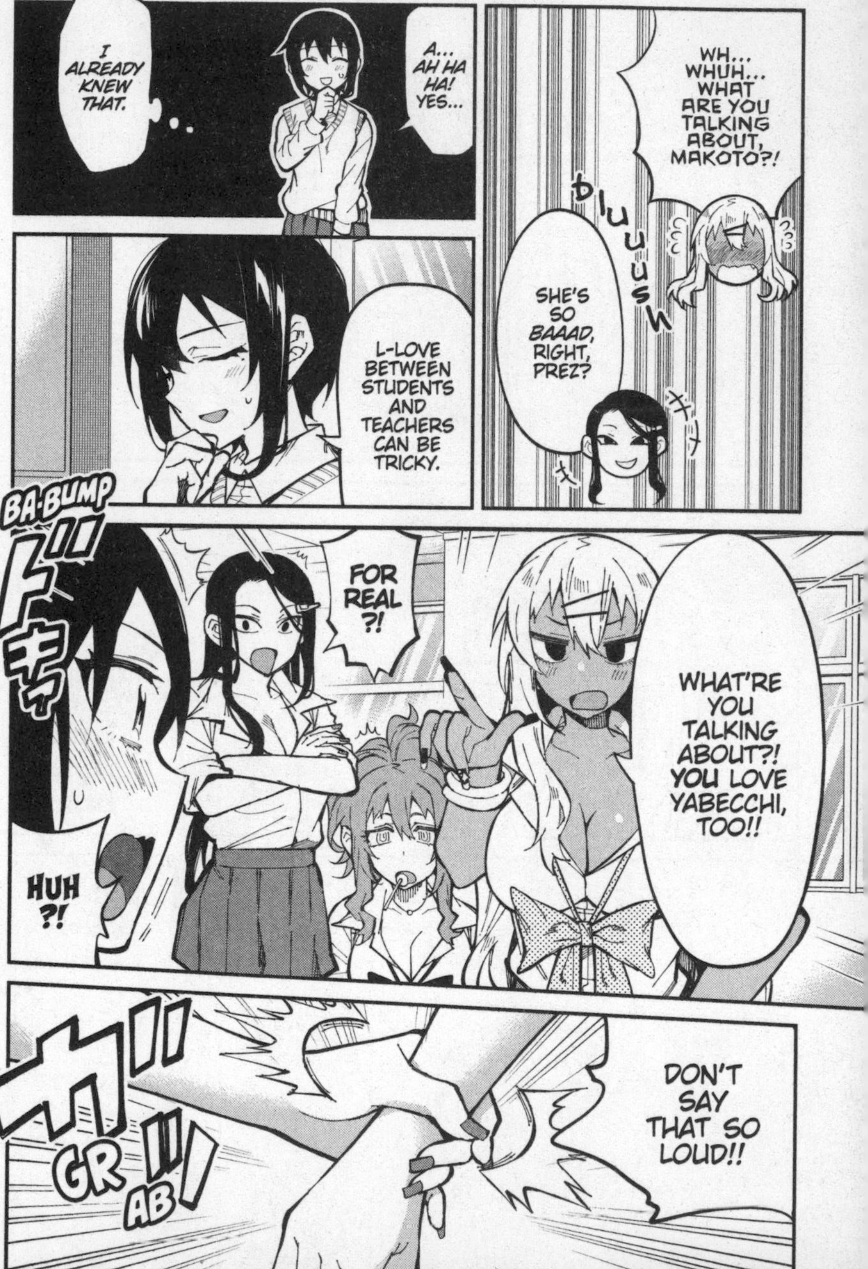
WH... WHUH... WHAT ARE YOU TALKING ABOUT, MAKOTO?!
SHE'S SO BAAAD, RIGHT, PREZ?
A... AH HA HA! YES...
I ALREADY KNEW THAT.
L-LOVE BETWEEN STUDENTS AND TEACHERS CAN BE TRICKY.
WHAT'RE YOU TALKING ABOUT?! YOU LOVE YABECCHI, TOO!!
FOR REAL?!
BA-BUMP
HUH?!
DON'T SAY THAT SO LOUD!!
GRAB

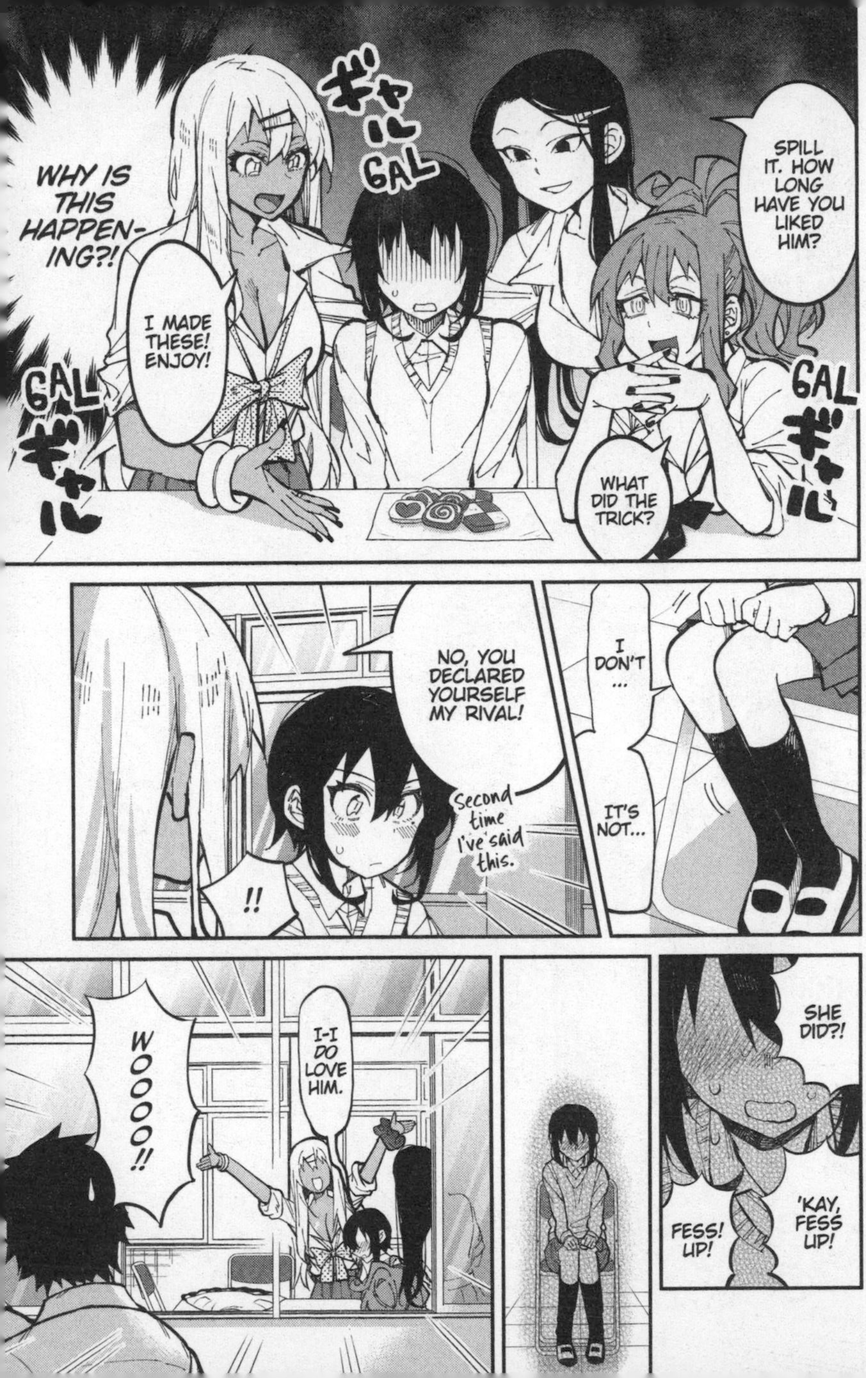
SPILL IT. HOW LONG HAVE YOU LIKED HIM?
ギャル GAL
WHY IS THIS HAPPEN-ING?!
GAL ギャル
I MADE THESE! ENJOY!
WHAT DID THE TRICK?
GAL ギャル
I DON'T ...
IT'S NOT...
NO, YOU DECLARED YOURSELF MY RIVAL!
Second time I've said this.
!!
SHE DID?!
'KAY, FESS UP!
FESS! UP!
I-I DO LOVE HIM.
WOOOOO!!

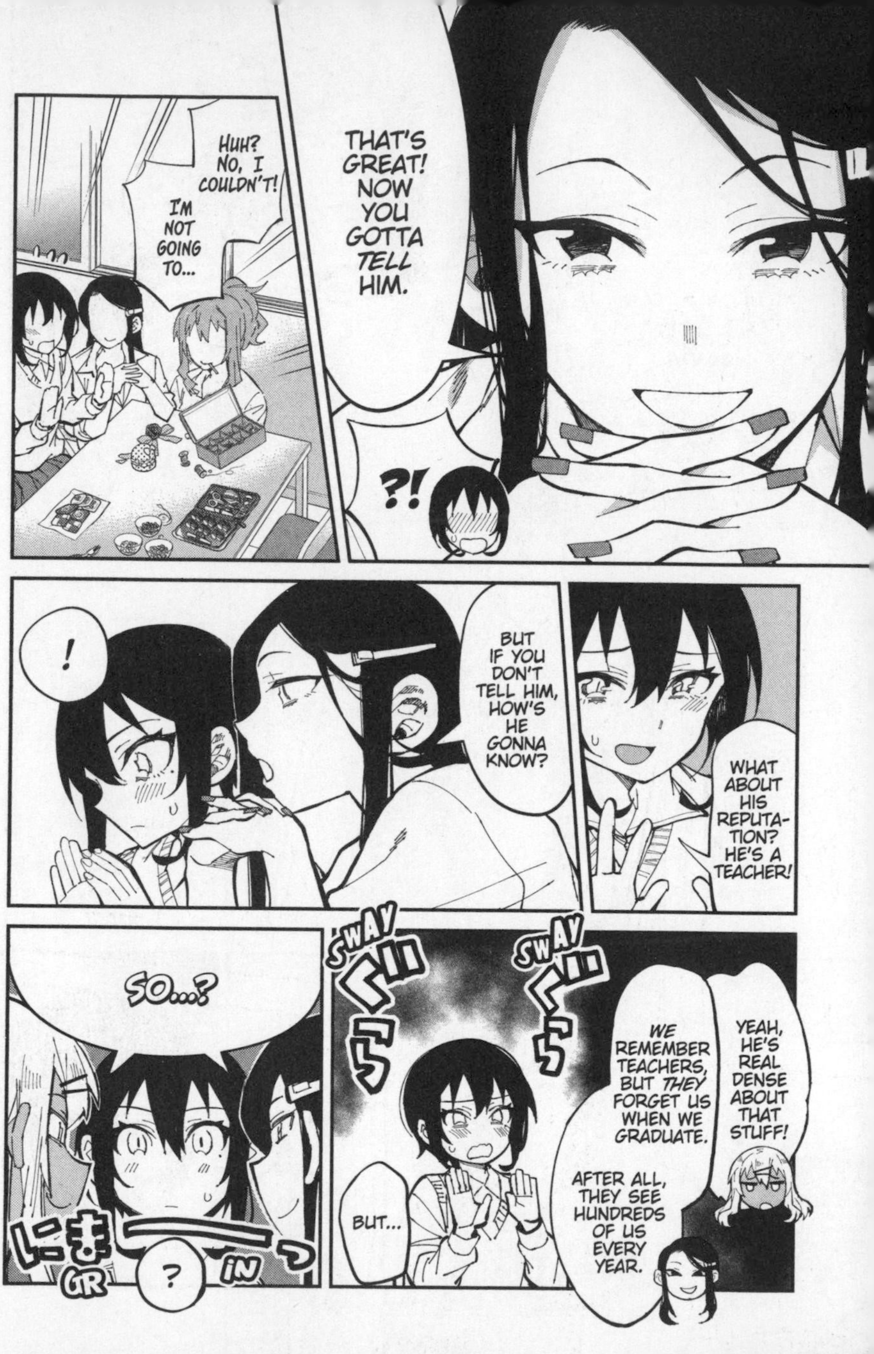
THAT'S GREAT! NOW YOU GOTTA *TELL* HIM.
?!
HUH? NO, I COULDN'T!
I'M NOT GOING TO...
WHAT ABOUT HIS REPUTATION? HE'S A TEACHER!
BUT IF YOU DON'T TELL HIM, HOW'S HE GONNA KNOW?
!
SWAY
SWAY
YEAH, HE'S REAL DENSE ABOUT THAT STUFF!
WE REMEMBER TEACHERS, BUT *THEY* FORGET US WHEN WE GRADUATE.
AFTER ALL, THEY SEE HUNDREDS OF US EVERY YEAR.
BUT...
SO...?
GRIN
?

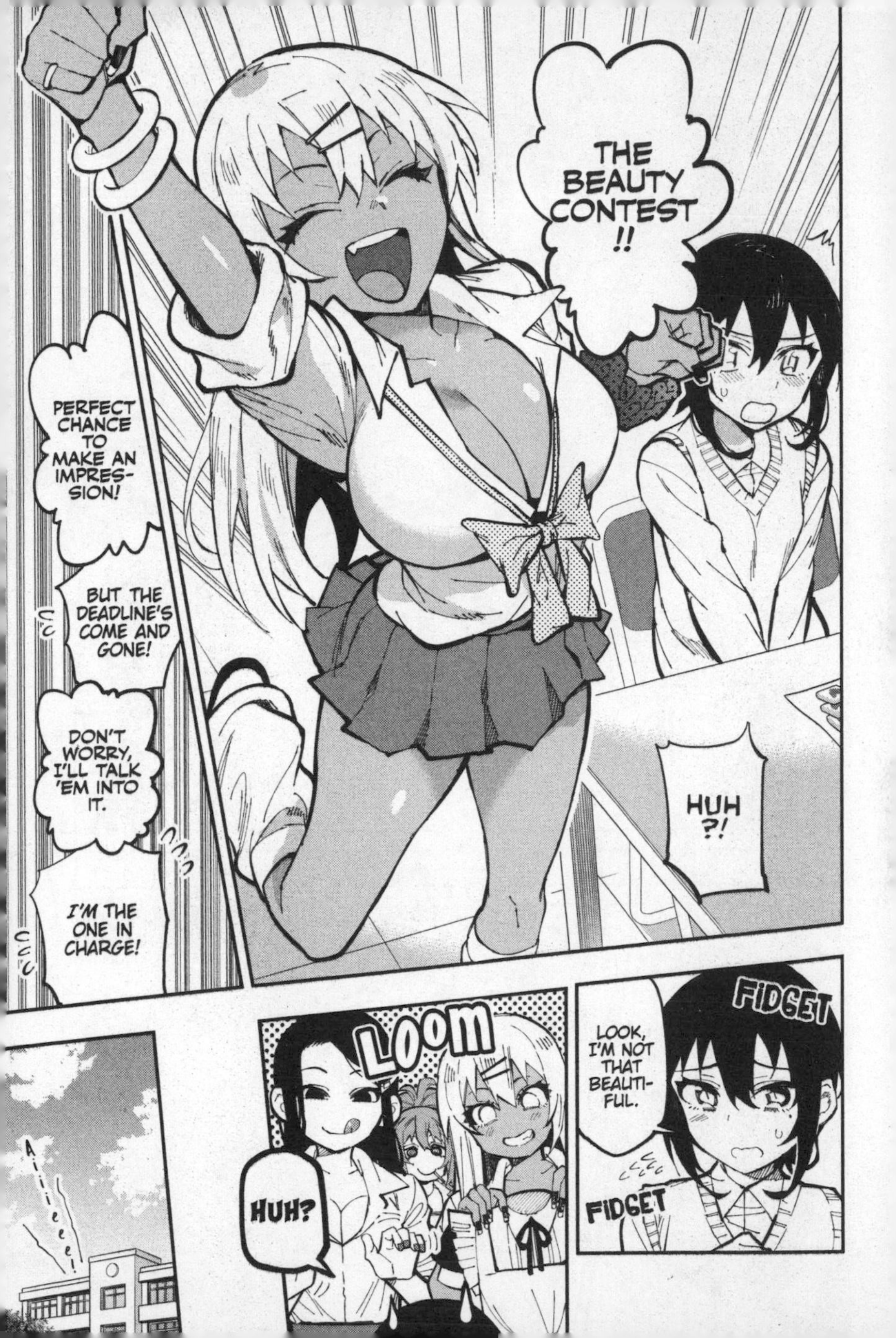
THE BEAUTY CONTEST!!
HUH?!
PERFECT CHANCE TO MAKE AN IMPRESSION!
BUT THE DEADLINE'S COME AND GONE!
DON'T WORRY, I'LL TALK 'EM INTO IT.
I'M THE ONE IN CHARGE!
FIDGET
LOOK, I'M NOT THAT BEAUTIFUL.
FIDGET
LOOM
HUH?
Aiiieee!

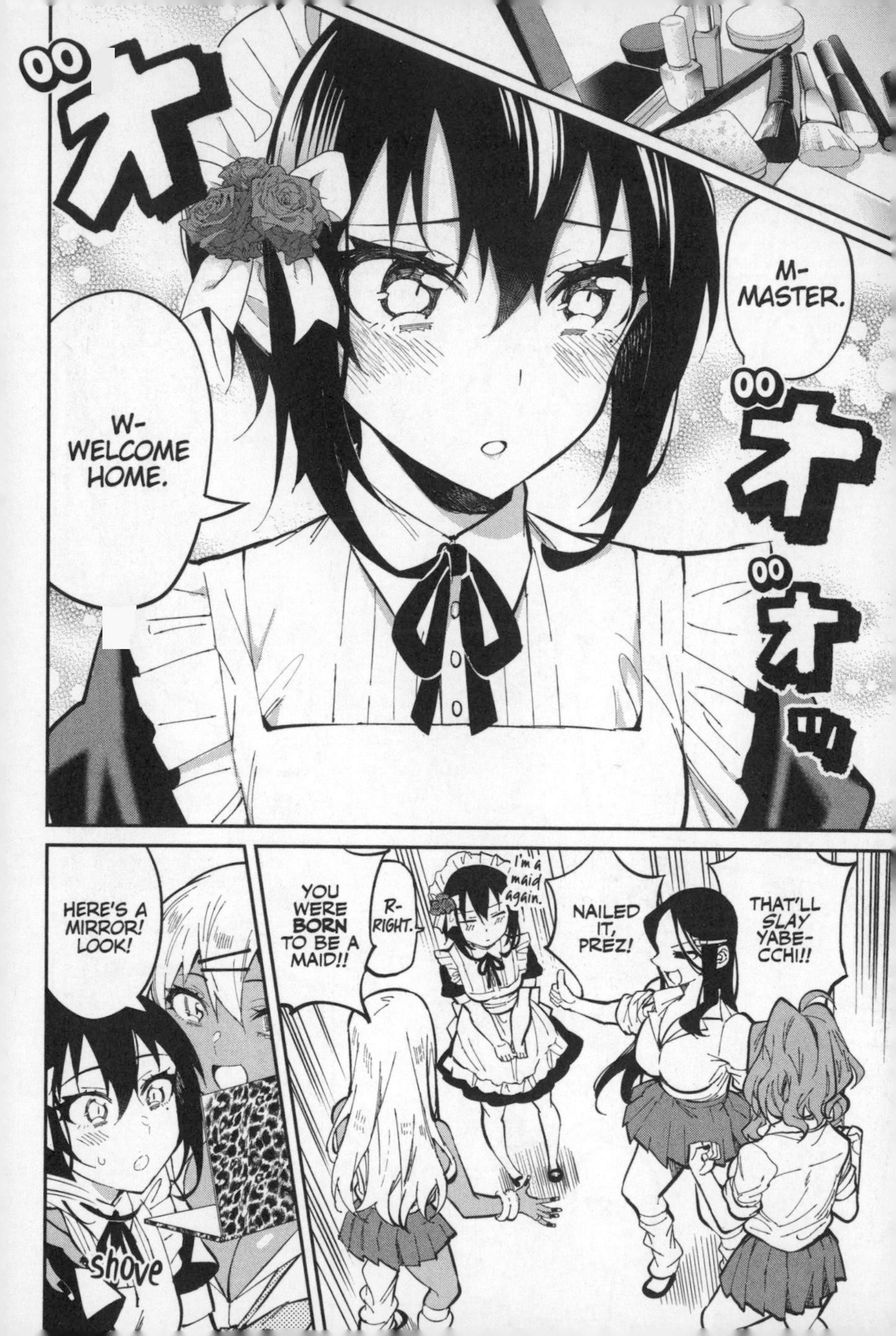
M-MASTER.
W-WELCOME HOME.
THAT'LL SLAY YABECCHI!!
NAILED IT, PREZ!
I'm a maid again.
R-RIGHT.
YOU WERE BORN TO BE A MAID!!
HERE'S A MIRROR! LOOK!
shove

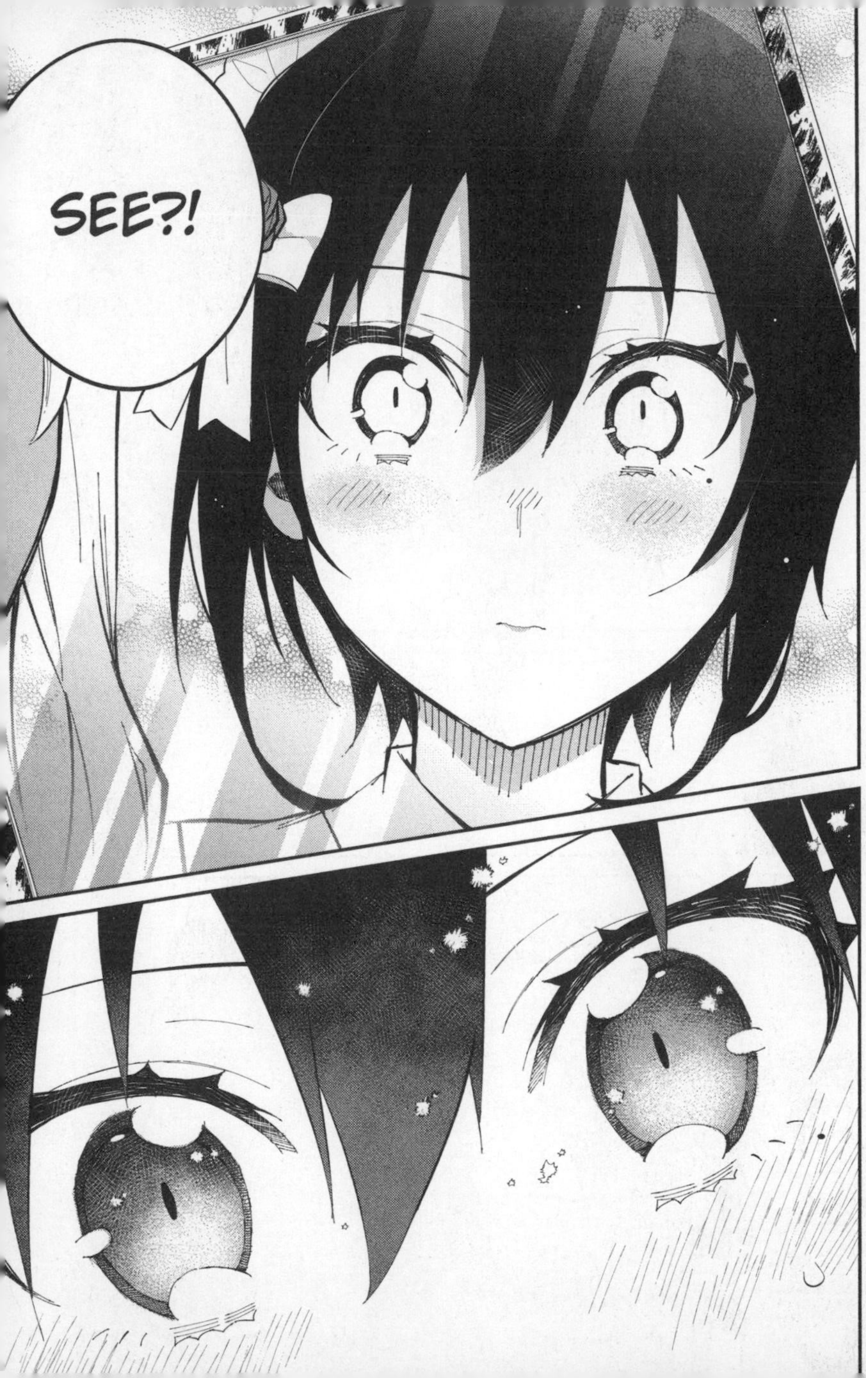
SEE?!

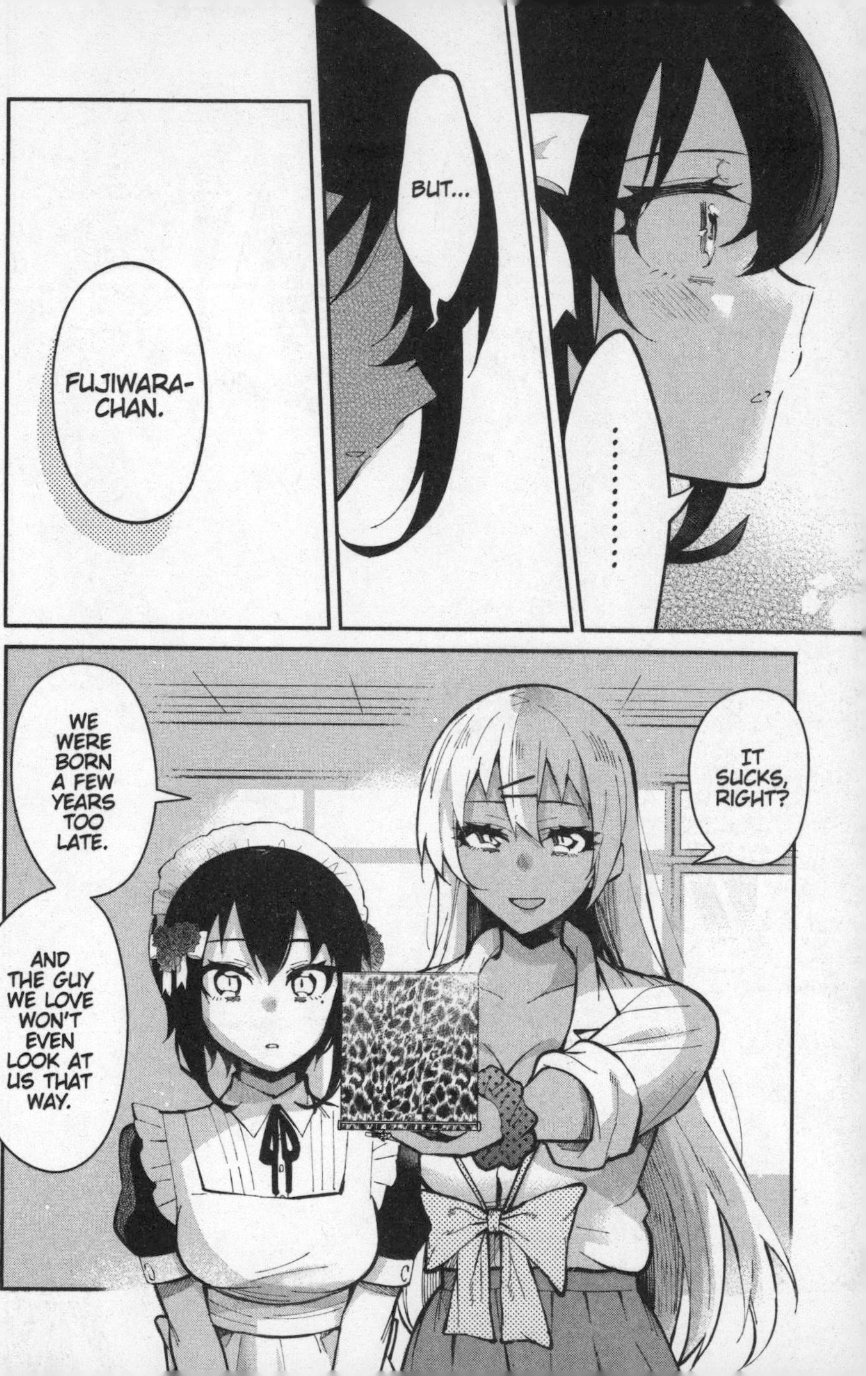
......
BUT...
FUJIWARA-CHAN.
IT SUCKS, RIGHT?
WE WERE BORN A FEW YEARS TOO LATE.
AND THE GUY WE LOVE WON'T EVEN LOOK AT US THAT WAY.

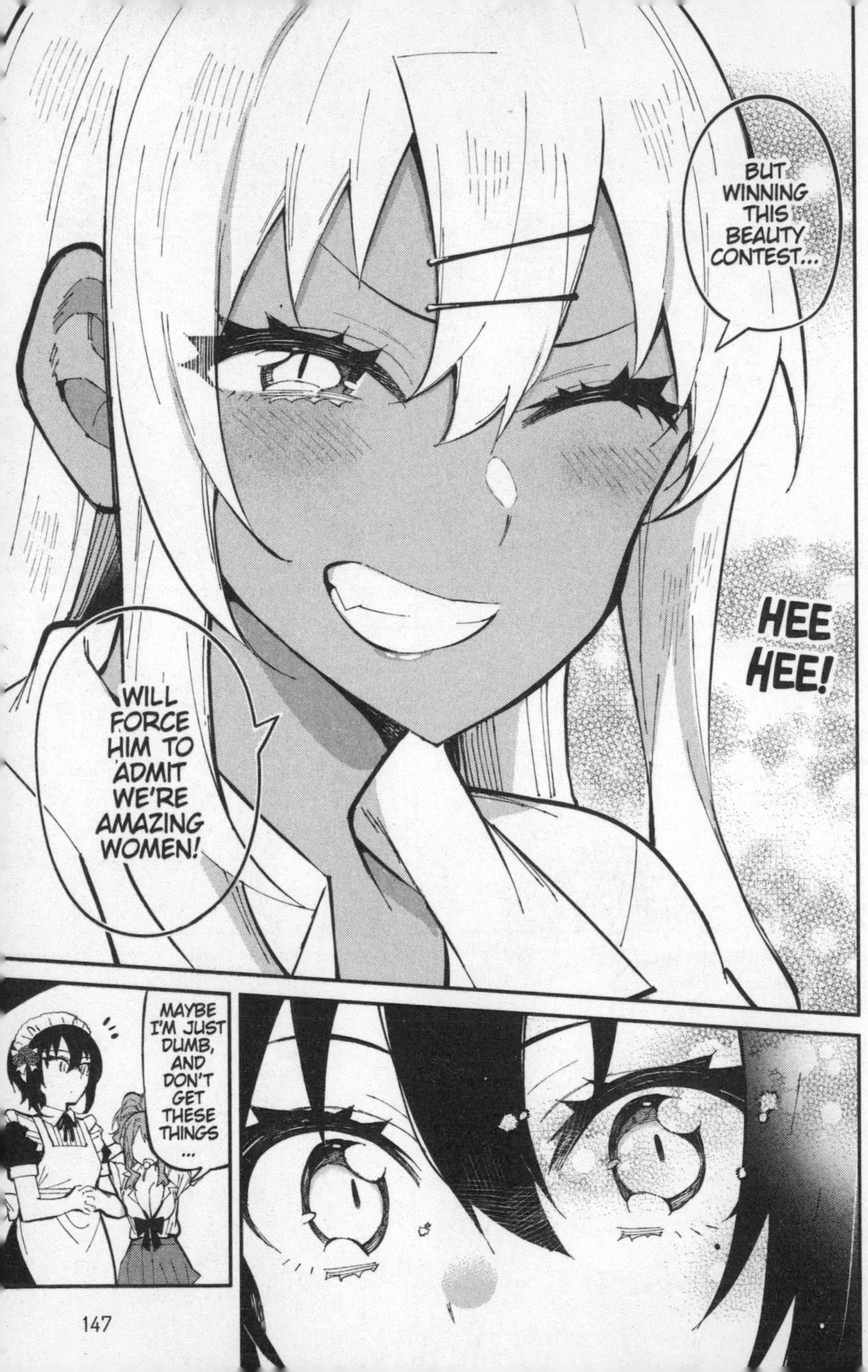
BUT WINNING THIS BEAUTY CONTEST...
WILL FORCE HIM TO ADMIT WE'RE AMAZING WOMEN!
HEE HEE!
MAYBE I'M JUST DUMB, AND DON'T GET THESE THINGS ...

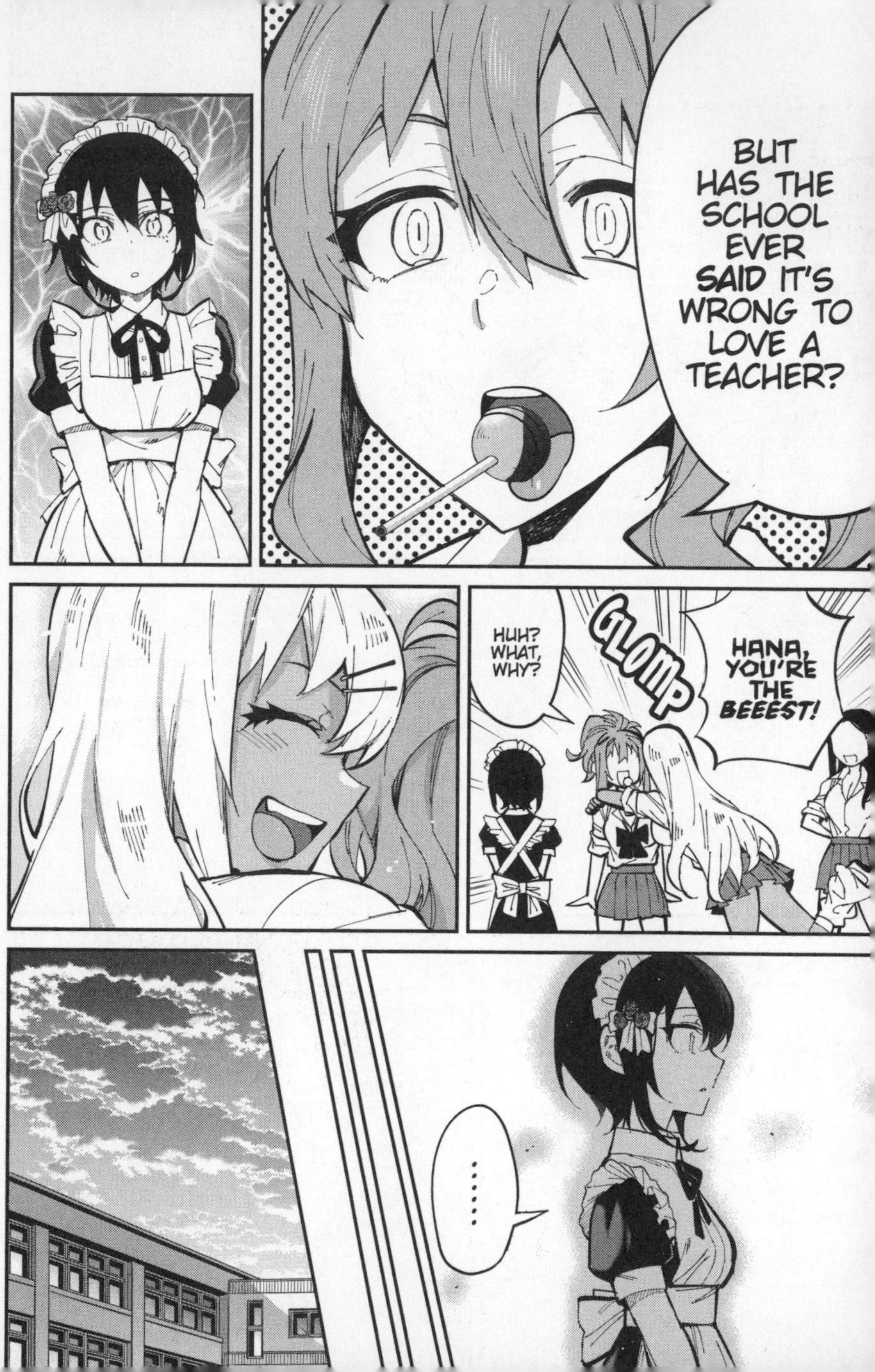
BUT HAS THE SCHOOL EVER SAID IT'S WRONG TO LOVE A TEACHER?
HANA, YOU'RE THE BEEEST!
GLOMP
HUH? WHAT, WHY?
......

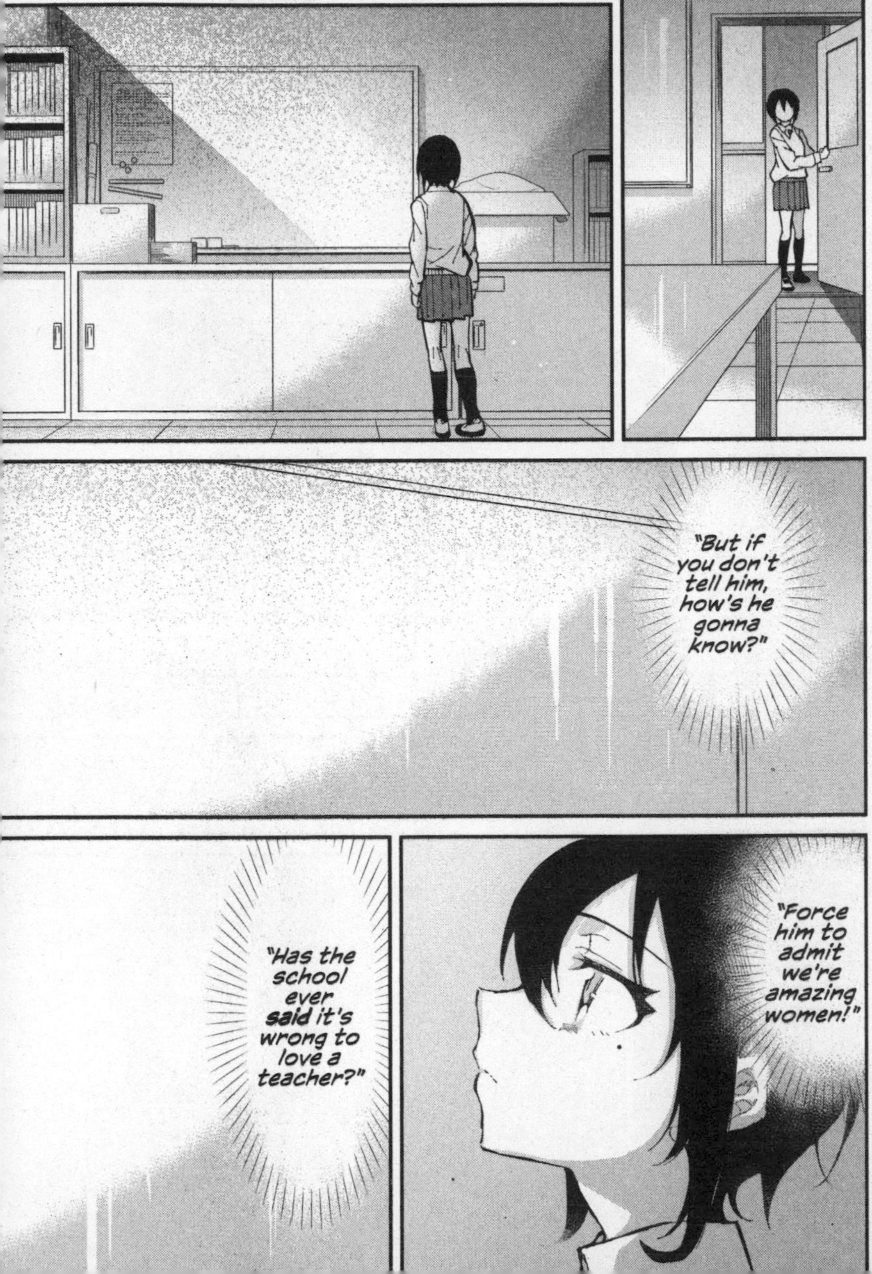
"But if you don't tell him, how's he gonna know?"
"Force him to admit we're amazing women!"
"Has the school ever **said** it's wrong to love a teacher?"

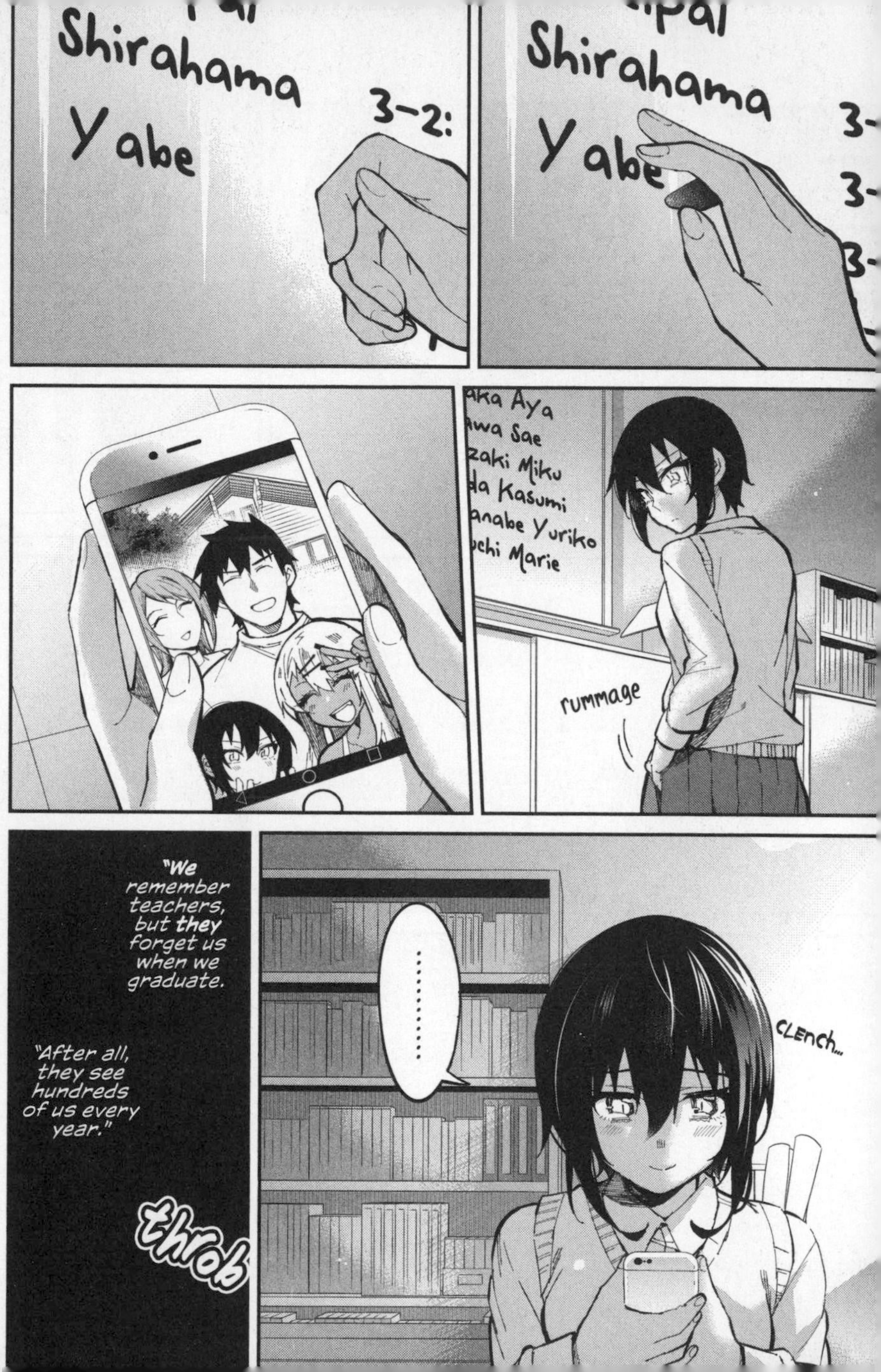

Shirahama
Yabe
3-
3-
3-
Shirahama
Yabe
3-2:
aka Aya
awa Sae
zaki Miku
da Kasumi
anabe Yuriko
uchi Marie
rummage
......
CLENCH...
"We remember teachers, but they forget us when we graduate.
"After all, they see hundreds of us every year."
throb

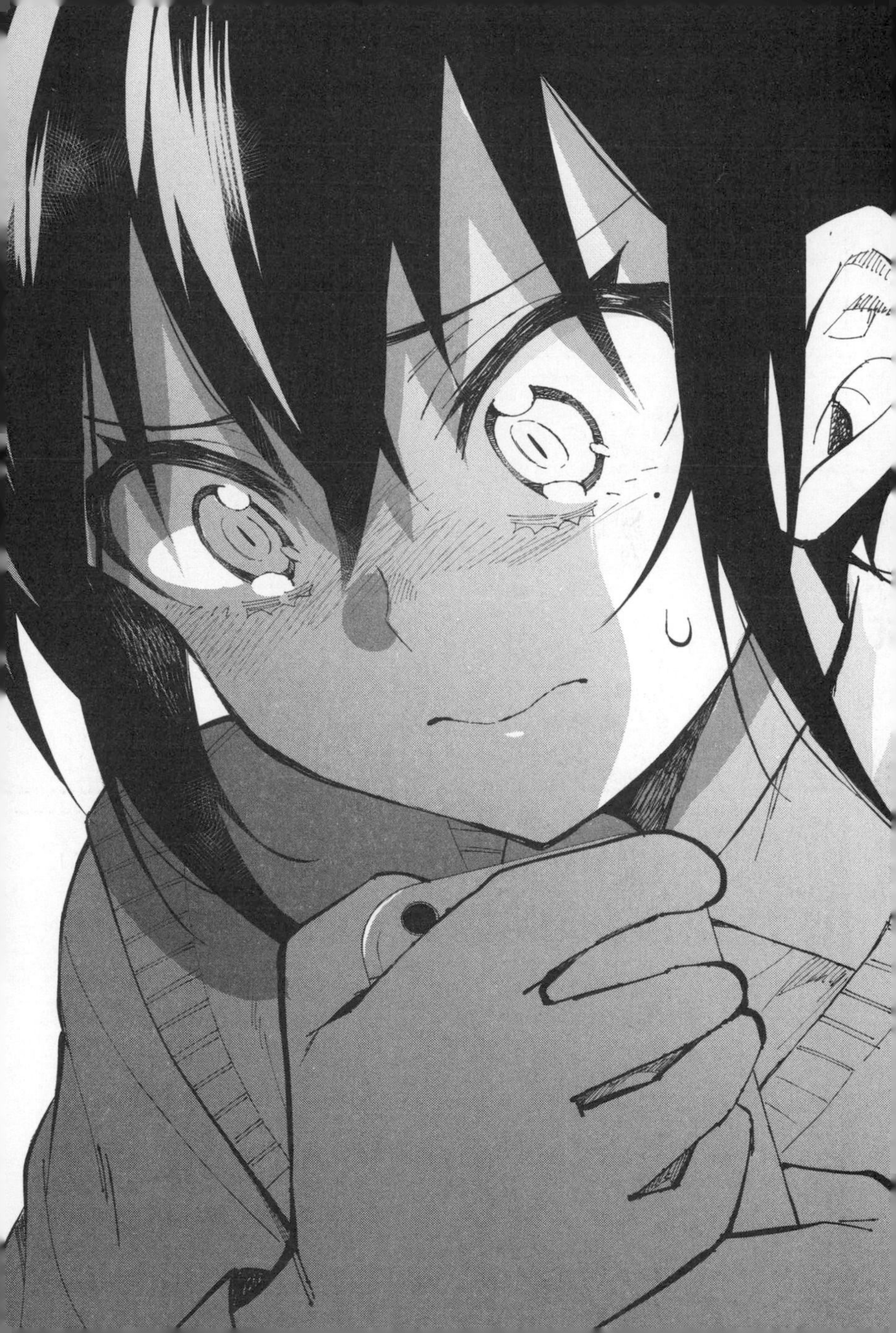

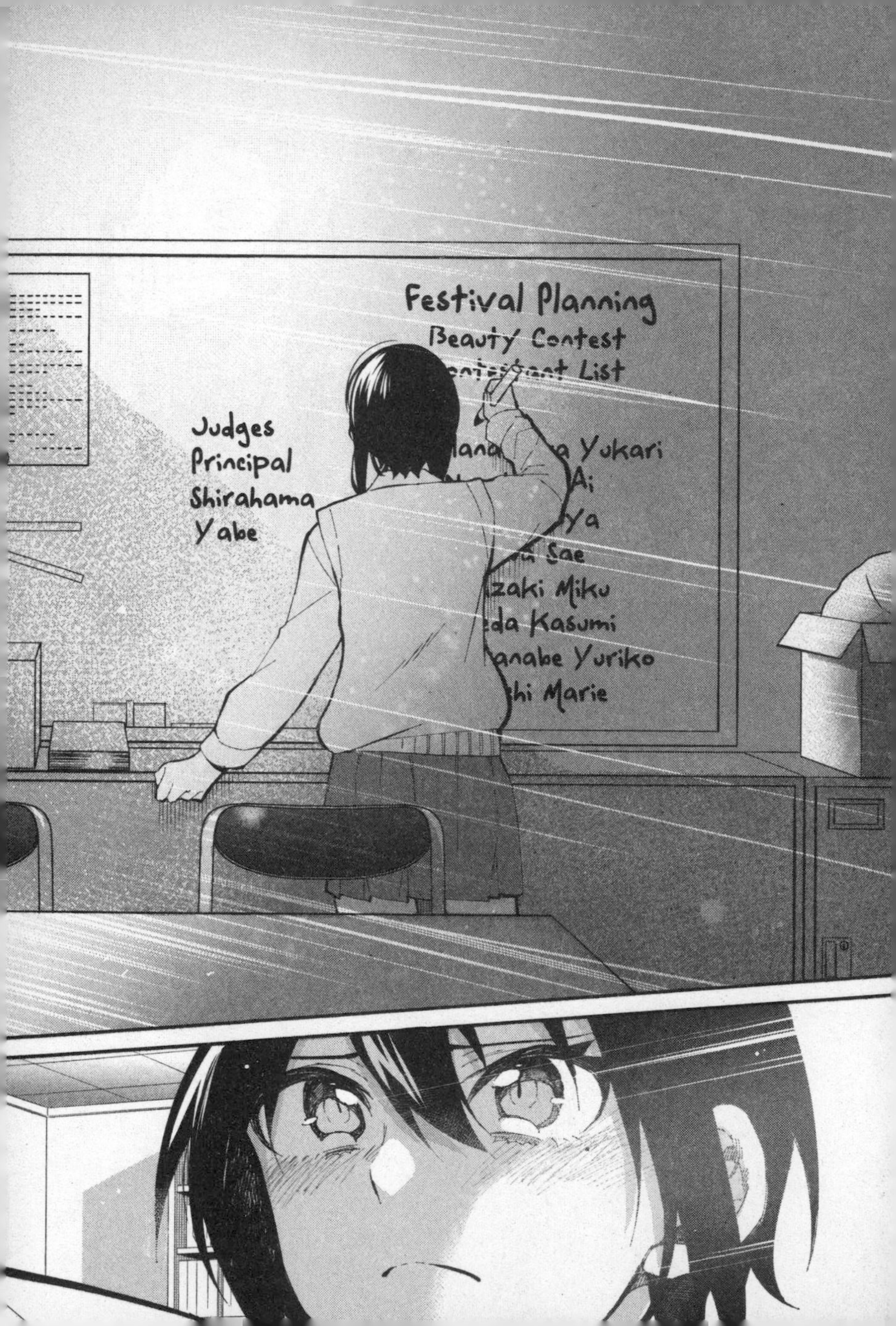
Festival Planning
Beauty Contest
List
Yukari
Ai
Sae
Miku
Kasumi
Yuriko
Marie
Judges
Principal
Shirahama
Yabe

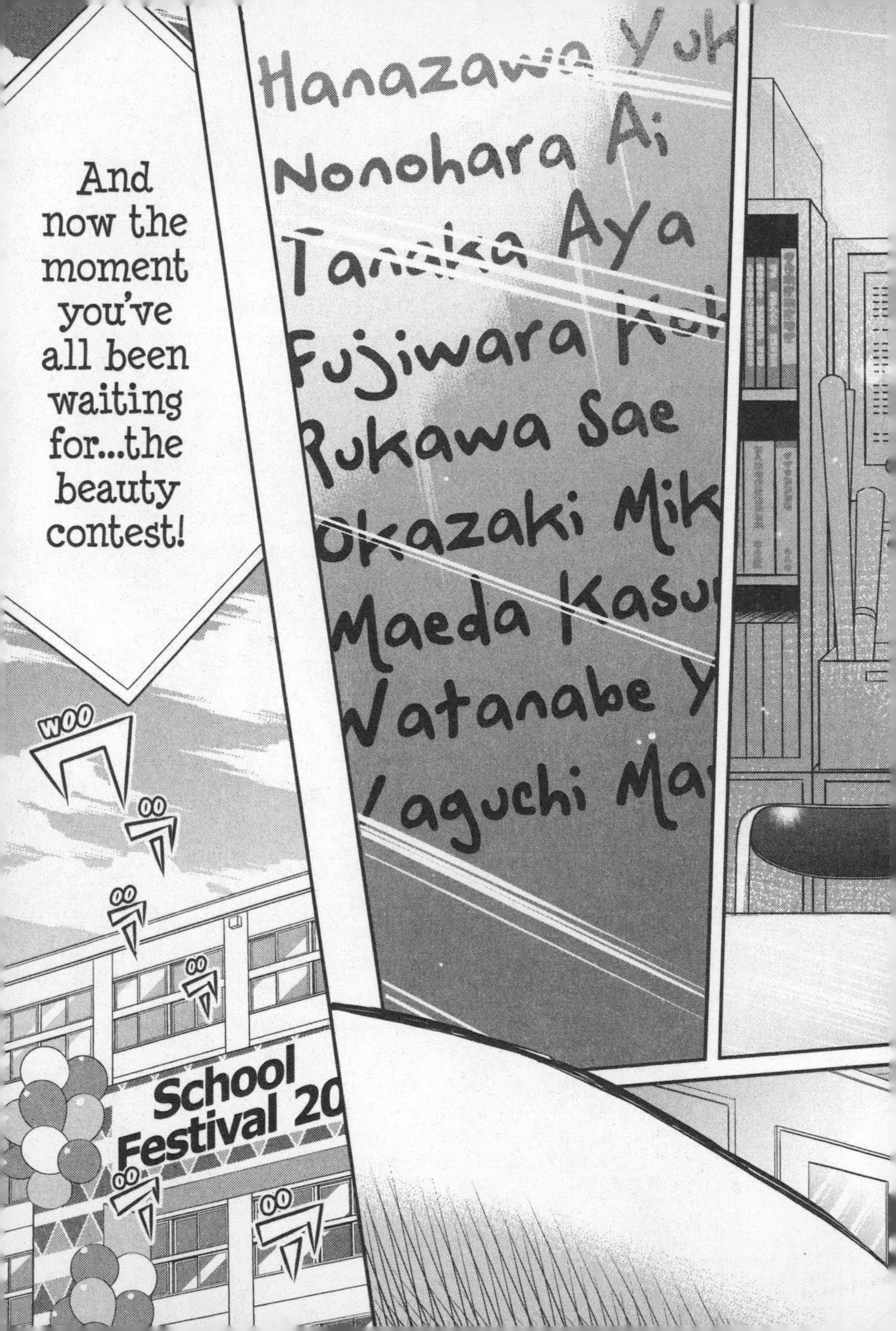
Hanazawa Yuk
Nonohara Ai
Tanaka Aya
Fujiwara Ko
Rukawa Sae
Okazaki Mik
Maeda Kasu
Watanabe Y
Yaguchi Ma
And now the moment you've all been waiting for...the beauty contest!
WOO
School Festival 20

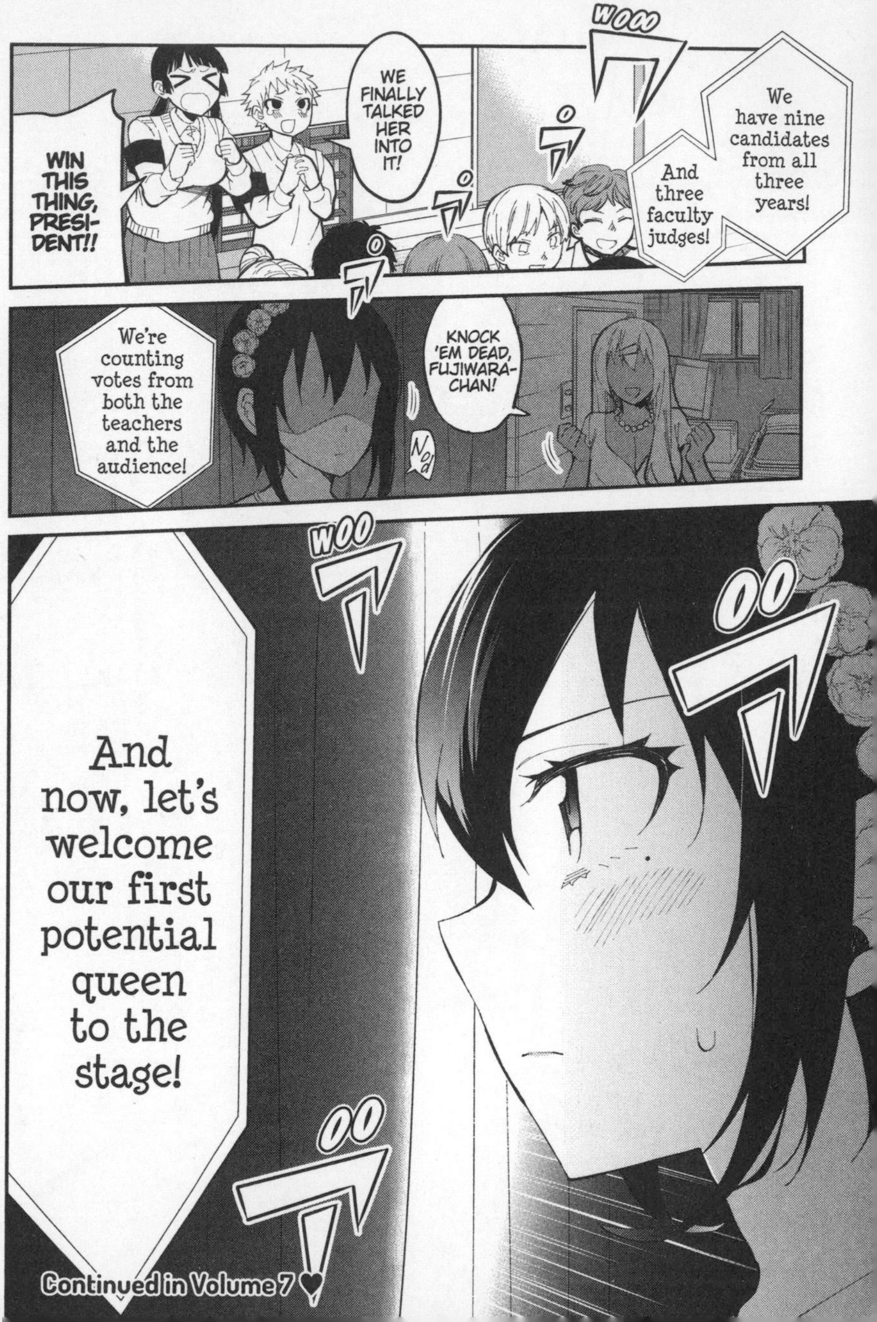
We have nine candidates from all three years!
And three faculty judges!
WOOO
WE FINALLY TALKED HER INTO IT!
WIN THIS THING, PRESIDENT!!
KNOCK 'EM DEAD, FUJIWARA-CHAN!
Nod
We're counting votes from both the teachers and the audience!
OO
WOO
And now, let's welcome our first potential queen to the stage!
OO
Continued in Volume 7 ♥

Gal
Gohan

AFTERWORD

Volume 6!
Thanks for buying!

Miku-chan finally did it...

She told him how she feels!

Ah...ah...   Yay!

The story is over the hump now, and as I write this afterword, I'm busy stressing over whether I'll be able to wrap everything up right.

I'd love it if you follow me all the way! Please keep supporting the series.

Also, I sometimes upload sketches to @taiyoumarii so please follow me there!

See you in Volume 7! ♪

The next page is a report on the talk show held at the Osaka Loft PlusOne West.

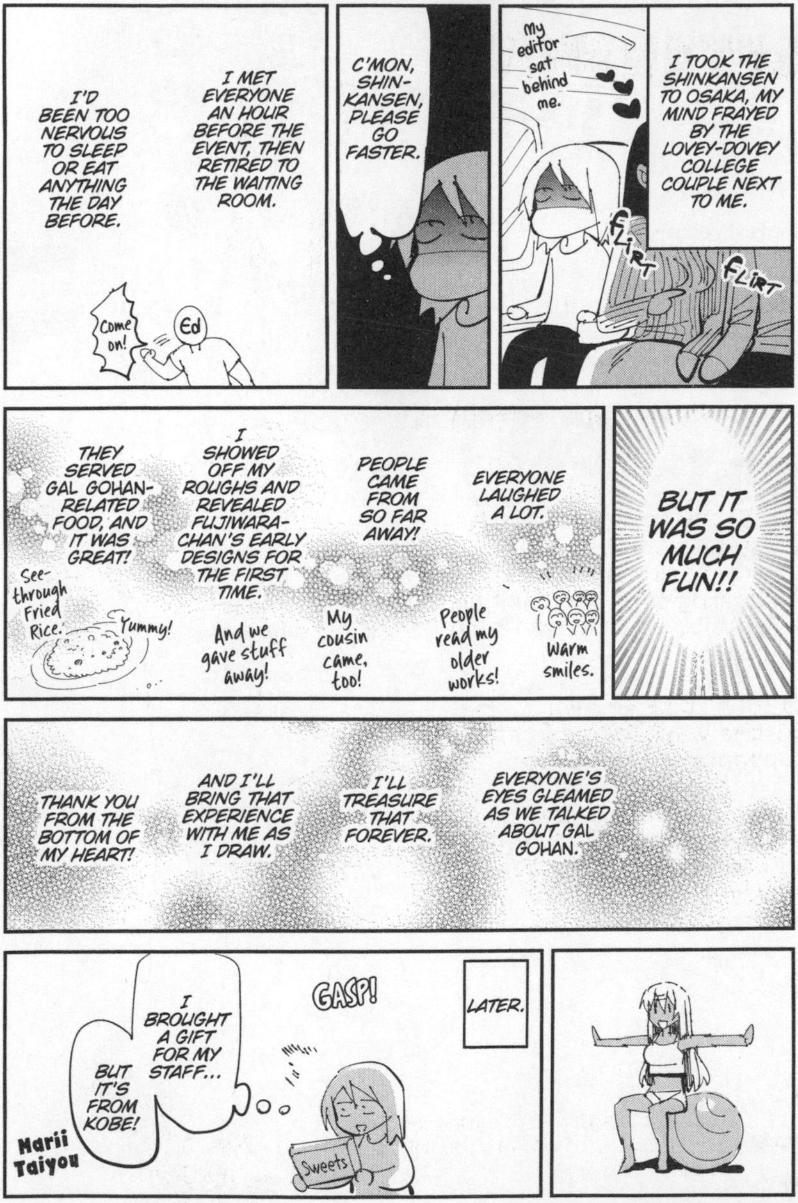
I TOOK THE SHINKANSEN TO OSAKA, MY MIND FRAYED BY THE LOVEY-DOVEY COLLEGE COUPLE NEXT TO ME.
My editor sat behind me.
FLIRT
FLIRT
C'MON, SHIN-KANSEN, PLEASE GO FASTER.
I MET EVERYONE AN HOUR BEFORE THE EVENT, THEN RETIRED TO THE WAITING ROOM.
I'D BEEN TOO NERVOUS TO SLEEP OR EAT ANYTHING THE DAY BEFORE.
Ed
Come on!
BUT IT WAS SO MUCH FUN!!
EVERYONE LAUGHED A LOT.
Warm smiles.
PEOPLE CAME FROM SO FAR AWAY!
People read my older works!
My cousin came, too!
I SHOWED OFF MY ROUGHS AND REVEALED FUJIWARA-CHAN'S EARLY DESIGNS FOR THE FIRST TIME.
And we gave stuff away!
THEY SERVED GAL GOHAN-RELATED FOOD, AND IT WAS GREAT!
See-through Fried Rice.
Yummy!
EVERYONE'S EYES GLEAMED AS WE TALKED ABOUT GAL GOHAN.
I'LL TREASURE THAT FOREVER.
AND I'LL BRING THAT EXPERIENCE WITH ME AS I DRAW.
THANK YOU FROM THE BOTTOM OF MY HEART!
LATER.
GASP!
I BROUGHT A GIFT FOR MY STAFF...
BUT IT'S FROM KOBE!
Sweets
Marii Taiyou

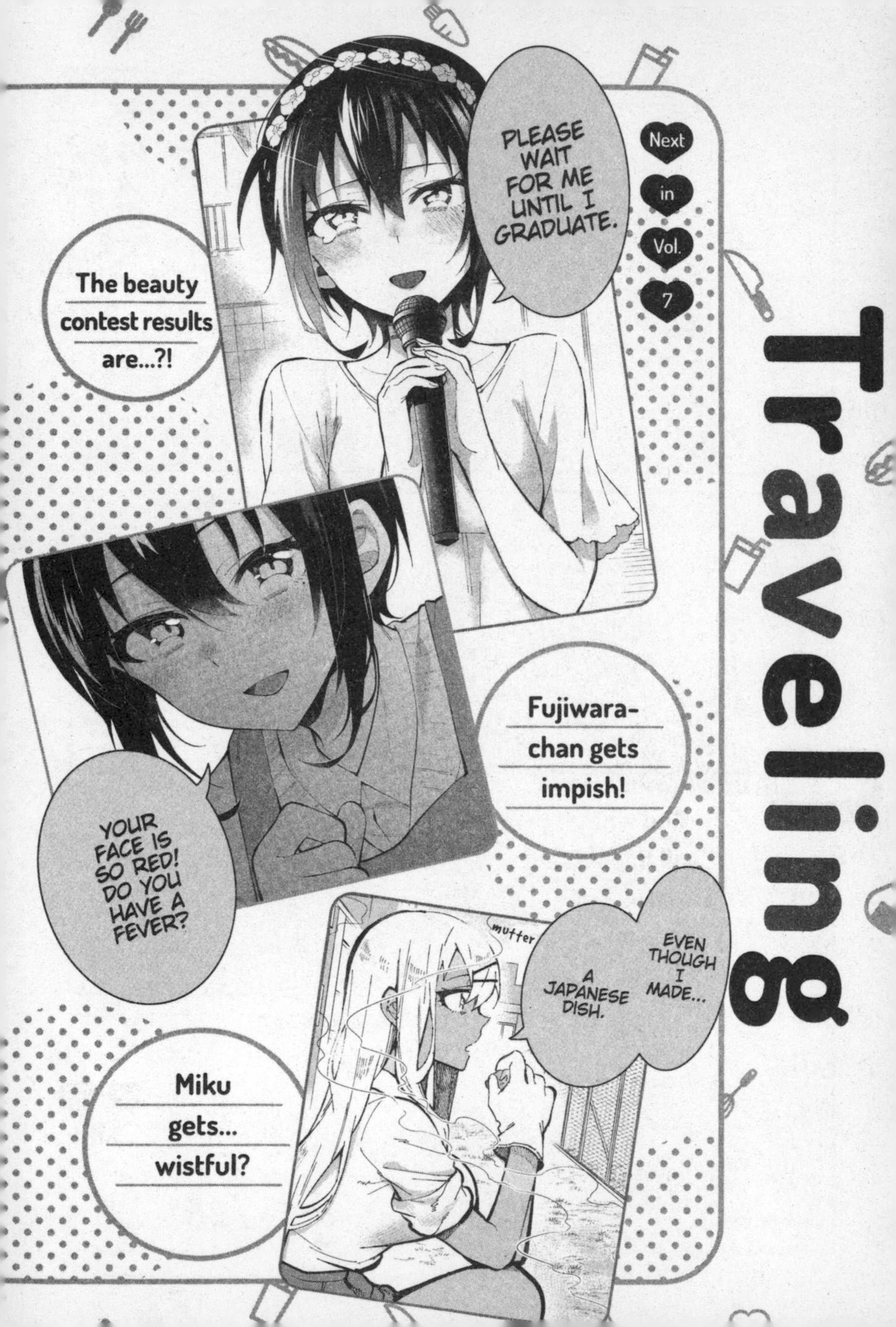
Traveling
Next in Vol. 7
PLEASE WAIT FOR ME UNTIL I GRADUATE.
The beauty contest results are...?!
Fujiwara-chan gets impish!
YOUR FACE IS SO RED! DO YOU HAVE A FEVER?
mutter
EVEN THOUGH I MADE...
A JAPANESE DISH.
Miku gets... wistful?

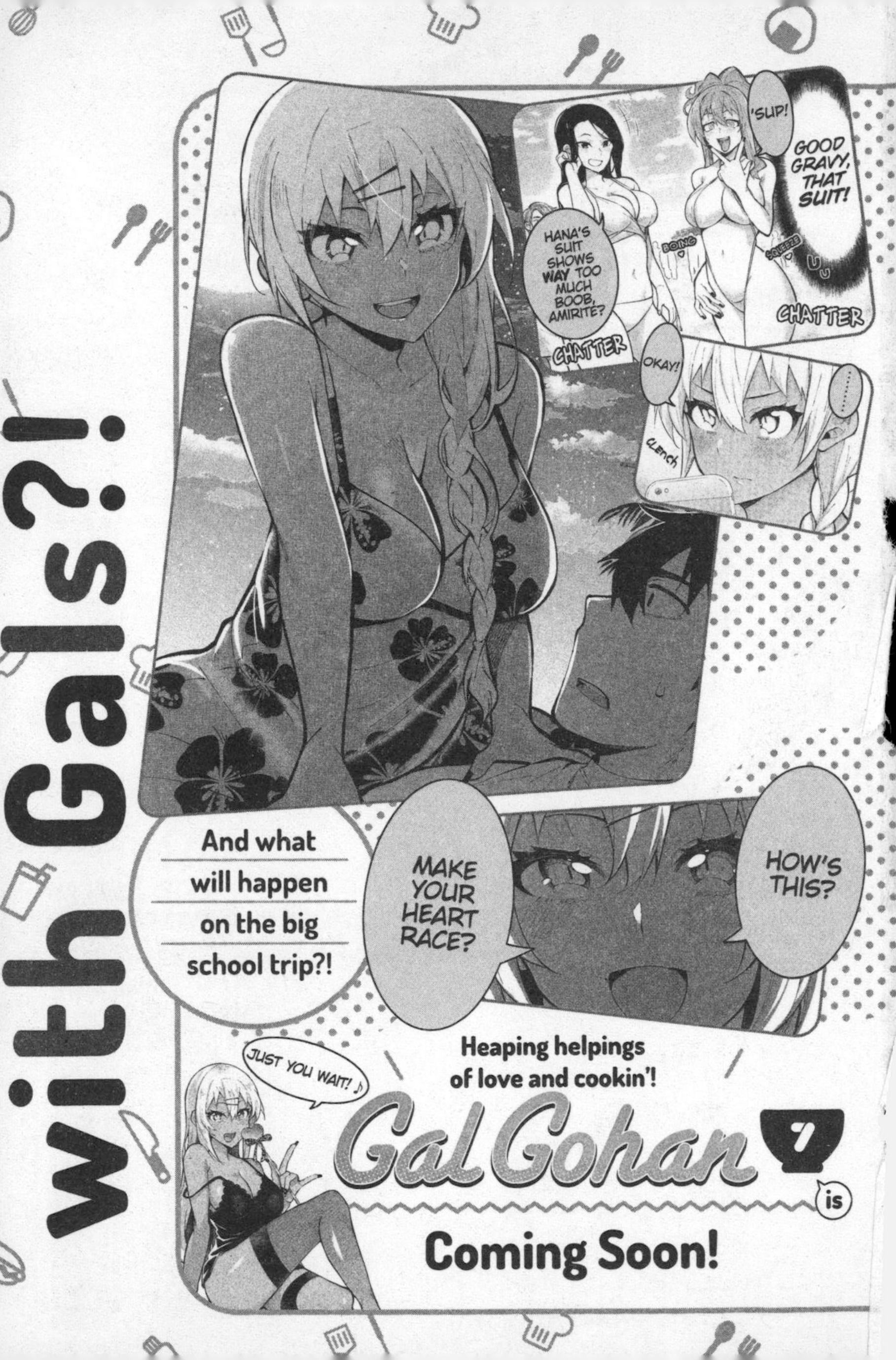
'SUP!
GOOD GRAVY, THAT SUIT!
SQUEEZE
CHATTER
HANA'S SUIT SHOWS WAY TOO MUCH BOOB, AMIRITE?
BOING
CHATTER
......
OKAY!
CLENCH
HOW'S THIS?
MAKE YOUR HEART RACE?
And what will happen on the big school trip?!
with Gals?!
JUST YOU WAIT! ♪
Heaping helpings of love and cookin'!
Gal Gohan 7 is
Coming Soon!

SEVEN SEAS ENTERTAINMENT PRESENTS

Gal Gohan

story and art by **MARII TAIYOU** **VOLUME 6**

TRANSLATION
Andrew Cunningham

ADAPTATION
Bambi Eloriaga-Amago

LETTERING
Carolina Hernández Mendoza

COVER DESIGN
Kris Aubin

PROOFREADER
Dawn Davis
Brett Hallahan

EDITOR
Shanti Whitesides

PREPRESS TECHNICIAN
Rhiannon Rasmussen-Silverstein

PRODUCTION MANAGER
Lissa Pattillo

MANAGING EDITOR
Julie Davis

ASSOCIATE PUBLISHER
Adam Arnold

PUBLISHER
Jason DeAngelis

First published in Japan in 2019 by HAKUSENSHA, INC., Tokyo.
English language translation rights in U.S.A. arranged with HAKUSENSHA, INC., Tokyo through TOHAN CORPORATION, Tokyo.

Seven Seas press and purchase enquiries can be sent to Marketing Manager Lianne Sentar at press@gomanga.com. Information regarding the distribution and purchase of digital editions is available from Digital Manager CK Russell at digital@gomanga.com.

ISBN: 978-1-64505-964-6

Printed in Canada

First Printing: January 2021

10 9 8 7 6 5 4 3 2 1

FOLLOW US ONLINE: ***www.sevenseasentertainment.com***

READING DIRECTIONS

This book reads from ***right to left***, Japanese style. If this is your first time reading manga, you start reading from the top right panel on each page and take it from there. If you get lost, just follow the numbered diagram here. It may seem backwards at first, but you'll get the hang of it! Have fun!!

1
2
3
4
5
6
7
8
9

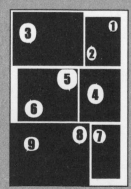